THE ART OF
MICROWAVE COOKING

THELMA PRESSMAN

Contemporary Books, Inc.
Chicago

Library of Congress Cataloging in Publication Data

Pressman, Thelma.
    The art of microwave cooking.

    Includes index.
    1. Microwave cookery.   I. Title.
TX832.P7   1983   641.5'882   83-19001
ISBN 0-8092-5866-8

Copyright © 1983 by Thelma Pressman
All rights reserved
Published by Contemporary Books, Inc.
180 North Michigan Avenue, Chicago, Illinois 60601
Manufactured in the United States of America
Library of Congress Catalog Card Number: 83-19001
International Standard Book Number: 0-8092-5866-8

Published simultaneously in Canada by Beaverbooks, Ltd.
195 Allstate Parkway, Valleywood Business Park
Markham, Ontario L3R 4T8 Canada

CONTENTS

When women writers dedicate the culmination of the hours of testing, retesting, and agonizing over the final recipes to be included in their masterpieces to their wonderful, adoring, supportive, mates, who ate *all* of their offerings with love and affection, and never complained, I am filled with envy!

I would like very much to dedicate this long awaited book to my sweet, adorable husband of many years—but it would be a lie! He would never eat my slaved-over original offerings if in anyway they did not meet his high standards of what should be served to him. He would not dine on the microwave cook's newfound, greatly touted, easily cleaned-up paper plate. Nor would he be kind and gracious in his critique. One would think he was of royal birth, which believe me, he is not!

So there I was, with my newfound technology in my very own kitchen, with all the input that came with it. Easy cooking on paper plates; put brown sugar on everything so it will be brown; don't stand too close, or you will become sterile; turn the plate every two seconds so it will cook evenly. And of course I was surrounded by the unappetizing foods that were prepared in the very early years of pioneering.

Still, I was determined to make this TV set look-alike cook to please the family and, like many early microwave pioneering cooks, I began to discover and use those techniques that worked. To justify and prove my interest in advanced technology in the kitchen, and to avoid rejection, I began to think in terms of "presentation" and from that concept developed cookware that not only enhanced the cooking of foods in the microwave, but went to the dining table with style.

In all fairness, if it were not for my husband's shock and disbelief at my early microwave cooking attempts, I might never have achieved the high standards of quality I strive for.

So—dedicated to my favorite male chauvinist, husband, golfing companion, and most of all my good friend, Mo.

ACKNOWLEDGMENTS

Since this book is about teaching, it seems appropriate to remember the teachers who have influenced me. Dr. Bob Decareau made it possible for me, as a teacher, to interact with the scientific community. Ralph Wegman, my other mentor and good friend, translated and spoon-fed to me the enormous amount of new information coming through the scientific channels.

I acknowledge and thank my students, who demanded only the best and who then became the teachers who spread the microwave word with style. Without their constant prodding, encouragement, and support the Microwave Cooking Center would never have happened. There have been thousands of students who allowed me to practice my craft. Many have become lifetime friends. Harris Goldstein said, "What the world doesn't need is another microwave cookbook. What is needed is a book on microwave that tells it like it is. Bring the classroom to the students, just as you do it in class." Andrea and Harris, if you find anything in your class notes I forgot to include, don't call me . . . it is too late! Believe me, I tried to remember everything, and writing is harder than talking.

It would be impossible to give special attention to all those responsible for my professional growth. Among them are: Sylvia White, now Dr. Sylvia Weishaus, my first "boss" in the field of Consumer Education and Affairs; Joyce Perlstein, who translated 12 hours of Bon Appetit's taping of my 4-week microwave workshop, and Ed Pearlstein, who found time in his busy schedule to give me advice when it was needed; Bon Appetit's Managing Editor, Marilou Vaughan, whose confidence in me is greatly appreciated; Barbara Varnum, whom I thank for being a "tough editor"; Elizabeth James, a colleague and friend with a talent for food that is bigger than she is; Barbara and Bob Kassel and Bill Morgan who showed their faith by inviting me to design the innovative microwave cookware line for Blisscraft; Bill Gould, president of American Family Scale, who manufactured the line; and Rosemary Walbert and Anne Marchiony for their devotion and interest.

I am also grateful to Natalie Haughton, food editor of the Daily News, for her early recognition of my work and making me feel I was making an important contribution to my community; Kit Snedaker, food editor of the Herald Examiner, a writer with a great sense of humor who gave me the title "The Susan B. Anthony of modern cooking"; the Los Angeles Times, for its coverage of our Microwave Contest Events, and encouragement of microwave technology through food editor Betsy Balsley, and writers Minnie Bernardino and Barbara Hansen; Marsh Industries for many years of pioneering and allowing me to experiment until I got it right; Rick Lapine for his talent and drive and for his belief in my concepts; Ira Lifland for the years of support and encouragement, when I needed it most; Alain Karyo for design and beauty and all the things yet to come; and to Sanyo Electric, Inc., for the years of exciting technological developments. I consider myself fortunate to have had the opportunity to interact with the quality, intelligent, respectable people in my profession.

I also thank my dear family, to whom I am eternally devoted: my mother, who made love and food synonymous; my sister Sydelle and her husband Raymond, who carried on the family tradition with great style; my supportive and beautiful children, Richard, who watched me with amazement, and Paul, who has long since surpassed my cooking ability and has developed a style of his own; their lovely wives, Denise and Roberta, the daughters I finally had, who took over where I left off and are making their own mark in the field of microwave; and the emerging new microwave cooks, my grandchildren, Amanda, Gretchen, and Chris—I hope that they will also become interested in new technology and become an active influence in the world.

INTRODUCTION

This book is about cooking. For that reason I have chosen not to use terms like *micro-cook*, which I find a rather unpalatable expression.

While writing a cookbook for a microwave convection oven several years ago, the publisher "corrected" my manuscript from my use of the word *cook* to read *micro-cook*. I sent it back with this message: "When cookbooks begin to use instructions like *Gas* onions for 3 minutes or *Electrocute* celery for 5 minutes, I will agree to the use of *micro-cook*!" By return mail I received their reply—they all conceded that cooking is cooking, no matter what appliance is used.

No one kitchen appliance is designed to do everything. What makes the difference between success and failure in the use of an appliance is taking the time to learn the technique needed to properly enjoy the product and its unique function.

If you decided to become proficient in French cooking, you would find a good teacher, an accredited school, or a quality cookbook to instruct you. The same with Italian or any other fine cuisine. And if you were fortunate enough to grow up in a family where good cooking was the order of the day, you would have absorbed not only the wonderful fragrances of the kitchen, but also a rich foundation to draw upon later in developing a cooking style of your own.

In microwave cooking, however, no foundation has been laid—everyone starts from scratch. You cannot call your mother, a favorite aunt, good friends, or neighbors to get recipes and help in avoiding errors, as you probably did many times when cooking conventionally. While in the past you might have ruined a roast or cake, you didn't blame it on your oven. However, as a microwave beginner, if you ruined a roast once you might never try again—and the microwave you purchased with such high hopes would spend most of its time on the shelf.

In spite of the "food experts" who ignore its potential, over 40 million microwave ovens have now been sold—a penetration in our homes never dreamed of by those skeptics. The microwave is no longer just a gadget for affluent trend-setters but is a practical and very convenient appliance.

With microwave sales increasing daily, the "outside" world has finally begun to pay attention to the microwave cook—and it is about time!

In our culture with all the responsibilities we assume in our present lifestyle, with education and career options available as never before, with mobility which allows us to go in many directions, and with household help a luxury few of us can afford, we need and deserve all the help we can get.

Microwave ranges, like the food processor, can replace help in the kitchen because they remove drudgery. I often wonder what the first woman who allowed her husband to bring a gas pipeline into her kitchen was like. She must have been a brave soul—and probably had a lot of neighbors standing around telling her it would never work. But maybe she had a pioneering spirit—and was tired of chopping wood.

I must admit that I did enjoy the early years of microwave pioneering, as lonely as it was. But I still do not believe that interest would have developed without the schools and teachers who brought microwave cooking to the public. Without their help, who could have believed that a box that looks like a TV could produce a juicy prime rib, or an attractive quiche Lorraine? But it does! With more and more fine cooks experimenting in and building this newest cuisine, we are just beginning an exciting new era in the kitchen.

Not too many years ago, the frozen food and convenience food industries were complaining that they could not attempt to design foods for the microwave cook until the microwave manufacturers got their act together and standardized cooking power wattages. Not until microwave ownership reached 35–40 percent of all households did they wake up to the fact that there existed a significant market for microwave foods. Now we go to our supermarkets and see row upon row of frozen foods with microwave instructions on the back—even though the microwave industry still has not achieved standardization! To cope with this lack of standardization, frozen food manufacturers are using the same system they have always used for conventional cooking: they give the cook flexible timing.

As with microwave ranges, conventional ovens often vary. Much depends upon how your microwave or conventional oven is manufactured. My mother insisted on baking in her own kitchen, rather than mine, because her oven cooked differently from mine. I think all of us experience this difference when we change equipment.

Lois Dwan, restaurant editor of the *Los Angeles Times*, wrote in her restaurant guide that "Education is achieved when a subject is mastered to that point where further thinking is all one's own—thoughts that no one else ever had." Something of the same holds true for cooking. In order to achieve this individuality and draw from your own background and experience, you must understand the appliance and how it relates to food. Unless you know what is happening, you are not free to produce your own recipes and adapt your favorites.

Instead of only suggesting that you find a recipe in the book similar to one you wish to try (which is a fine idea and lets the writer off the hook) this book (even at the expense of repeating) will detail with each recipe the reasons why food is placed in a certain way, why a specific dish is used, and why a certain level of microwave energy is used for a specific food.

One of the restricting things about the early pioneering days of microwave teaching was the poor quality of the cookbooks—everything was covered with brown sugar! If the early writers could have found a way to get the public to accept a prime rib covered with brown sugar to mask the fact that the meat did not look the same when cooked by microwave, they would have.

In my early days of adapting recipes to the microwave, I found a delightful stuffed breast of chicken recipe in a fine French cookbook, with a picture in color. I chose it because the chicken was pure white, as was the delicate sauce.

The only touch of color was in the fresh mushrooms and a bit of chopped parsley. When the recipe was used for a workshop the students loved it, however (as I have learned to expect), one voice exclaimed, "But it doesn't brown does it? What if I wanted it to be brown?"

There is a sign in my school made for me by a delightful PR man about 10 years ago. I was approached by a very fine, old bank in Burbank that wanted me to provide entertainment during their quarterly interest review. Their clients were mainly retired professionals who reinvested their interest each quarter and usually had to wait their turn to meet with an advisor.

As we discussed arrangements for publicity and setting up a cooking area in the bank, the PR man asked me what I would like to get over to the public about microwave cooking. My answer was as it has always been: Though we finally have an appliance to take the drudgery out of cooking, it is usually difficult to get this across in public due to the many misconceptions the public has. As he pressed me further I finally said in frustration, "If one more person watches me cook a prime rib to perfection in the microwave, beautifully brown on the outside, and still blurts out, 'But it doesn't brown does it?' I may not be responsible for my actions!"

When I arrived the following month, there was a lovely cooking area arranged in great style: red carpeting, an elevated area roped off with royal thick gold braid, a huge work table, overhead mirror, and this huge sign that read, "BUT THELMA, IT DOESN'T BROWN, DOES IT?" It has been with me ever since, reproduced in stitchery by one of my students, and is placed in a strategic location in my school.

NEW TECHNOLOGY AND THE KITCHEN

While we may have come a long way with technology in our office environment, when it comes to our kitchens, we are often still using archaic equipment.

When we go into our modern offices, we use spin-off technology from the space program. Tiny computer chips record and send signals. We use solid state—which means no moving parts to wear out—rather than timers that move and have limited capabilities. Typewriters erase, word processors send out information from stored memories, and the secretary simply touches a button. Then she goes home and uses obsolete equipment in her kitchen designed with obsolete engineering technology.

All of this stems from a lack of technical awareness. With the majority of "food experts" who lead the way in food trends against the microwave, it's amazing that microwave cooking has mushroomed as fast as it has around this country. I'm convinced that as we develop greater expertise and better recipes, and as the technology continues to improve, we will achieve a kitchen that is equipped with the very best our engineers can produce. *We deserve it!*

The microwave is the forerunner of this trend, bringing us into the twentieth century with new thinking and reexamined options. I am not insisting that a microwave is an all-purpose appliance, but so far it is the best the engineers have given us. It is a giant step in the right direction. Now, like the Wright brothers, we can begin to enjoy the excitement of change.

THE TOTAL KITCHEN, UPDATED

The ideal kitchen should provide all available methods for cooking. After all, no one appliance is designed to do it all. A flaky pastry belongs in a hot, dry oven, a steak belongs on a barbecue, and all the rest belong in a microwave!

A bit oversimplified, but the point is, we must rethink our alternatives. Just as prop airplanes gave way to jet propulsion and the old-fashioned adding machine to computers, microwaves will make the conventional oven obsolete, because they are more efficient. And along with the microwave should go all of the other new technology to make the kitchen function for us in the best way possible.

Your kitchen should have appliances that reflect your particular needs: a food processor, a microwave sized to fit your household, a toaster oven, cook-top burners, some type of barbecue (even a portable gas), freezer space, and a well-designed storage and work area.

Food Processor

The introduction of the *food processor* made possible in seconds the chopping, blending, shredding, and mixing of ingredients to prepare the most involved recipes. But it could not have achieved its current success in the marketplace had it not been for our sustained interest in good food preparation, the difficulty and expense of securing good kitchen help, and the large number of working women.

Many years ago, when wives were locked into their homes without cars, what creativity was available except to make certain that the silver shone, you could eat off their floors, and that their food was the best in town? Activity away from home was limited by the lifestyle of the times.

Our lifestyles are different today, but eating still goes on. And we can choose between ordinary and exciting. If a child eats mostly fast-food takeouts, he will grow accustomed to that. On the other hand, if appliances in the kitchen make quality food preparation possible with a minimum of fuss and cleanup, the whole scene changes.

What we have is an ongoing change in our eating patterns. And we have a lot to learn. Cooking schools are very much in fashion because people who have not learned the skills at home are out there trying to master them. But what good is a course that teaches long, involved recipes that take long hours and many pots and pans if we do not have the time to prepare them.

Microwave Range

Microwave ranges are selling because they offer people a viable alternative. I can make the fastest treats on the block for my grandchildren in a microwave — or better yet, they can program it themselves, since it is not only easy, it is safe. Although more children are injured each year in kitchen accidents than any other room in the house, it is *never with a microwave.*

Toaster Oven

When I first suggested the use of a *toaster oven* to crisp a potato I had just cooked in a microwave. I was amazed to learn how many of my students were still purchasing pop-up toasters. For the same amount of counter space, you can have an appliance that functions in so many ways besides making toast. It grills sandwiches, bakes refrigerated biscuits, reconstitutes TV dinners, crisps foods — and comes in sizes that will accommodate all families, from small to large.

To zero in on the frozen food market, the microwave and the toaster oven provide the needed combination for reconstituting these foods. Since most frozen foods are used by one or two people at each meal, the large, conventional oven is not your best choice. It takes approximately seven minutes to preheat a conventional oven to 350°. That is just the oven itself — then after heating the platter, the heat begins to penetrate the food. Much energy is wasted in this method. The oven is large and requires hot air space surrounding the food. If you attempt to cook a pie in your regular oven and place it in the center of the oven on the center rack, in order to achieve proper cooking you cannot place another pie beneath it. The second pie will block the heat source and the bottom of the first pie cannot cook; only the top will get done. So even though the oven has a large cavity, the space is not efficient, since you cannot use it all at once for all foods.

The smaller cavity of a toaster oven provides speed in heating the food, making it a more efficient appliance. And the improvements in toaster ovens over the past few years are keeping pace with the lifestyles of today's living.

Magnetic Induction Cook-Top

Are you aware of the *magnetic induction cook-top,* which only heats the metal pans and which can be wiped off with a paper towel during cooking should there be a spillover? Nothing drips underneath, there is no spill bowl to clean, and no grates! It has been around for over 10 years — a bit expensive right now, but with consumer acceptance the price will drop.

The Cooking Bag Sealer

Another product that uses your resources to good advantage is the *cooking bag sealer.* By freezing your leftovers in these bags while the food is still fresh, you can make efficient use of your freezer space and provide yourself with the best possible food for your own TV dinners. The ability to restore these frozen leftovers by cooking them in their pouches makes food preparation easier and the cleanup a matter of tossing an empty bag into the trash.

Don't make the mistake of expecting a sandwich bag or zip-lock bag to become a cooking bag. It is not made of the same material and should not be used in the microwave for food. A cooking bag, which is the same variety as the type that comes in the frozen food section, is a bag designed specifically for cooking. Plastic should only be used if they state they are made for microwave cooking. Why? Because plastics (such as polyvinyl chlorides) can give off gas and be toxic when heated. I repeat: there are many plastics available; only those marked "for microwave" should be used.

1

LET'S GET TECHNICAL

This Room Is Equipped With

Edison Electric Light.

Do not attempt to light with match. Simply turn key on wall by the door.

The use of Electricity for lighting is in no way harmful to health, nor does it affect the soundness of sleep.

Special thanks to the Madsen Electric Museum for the discovery, background and history of this sign.

Signs such as this first started appearing in 1892 with the advent of the installation of electricity in hotels and public buildings. The sign was in use for approximately 20 years to inform guests and visitors on the use and safety of electrical lighting.

Most people who have succeeded in microwave cooking have either been to a good class with a dedicated teacher, or have had a good book on the subject. I hope you will find this book fun to read and a good learning experience.

For several years I took over 7th, 8th, and 9th grade classrooms to bring microwave cooking into focus for these young students. In the science classes, the majority of students were boys. I was amazed at how quickly they grasped the microwave concept. It made me realize how much technology is in their world. They understand it completely—after all, music, stereo, TV, and radio are all utilizing the very same concepts used in microwave cooking technology. After this experience, if a new microwave recipient phoned me, telling me they had just received a touch panel microwave and didn't understand its operation or could not set the clock, I would find myself asking if there was a teenage boy in the house. The answer often was, "Yes, but he is not allowed to use the microwave yet." My response was to ask them to reconsider, since they would probably need his help—and to put him on the phone. In just seconds, he would grasp the concept and leave the phone to program the panel. (This is not to say girls do not also have this ability; it is that we do not as readily encourage it in our girls as we do our boys.)

Our children do not have any preconceived concepts. They have the freedom to express their ingenuity and become quite innovative in their cooking approach. I expect in the years to come, as our kitchen grows into the twentieth century, it will be this generation that will truly make it the exciting room it deserves to be.

I happen to believe in clothes washers and dryers, dishwashers and garbage disposals, induction cook-tops and convection concepts. Microwave systems need to be explored and developed to bring them into full bloom and simplify our cooking. We can then bring an abundance of fresh and fresh-frozen foods to our table, to enhance our lifestyles with good nutrition and wonderful dining.

If we make our kitchens more efficient, both in food preparation and with a minimum of cleanup, perhaps the fast-food industry will not be so tempting.

In the next few pages, you will find simple explanations for the questions I have been asked most often about microwaves. (Also, for those who would like to read further, more technical information.)

MOST-ASKED QUESTIONS

1. What are microwaves?
Microwaves are invisible electromagnetic waves that travel at the speed of light. They are a form of nonionizing radiant energy, and are absorbed, reflected, or transmitted, depending on the substance with which they come in contact.

2. What frequencies are used for cooking?
The FCC (Federal Communications Commission) has assigned 2450 Mhz and 915 Mhz for cooking. Mhz is the symbol for megacycles, 2450 Mhz means 2,450,000,000 cycles per second.

3. How do microwaves cook?
Microwaves reverse the position of the food molecules. The reversals, at 2,450,000,000 cycles per second, produce friction which produces heat. Literally, when exposed to microwaves, the food vibrates itself hot.

4. Is the user of a microwave oven ever exposed to dangerous radiation?
No, the microwave energy is confined within the food cavity by the door and the door seals. Opening the door stops the microwave feed instantly.

5. What if my hand were exposed to a high level of microwave energy such as the inside of the food cavity?
First of all, you cannot get your hand into the cavity while the microwaves are being generated because of double safety interlocks. If you could, however, you would quickly move your hand elsewhere as you would experience a burning sensation within five seconds.

6. Is there any danger from microwave energy leakage?
There has never been a known injury from energy leakage from a microwave oven. In millions of hours of use, there has never been a case of injury to humans, nor will there be as long as microwave ovens meet present federal safety standards.

7. What makes the microwave oven so safe?
First, the door seal—it is designed to keep microwaves in. Second, the door latch, which positively compresses the seal against the food cavity. Third, two electrical interlocks—one operated by the movement of the latch, the other operated by the movement of the door. With this arrangement, the microwave energy is shut off before the door seal separates from the food cavity.

8. Does the food retain any radiation?
No. Food, or for that matter, any part of the range itself, is incapable of storing microwaves. When the power is off, the microwave output stops.

9. How much faster is microwave cooking than conventional cooking?
   The speed varies with the size and kind of food. Most foods require only about one-fourth the cooking time; however, small single items can become piping hot in as little as one-fiftieth of the time.

10. Why is the microwave oven vented? And can the vent leak microwaves?
    It is vented so that moisture and odors can be exhausted out of the cavity, just as in a conventional oven. The vent is not in contact with the microwave energy, thus the moisture expelled is harmless.

11. Why does it take longer when you add more food, such as two potatoes?
    There is a fixed amount of energy that comes into the cavity. If there is a small amount of food, all of the energy is absorbed by the small item. When larger amounts are cooked, they will take longer to heat because the energy is dispersed among the items.

12. Why is it smaller than a conventional oven?
    The design concept is based on the cooking which the microwave performs. The very nature of microwave cooking limits the size of the food item being cooked. You also eliminate the need for a large cavity because hot air does not need to circulate around the food; microwaves are directly absorbed by the food.

13. Will I damage the magnetron tube if I cook a frozen TV dinner in its metal tray?
    Since metal does not allow microwaves to penetrate, it is inefficient to use metal. By cooking the food from the top only, it slows the process. It is best to use the new microwave TV dinners packaged in nonmetal presware trays.

14. Why is the door panel perforated and why are these perforations covered with glass?
    Microwaves cannot pass through this perforated screen,. as they would an ordinary window. The glass is placed there for ease of cleaning.

15. Is the microwave self-cleaning?
    No. Self-cleaning is a wonderful feature designed to clean the oven of burned-on food soils. Microwave food soils cannot burn on since the walls do not get hot enough to cook anything.

16. How do you clean the cavity?
    Wipe it with a damp soft towel and liquid detergent. Nothing abrasive is necessary. If there should be an odor at any time, boil a tablespoon of vinegar in a cup of water for two to three minutes.

17. Is a person wearing a pacemaker affected by microwave ovens?
    Microwave ovens do not pose a threat to pacemaker wearers; there is no federal law that says a sign must be displayed where they are in use. All pacemakers today are designed to guard against outside interference, whether it comes from television and radio broadcast signals or faulty ranges.

18. Is there any change in flavor or nutritional value of foods?
    Food tastes the same as when cooked conventionally. Some foods taste even better. Studies have indicated foods cooked by microwaves retain more vitamins and food nutrients because of the speed of cooking.

19. How do you know when to cover food or not?
    Depending on the effect you want, the rules are about the same as for conventional cooking. Vegetables, for example, should be steamed and would be covered. Chicken with a crisp coating would not be covered because it would create steam.

20. Articles in the press have indicated that individuals should stand an arm's length from the oven when it is operating. Is this necessary?
    No. Microwave energy dissipates very rapidly as the distance from the range increases. Thus, just a few inches from the unit, the safety factor already built into the product is increased by many times.

21. Have microwave ovens caused cataracts or sterility?
    There is no known case of cataracts or any other effect such as sterility recorded from the use of a microwave cooking appliance.

DISPELLING THE MYTHS

In the past few years many of the myths and misinformation about microwave cooking have been dispelled, but some are still with us. If you can discover where these myths started, it sometimes helps you to understand the situation better.

In reading a popular microwave cookbook, I was amazed to discover I could get a brown pie crust shell if I simply used an amber or dark-colored pie plate. I immediately tested three pie shells, one in my dark Corning pie plate, one in my white Marsh porcelain, and one in my Anchor Hocking amber. After they cooled, I removed all three—none were brown. I finally realized what she must have meant: looking *through* the dark colored pie plates the pie shells were definitely browner; however, from the top, they were all still the same light color. I guess it is all in the way one looks at things!

To Salt or Not to Salt?

One of the most persistent myths has been not to salt the food before cooking. Although this appears in the introduction of every microwave cookbook I have ever read, salt still seems to be an ingredient in many of the recipes, with no ill effects to the food.

The origin of this myth goes back to a research project conducted at one of the universities in the 1960s. A book was written describing the findings. Observations made in the laboratory testing of food in microwaves indicated that salt on the surface of the food would deflect the microwaves—therefore they concluded that food cooked in the microwave should not be salted.

In my early microwave cooking I added salt *after* cooking as recommended, but did not find the flavor of the food to my liking. My own testing soon proved that presalting made no difference at all in how the food cooked. Therefore, it is my feeling that salting food is as normal in microwave cooking as it is in any other method.

How the "Microwaves Cook from the Inside Out" Myth Began

Microwave ranges have revolutionized the kitchen and it seems appropriate that it all started with a Hershey bar. In 1946, Percy Spencer, a Raytheon scientist working with radar (ultrahigh-frequency radio waves), noticed that a chocolate bar in his pocket had melted. It was his curiosity that began the investigation that resulted in the first microwave cavity.

A galvanized refuse can was set up to test the remarkable ability of the magnetron tube, using short wave frequencies, to interact with food so that the food would cook itself.

Hot dogs, popcorn, and other small bits of food were placed into the cavity. Because of the wave length of the frequency used and the small quantity of food, they thought that microwaves either cooked the food from the inside out, or penetrated the food all at once. And so the myth began.

It is important to understand that these tests were done with no concern about radiation: hands reached in and brought out cooked food, and although they

did experience warmth, no injuries took place—the scientists lived on to ripe old age, and raised healthy families.

We know now that microwave cooking takes place from the outside in, but the myth dies hard, and we still bump into the occasional person (often an engineer!) who repeats this misinformation.

Your Microwave Is Safe

Few questions have been the subject of as much controversy and misunderstanding as the safety of the microwave range. Some "scare" stories have been spread by overly zealous news media seeking the sensational; others have been pure misunderstandings.

In the 25 years that microwave ranges have been in use, there has not been a single injury associated with them. The truth is that it is one of the safest appliances in your home. Manufacturers must meet strict government codes to ensure safety.

Some of the misconceptions began in 1968 when the U.S. Senate held well-publicized hearings on potential radiation-producing appliances. There was never any doubt in the minds of experts about the safety of the microwave range even then. However, the Senate decided to include the microwave simply to cover all bases in its hearings. The hearings resulted in the Radiation Control for Health & Safety Act of 1968. No one can reasonably argue against the preventative measures contained in this Act, but unfortunate misunderstandings concerning microwave ranges were created during these hearings.

Dr. J.M. Osepchuk of Raytheon Research Division discussed the problems that emerged in an article in *The Journal of Microwave Power*. Osepchuk said, "It should be stressed that the microwave oven was included in the Act not because of demonstrated injury or hazards, but as part of an umbrella policy of prudence...by the Act, Congress blurred the meaningful differences between the more potent hazards of ionizing radiation, and the more benign nonionizing radiation, which includes microwaves."

In order to cash in on this ungrounded fear, many so-called "calibrated testers" have cropped up. These range in price from about $5 to $50. You might as well throw your money in the street for all the good these testers can do for you.

In my early years of microwave testing and teaching, I spent much time doing teachers' workshops at the Department of Water & Power facility in Los Angeles. They had a built-in $1,500 microwave, one of the early designs for home use. It had a full-powered broiler, operated on 220 volts, which could be used simultaneously with the microwave system. Several times I observed the engineers on their staff testing for leakage (the scare was on then—about 1969) using a small four-watt fluorescent tube, which they simply held against the door crack while the microwave was in use. I used this same method to show my classes how to test for leakage without having to obtain an expensive testing system.

In those days we did not have interlocking systems, and could crack the door during its operation to get the fluorescent tube to light up. It takes very little microwave energy to light the tube. The fluorescent tube test, however, was not a scientific test, and was only used to pick up any potential problem. I did discover one countertop model with a leak in a corner—because the unit had been dropped and was damaged. In all the years since, I have tested with a quality Holiday testing device and have never encountered one leaky door.

I do have a tester that goes with me wherever I am. It is my finger, which I frequently run around the door crack as the microwave is in operation to show my audience that it does not leak. (My body is made up of moisture cells, just like food; if my finger came in contact with microwave energy, my finger would feel a burning sensation, and my hand would jerk away instantly.)

Pacemakers: Are They Safe Around Microwaves?

Not too long ago, I received a call requesting I contact a woman who had just had a pacemaker installed and was told to stand a long distance away from her microwave while she was cooking. She was not only an avid user of the microwave, she was also an intelligent consumer, and wanted to know *why*. When none of the questions she asked of the medical profession gave her the answers, she called the manufacturer of her microwave.

In the interest of good consumer information, many years ago I did a study on pacemakers to better understand why they were even suspected of becoming a problem. And since there is no federal law requesting signs be posted where microwaves are being used in public facilities, I was pleased to learn why this position had been taken by the government many years ago (see previous section: "Your Microwave Is Safe"). Signs are still posted by those who really do not even know what the reasons are.

First, let us examine how a pacemaker restores rhythm to the heart. The heart is remarkably small for the amount of work it performs. About the size of your clenched fist, your heart is a special muscle that pumps nearly 5 quarts of blood throughout your body every minute. It does this steadily and rhythmically.

To do its work, the heart is equipped with its own natural pacemaker. This pacemaker produces steady electrical impulses. Each impulse causes the entire heart muscle to contract (or beat). A healthy heart will keep a steady rhythmical pace of about 60 – 80 beats per minute—or higher, depending on your level of activity.

Sometimes the heart's natural rhythm is interrupted or becomes irregular. It may be that the heart's natural pacemaker sends out electrical impulses too slowly, or that these impulses are blocked along the pathway through the heart, resulting in a condition called "heart block." Your heartbeat then becomes very slow or unsteady. With a low heart rate a person may feel tired much of the time; physical exertion like climbing stairs can cause shortness of breath. If left untreated, the condition may even trigger fainting spells.

But rhythm disturbances are treatable. With an artificial pacemaker, a steady flow of electrical impulses is restored to the heart.

A pacemaker is comprised of three basic parts. A small container called the pulse generator houses the battery and circuitry. Energy from the battery is converted into tiny electrical pulses inside the circuitry. Functioning like a minicomputer center, the circuitry also controls the timing of electrical pulses sent to the heart. There is also an insulated wire called a lead, and the contact with the heart, the metal electrode at the end of the lead. Through this electrode the electrical pulses stimulate the surrounding heart tissue, causing the heart to beat.

Most wearers have a pacemaker which stimulates the lower, primary pumping chambers. In some cases, however, it is more advantageous to use a pacemaker which stimulates the upper chambers, or one that paces both sets of chambers in sequence. All of these pacemakers have the same basic function of maintaining the heartbeat and preventing slow and irregular rhythms.

In many heart block conditions, the heart still beats normally part of the time. To allow the heart to work on its own, a special kind of pacemaker has been developed called a "demand" pacemaker. It sends out electrical pulses only when the heart fails to beat by itself. When the heart is beating normally, the circuitry refrains from sending out pulses and simply listens until it detects a missed beat. In this manner, the pacemaker works on "demand" from the heart. The majority of pacemakers implanted are of this type.

Pacemakers have now been produced that have built-in features to protect them from interference produced by other electrical devices. Most electrical items that are encountered in an average day are perfectly safe for these pacemaker wearers, posing no threat. The following items are listed as safe in a manual given to wearers of the pacemakers manufactured by Medtronic, Inc.: televisions, FM and AM radios, stereos; tabletop appliances such as toasters, blenders, electric can openers; hand-held items such as hairdryers, shavers; *microwave ovens;* and others.

The brochure goes on to suggest the following: If you suspect interference with your pacemaker, simply move away from or turn off the offending electrical device. Your pacemaker will not be permanently affected and will resume normal operation. However, it advises that you should consult your doctor for special situations, which might include: working with high-current industrial equipment and powerful magnets; or working in areas near transmitting towers, and antennas transmitting over 100 watts.

Anyone who has a pacemaker installed should request from his doctor a booklet by the manufacturer of the pacemaker, explaining exactly how it is built to perform. It is too important a situation not to be well-informed. (The booklet I have from the pacemaker manufacturer shows a woman standing in front of a microwave and cooking.)

The purpose of supplying this information is to help you avoid the type of concern expressed by the woman who requested information and was unable to receive it. After sending her a copy of the brochure and the reassurance that it is almost an impossibility for her to receive microwave interference from cooking, she wrote me a letter I treasure.

The letter indicated that she had learned more from the information she received from me than from the medical team who were treating her. She was very grateful, because, with her limited health at that time, the microwave was her greatest helper.

I hope this information becomes useful for those of you who wear or have someone in your household who wears a pacemaker—and who would like to enjoy the many advantages of the microwave range.

HOW TO SELECT A MICROWAVE

It is not unlike buying a new car for the first time. Each manufacturer offers many options, many designs, and features you have never been aware existed, let alone planned to use. It can be a most confusing experience—and you certainly want to avoid "buyer's remorse"!

In the early years of microwave ranges, I had no problem helping people who called me for advice. Because of my years with Waste King Corporation, I often received calls from couples interested in kitchen appliances and kitchen design for their new homes. I was comfortable with that field, as I was with the early microwave designs—there was little to choose from.

Now, advising the callers is a major operation. I need to know their lifestyle, if the microwave is going to be used by a large family or a single person, where will it be placed—a multitude of things. And I really get upset with the people who are only interested in defrosting and reheating—because there is so much more to a microwave than that. It is such a pity for them not to take the time to understand the wonderful quality of food they can prepare in the microwave. Unfortunately, with their limited use of this equipment, they are apt to reject it entirely if they experience a failure or two. What a waste!

Time marches on in the kitchen, as well as the other rooms in our houses. Electronic devices surround us: burglar alerts, smoke alarms, cable TV, telephones with microwave beaming, cordless telephones, CB radio transmitters—would anyone install these remarkable devices without learning how they operate or without knowing what the choices are?

The consumer now has close to 200 models of microwave ranges to choose from, produced by about 40 manufacturers. The choices vary, but basics are fairly consistent. When you shop, you will discover the following options:

Size of the Cavity

The size of the cavity can range from large to small compact.

The top-of-the-line large cavity unit has available all of the top-of-the-line features. These include options such as sensor probe, and power levels from 600–700 watts down to below 100 watts to give the user a wide range of cooking choices, just as you have on your cook-top or in your conventional oven. However, with the introduction of smaller cavity units a number of years ago, and a new interest in the smaller units because of restricted kitchen space, we now have top-of-the-line features in smaller units, also, along with a High power of 600 watts, instead of the 450 watts that most smaller units offered as High power until now.

So the size of the unit no longer brings the assumption that it has or has not all of the features you might enjoy.

Select the size that fits your needs. Then decide whether you wish to have the convenience (and expense) of additional options. But before you reject options, find out how they can make your cooking more interesting.

A word about the size of the cavity: In your conventional oven, you need a cavity large enough to provide air space around the food, so that the heat will be constant and cook the food. Depending upon the temperature you select, the thermostat will go on and off to maintain that temperature. In a microwave, however, there is no need to provide air space, since the air does not heat. It would be a waste to have a large cavity for a 2450 frequency microwave system in its present form. So the design of this unit is smaller, in keeping with the amount of cooking energy available.

Timers: Manual vs. Electronic Touch

A manual timer is a dial which turns the unit on and sets the time to cook. It should have well-defined designations for minutes. To me, however, it is important to be able to reheat small items, such as a roll, accurately. Can a manual timer set 45 seconds, for example, and be accurate?

An electronic touch model is designed to mark time by seconds, since it counts down. It is therefore more accurate than the manual timer for shorter timings. It is solid state, which to me has another advantage: should it ever need servicing, the serviceman simply removes the panel and places a new timing unit inside—a much simpler and less time-consuming repair. It makes sense to me to use our new technology whenever possible. Manual timers never made it to the moon!

How do the electronics work? Very simple—usually you have a choice of two ways, just as you do with a calculator. Your first option is to tell the microwave what you want it to do. For example, touch the word *Time;* then tell it how many minutes you want—1 (1 second), 10 (10 seconds), 100 (1 minute), or 1000 (10 minutes)—then touch *Start.* The timer then counts backwards until it turns itself off.

The other option would be to first feed in the numbers for the timing, then feed in the word *Time,* then touch *Start.*

The same method is used for all microwave functions, such as setting the *time-of-day clock,* telling it to use the *probe,* telling it what *power level* to use, and so on.

Turntables vs. Cavity Space

To understand the turntable option, you must first understand how microwaves are used inside the cavity.

Cavity space. The manufacturer has options on how to feed microwaves into an effective cooking pattern in the cavity. Since microwaves travel in a straight line like a ray of light, a method had to be found to distribute the microwave energy throughout the food.

The majority of microwave manufacturers have selected a stirrer fan at the top of the cavity, which breaks up the straight patterns of the microwaves as it moves back and forth against the metal walls, and engages the microwaves with the moisture in the food.

Other manufacturers split the energy source and bring it in from the sides and/or bottom, as well as the top. These two feeding methods appear to work about the same.

Turntable. How does a turntable differ? On turntable models, the microwaves enter from the top of the cavity in a single straight line, and the food rotates on the turntable below to receive the microwave energy. Because the turntable dominates the center of the cavity, you must be careful to select dishes that will fit the system.

In all fairness to both systems, neither one is yet perfect, although the large cavity allowing more flexible use of dishes seems to be more popular at present. The main concern in using the turntable is that the center of the turntable may not be receiving microwave energy, which means you may need to rearrange food to avoid overdone or underdone spots.

Probes

When using a probe (also known as a sensor), you are concerned with temperature. This has been confusing to many people because they have been told that there is no heat in the cavity of the microwave—therefore we always cook by time. However, this is a most interesting option (though not necessarily new to cooking—we used the concept as a built-in thermometer, and still do, in many conventional ovens).

The microwave probe is not concerned with temperature in the cavity. It is used to "sense" the temperature of the food that is cooking. Another interesting feature in this system is that the probe can shut off the microwave energy when the food has reached the selected temperature, or it can hold the food at a *keep-warm* setting, by automatically dropping to about 10% (65 watts) and cycling on and off at this setting for 1 hour. This means not enough microwave energy enters the cavity for cooking to take place—just enough to maintain the internal setting that is preset. I find this very exciting and recommend it as a feature. However, this keep-warm feature is not available with every probe—just with some manufacturers.

The probe can also be used to advantages in reheating. Reheating time is always a challenge—that means, it is difficult to judge. By simply using a probe, you can set the internal temperature you wish the food to be when ready. Another option we use at home is to read the internal temperature of a casserole when it finishes cooking. Then to reheat the frozen or leftover casserole, the temperature is preset into the microwave using the probe, which will automatically bring the casserole to just the right eating temperature without over- or underheating.

If your microwave does not have a built-in probe, a quick-acting microwave thermometer is available for purchase and is an excellent piece of equipment to have on hand.

Variable Power Levels

Variable power means that you can change the amount of energy reaching the food. The higher the energy, the faster the cooking.

Let us pretend you are camping—you have one cast-iron frying pan and a single Bunsen burner and a very large, thick slab of hamburger steak. You would like it grilled, so you heat the fry pan with the largest flame possible. You place the meat on the pan and it sears it quickly and the browning suddenly turns to smoke and you realize it is burning. You turn the steak over and again the meat begins to burn—so you bring the flame down as low as possible. Fine, it has stopped burning, however, it has also stopped cooking, so you slowly bring up the flame until cooking begins again. It is no longer burning, but until you brought up the flame, it was also no longer cooking the center.

That is using variable power. Whether a cook-top, or an oven, or a microwave, cooking takes place when the food can be brought to a certain

temperature. Too low, no cooking; too high, the food can be overdone on the outside before the inside can catch up—just as it was with our example.

Microwave ranges can have many power settings, or as few as one. The earliest microwave units had one power only: High (about 600–650 watts). Then came Defrost at about 50% (300–350 watts); later came Defrost at 30% (200–250 watts) when it was apparent that the lower wattage did a better job of defrosting.

Power levels will vary with the manufacturer. When looking at power levels, look for the High power and the lowest power on the unit—then see how many settings it offers. The power levels are usually divided into equal amounts. If High power is 600 watts, 70% would be 420 watts, 50% would be 300 watts, and so on.

Many manufacturers use the numbers 1–10 for power settings, 1 being the lowest wattage and 10 the highest. The number usually corresponds to the percentage of power, i.e., 1 would be 10% of power (60 watts on a 600 watt unit), and 5 would be 50% of power or 300 watts.

This is my system for understanding microwave power levels. It is really quite simple. It just looks complicated because it is making you think new. Don't be intimidated. If a salesman does not explain a unit well enough to make you understand it, he probably doesn't understand it himself! Find a salesman who is knowledgeable.

Also helpful is the spec sheet which describes the unit in detail.

Automatic Defrost

This option will vary with the manufacturer. Most defrost systems are set at either 30% or 50% of power. They will cycle on and off, giving microwave energy to the frozen food for a short time, then turning off to allow defrosting to begin, then another spurt of microwave energy.

Some systems have charts designed to provide a graduated input of microwave energy. They also have charts showing the proper program to use for each different food category. If defrosting is your favorite way of using your microwave, this is a good way to go.

Browning Element

I would like to avoid comment on this, because I really dislike the concept. The browning element is simply a "calrod" unit similar to ones used in toaster ovens;

however, the wattage is not enough to broil or brown quickly, so the food cools off before any real browning takes place. It also takes the joy out of cleaning the microwave, which does not have a heat source, and normally can be wiped off with a paper towel. When you bring a heat element in, you eliminate this feature. I could accept it if it made any real contribution, but it does not seem to in its present form.

People who want this feature should purchase microwave convection ovens and do it properly — or simply use the broiler or oven in their conventional stove, which does a better job.

Electric Requirements for the Microwave

Your regular household current source of 115–120 volts is all that is needed. You should use only a grounded 15–20 amp outlet. An adapter plug should be used only as a temporary measure; have an electrician place a grounded plug in permanently as soon as possible to avoid overheating the outlet. Keep in mind the microwave needs all of that circuit — it should not share the electricity. You can only use a toaster oven or other appliance on that circuit when the microwave is not on. It will blow your fuse to have the microwave on the same circuit as a refrigerator or other appliance that goes on and off sporadically.

Your household current is the input power into the microwave. The microwave system then converts to a "receiving set" which will use microwave wattage to cook.

Metal Rack

Most people ask why a metal rack is used in the microwave when they have been told they cannot use metal.

The answer is that metal *can* be used in the microwave when it is properly designed for a specific use. For example, racks are provided for whole meal cooking, to divide the space and allow you to place many items in at once; however, these racks do not interfere with the microwave energy needed to cook the food.

Meals that are worked out by test kitchens have been designed to work in unison. Unless you are aware of how much energy each food will absorb, you may not get the results you want. Remember, you are cooking by time. When you place a specific food in, you can judge the time for that food, but each time you add another food, you must add more time.

The entire meal concept, then, is to add up the times required by each food, and use that as the total cooking time. The important thing to know is when to add foods that may require just a small amount of time (like rolls or desserts), and where to place the food in the microwave so that the longest-cooking food will receive the most cooking energy. Usually, this is on the top shelf.

I find whole-meal cooking an interesting concept. It requires some effort on the part of the cook, but once understood, it can be helpful.

Glass Tray

Glass trays are expensive and are usually made of a tempered glass which can handle hot foods or browning dishes. Some even absorb microwave energy if you happen to make the mistake of running the microwave empty.

I find this to be a nice option. I like to have any spillovers go on a tray that I can remove to the sink to wash, rather than have the spillovers run out the microwave door. So my vote would be in favor of a removable tray.

HOW MICROWAVES WORK

Microwave energy is widely used in telephone relays, in CB radio transmissions, in radio, in TV, and also in medicine as the source of the deep-heat penetration therapy known as diathermy. Without the ability to transmit microwaves through the air there would be no space programs or satellite beaming of TV specials.

In radar, a microwave beam goes out into the sky — always in a straight line, since that is how microwaves travel, like a beam of light. If you could see the microwave beam, it might be comparable to a searchlight, which travels until it reaches an object that reflects the light. Because microwaves cannot penetrate metal, when a radar beam is sent to track aircraft, it bounces back to its source when it contacts the aircraft; that is how they know where the aircraft is.

It is this unique quality that led to development of a metal box to contain the microwave energy and use it to cook food: the microwave range.

The heart of the microwave is the magnetron tube (a vacuum tube). When plugged into a 115–120 volt household outlet, the household electricity is converted by the magnetron tube to microwave energy.

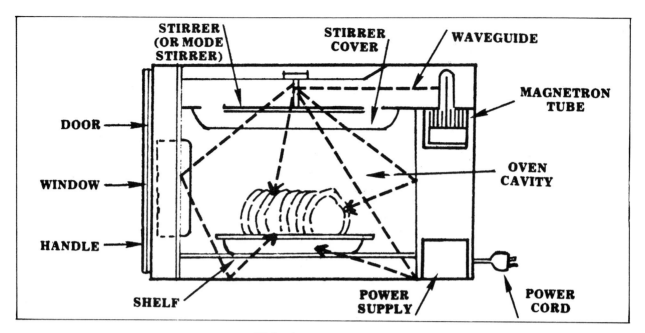

MICROWAVE RANGE

How Microwave Ranges Cook

Microwave energy is directed through a wave guide (a metal tube) to the entrance of the microwave cavity. Microwaves are fed to the food in one of two ways: They are either dispersed by a rotating stirrer fan or blade throughout the cavity, and penetrate the food from all sides, top and bottom; or they may be fed into the cavity in a straight line onto a rotating turntable that holds the food. Because the walls of the microwave cavity are metal, the microwaves are kept within and keep bouncing around until absorbed by the food.

Foods are cooked through the absorption of microwave power. The water molecules in the food tend to align themselves to the energy field—similar to placing a magnet on each side of a molecule, which would then try to stand up straight while the magnetic force is creating rotation.

Microwaves vibrate water molecules at the rate of 2,450 million times per second. This constant and rapid movement causes the food to cook from the outside in by conducting heat to the layers of food underneath, just as in conventional cooking.

One of the easiest ways to get children to understand this concept is to suggest that they rub the palms of their hands together as rapidly as possible. If you try this, in a short time your hands will begin to heat up. If you could continue as fast as the microwave, you could cook—it is only the vibration that creates the heat that cooks.

Microwave cooking has three basic principles that are important to understand:

1. *Absorption*. The moisture in food absorbs microwave energy and the rapid movement of the moisture in the molecules heats up the food and cooks it.
2. *Reflection*. Metal surfaces, such as the walls and the mesh inside the door, reflect microwave energy and do not absorb it.
3. *Transmission*. Glass, paper, ceramic, and microwave-safe plastic containers are transparent to microwave energy, thus allowing the waves to pass through to the food.

Because microwave energy generates heat only within the food itself, the surrounding walls and utensils do not absorb microwave energy and stay cool, leaving the interior of the cavity clean. A plate of food taken from the cavity can sometimes be quite hot, but this is only because the food on it has transmitted this heat to the plate. The microwaves themselves are not warm at all.

Operating the Microwave Empty: What Happens?

Operating the unit empty, we are told, might burn out the magnetron. In the absence of a load (such as food or a browning dish) to absorb the energy, the electric field tends to concentrate on anything else that might be there to absorb it, such as the glass tray in the microwave. Or this same energy might find its way to the magnetron tube. Even though the tube is constructed of metal and ceramic, it is not inconceivable that it might be damaged by protracted operation of an empty oven.

Microwave Frequencies

The FCC (Federal Communications Commission) controls the use of microwave systems. In order to keep all the frequencies from interfering with each other, the FCC assigns to each industry the frequency it may use. Otherwise, when you turn your microwave on, your TV or CB radio could begin to operate.

Two frequencies assigned to the microwave industry are 2450 MHz and 915 MHz. At present we see only the 2450 band being used, because it has a shorter wavelength and works best with smaller amounts of food. This frequency allows microwave penetration into the food to about 1½–2 inches. From that point it heats in layers toward the center by conduction, similar to conventional methods— except it happens much faster. A 2450 wavelength is about 4 inches long. The 915 MHz is about 12 inches long and penetrates the food to a much greater depth. If you had a ¼ pound of butter you were trying to melt, it might never find it!

Of course, the ideal system for mass feeding would be the use of both frequencies in a large cavity. This is being used at present. It is most successful when used for custom cuts of meat that can take advantage of its design.

Microwave Cooking vs. Other Methods

Other cooking methods currently being used include:
1. *Conduction.* Transfer of heat by contact, such as on a conventional cook-top. The burner is turned on; the hot metal burner or electric coil conducts heat to the pan, which in turn conducts heat to the food.
2. *Convection.* Transfer of heat by circulating heated air, such as in a conventional oven. The oven is turned on; the air in the oven heats and circulates around the cavity. The hot, dry circulating air then conducts heat to the food.
   Those ovens currrently referred to as *"convection ovens"* have added a fan to increase air circulation, providing faster and more even heating. Used in restaurants for

over 25 years, they were introduced into the home market in Europe several years ago as an energy-saving device.
3. *Radiation.* Conversion of radiant energy into heat energy. It is similar in nature to light traveling through space and converting back to heat when absorbed. The sun heating your back at the beach and the heating elements in the toaster toasting your bread are examples of radiant heating.

All of these methods of heat transfer have one thing in common: they heat the outer surface first, which then conducts the heat toward the inside.

In microwave heating we have a system completely different from conduction and convection. The microwaves are attracted directly to the food and have no affect on the surrounding environment.

For all of the above reasons, I have resisted the temptation to call this new cooking appliance an *oven*—in no way, shape, or form does it resemble any of the conventional oven systems. It gives the wrong connotation. For lack of a better term, I refer to it as a *range*.

The greatest advantage to a microwave range is, of course, speed. Since microwaves travel directly to the food, no time is lost in preheating a cavity. Another large plus is that no energy is wasted, since microwave ranges only use what is needed to cook.

If you have only one potato in the microwave range, all of the microwave energy is absorbed by the one potato, cooking it rapidly. However, if you have several potatoes in the range, the microwave energy is dispersed among the potatoes and cooks them more slowly. In both instances, *no energy is wasted*.

What's New?

Slow to get started, but a great new product, is the Microwave/Convection combination oven.

It is a regular oven, providing heat through a calrod unit that uses oven temperature settings—and it also has a microwave built in to the same cavity system. It can be used as a microwave range, as a convection oven, and—in the counter-top unit—will cycle on and off between the two systems to provide combination cooking.

For those with a limited amount of space, who long for conventional cooking but still want a microwave, the microwave/convection oven provides the best of both worlds.

Microwaves and Nutrition

The nutritive value of foods is determined to a large

extent by the system of cooking used. It is generally conceded that vitamins and other nutrients deteriorate with time and at elevated temperatures. Foods that are kept at steam tables for long periods of time suffer great losses in nutritive value.

More and more studies are available from such reliable sources as university research centers, confirming that vegetables cooked by microwaves retain more thiamine and ascorbic acid than by any other method tested. In microwave cooking, less water is required, the cooking action is contained within the food itself, and heating takes place in a short space of time—all bonuses for the consumer. A green vegetable cooked in the microwave has a wonderful texture and flavor, and still retains its bright green color.

I am convinced that those who do not enjoy vegetables have never tasted them properly cooked, with vitamins intact. They are almost as good as chocolate!

2

TIPS AND TECHNIQUES

Recipes by themselves do not teach us technique. A good cook begins in the classroom—so we have brought our classroom to you. Do read the many hints and reasons why you are asked to prepare recipes in a certain way. It is designed to give you insight—and expertise.

Although this section will deal with in-depth discussions of *how* and *why* we do things differently in the microwave, the recipes may repeat much of this information. But there is a reason for this repetition. After all, I can't be with you to discuss all of the variables as you cook, and if you are like many of us (myself included) the hardest thing to do is to read through all of this introductory material. However, as it has often been said, *When all else fails, read the instructions!* In thinking new, reading will help.

A NEW WAY TO UNDERSTAND MICROWAVE POWER LEVELS: COOKING WATTAGES

When a recipe that is to be cooked in a conventional oven calls for a power setting of 350°F., every conventional oven made (if it is accurately calibrated) is standardized to consistently heat to the same cooking temperature at this setting.

Unfortunately, we do not yet have this same standardization on power settings for the microwave range. A Consumer Appliance Section of the International Microwave Power Institute is working on this standardization, to be used by all microwave manufacturers. While they have agreed on a standard terminology—High is 100%, Medium High

about 70%, Medium about 50%, Medium Low about 30%, and Low about 10%—there is no standardization on the cooking wattages these power settings represent.

What is wrong is that not all microwave units have the same High wattage. For example, if you purchase a top-of-the-line microwave; the cooking wattage on High power is between 600–700 watts. On the other hand, smaller cavity units generally have a cooking wattage on High of about 400–500 watts. These units are becoming increasingly popular because their size permits them to go into smaller spaces—so that smaller cavity units are now also available with a High power cooking wattage of about 600 watts. It's no longer possible to assume the High power of a microwave by its size.

Power Levels to Guide You

If you would like to pioneer with me, I would like to give you a chart showing wattage settings compared to the common-use words like High and Medium and percentages of power such as 100% and 50%.

The purpose of this chart is to make it easy for you to take microwave recipes from magazines, cookbooks, and newspapers and use them on your microwave. I have also given you a second chart to help you find out what your cooking wattages are at each of your power settings.

This first chart is to identify the terminology now being used.

POWER LEVEL CONVERSION CHART

Possible Descriptive Term	Power Level	Wattage	Number Scale	Percentage of Power
Cook	High	600–700 watts	10	100%
Roast Bake	Medium High	400–500 watts	7	70%
	Medium	300–350 watts	5	50%
Simmer/Defrost	Medium Low	200–250 watts	3	30%
Warm/Low Defrost	Low	60–100 watts	1	10%

The microwave cooking charts will list a small cavity unit with a cooking wattage on High of 400 watts and a large cavity unit with a cooking wattage on High of 700 watts without taking the time to explain that High is not the same wattage on the two units. It makes no sense to me at all—and invalidates the charts.

Know Your Microwave Range

If you do not know the actual wattage for each of the power settings on your microwave, try the following:

- First, check your care and use manual, or the cookbook that came with your microwave.
- If this does not have the information, write to your manufacturer. What you should find out is: on High power (100%), what is the cooking wattage inside the cavity? (It can be anywhere from 400 watts to 700 watts.) On Medium High power (70%), what is the cooking wattage? (It can be anywhere from 300 watts to 500 watts.) And so on. Be sure to include the model number of your unit.
- If you can't get wattage information from the manufacturer, let me suggest a simple water test. Place an 8-ounce cup of cold tap water in a glass measuring cup inside your microwave range. Using High Power for the first test, watch and record how long it takes for the water to come to a rolling boil. Before repeating the test for each setting, allow the microwave cavity and glass cup to cool completely.

Follow the chart below to determine what your approximate wattages are at each setting:

To Determine Cooking Wattage at Each Microwave Power Level

If 8 ounces of water boil within this time:	Your cooking wattage is approximately:
2½–3 minutes	600–700 watts
3½–4 minutes	400–500 watts
4½–5½ minutes	300–350 watts
8½–10 minutes	200–250 watts
does not boil	60–100 watts

Since your tap water is not always the same, do not be concerned if there are slight variations in your tests. This is not a scientific test; it is just intended to give you approximate wattages.

Once you are aware of what each power setting on your microwave is in terms of cooking wattages, you can then cook by wattage numbers.

Should you discover that your Medium High, Medium, Medium Low, and Low cooking wattages are lower or higher than the one I have used in my testing, you can adjust by using slightly less time, or slightly more time. The difference 100 watts of cooking power makes is not too great—so do not worry if it is not exactly the same. The significant difference will be in the smaller units—and in the older models, which use 50% of power as Defrost instead of 30%, because that was all there was in the early days.

> *Please note:* All of the recipes in this book have been developed and tested using a High Power of 600–700 watts. If your range has a High Power of 400–500 watts, add 30 seconds to each minute of cooking time. If your range operates on a High power of 500–600 watts, add 15 seconds to each minute of cooking time.

It is very difficult for a major industry to reach out to the consumer with what appears to be, at first, highly technical information. But learning is an ongoing experience—it is fun, challenging, and easy, once you get the hang of it. And wattage numbers make it all sensible.

Perhaps with enough consumer support, wattages will become the common standard for power level settings on our microwave ranges.

WHAT THE MICROWAVE WON'T DO

Will we ever live to see the day when one appliance can do it all? Not yet—and probably never in my lifetime. And since this is always a popular question, perhaps we should discuss what the microwave cannot do.

What It Won't Do

- Flaky pastries, because a hot, dry environment is needed for the pastry to become crisp.
- Eggs cooked in the shell, because the tight membrane surrounding the yolk absorbs energy, which creates steam—and like a balloon, it can burst. (Quite a mess.)
- Deep-fat frying. Hot oil belongs on a cook-top, or in a proper utensil where it is stationary. It is not safe to move around, nor is it easy to work with inside the microwave cavity.

- Toasting, except for specific items like croutons.
- Home canning, because it is impossible to judge the temperature inside jars and there is no way to be certain you are preventing contamination, which you need to do for proper canning. Early microwave books contained canning information, but it has never been recommended by the industry.
- Angel food cakes and chiffon cakes, because they need a hot, dry environment for the honeycomb cells to dry out as they rise. In the microwave they rise, but no drying takes place—so they collapse.
- Heating bottles with small necks, like syrup bottles, because they do not allow enough steam to escape and pressure will build up.
- Large items, such as 20- to 25-pound turkeys. Microwave energy coming into cavity is too close to the bird and cannot cook it evenly.
- Pancakes and popovers do not do well in microwave, but reheat well.
- Popcorn *in a paper bag*. Dehydration of bag and dry corn may cause bag to catch fire. (However, popcorn *can* be cooked in the microwave; see index.)
- Paraffin will not melt in the microwave, since it does not contain moisture and microwaves pass through with no effect.

Other Nos

- Don't use egg cartons. The Egg Council has stated that since eggs are not washed before packing, they should be washed before using. Therefore, using an egg carton for cooking is not advised. It is not sanitary.
- Don't dry your wet newspaper in your microwave. The oil-based print may ignite, resulting in a fire.
- Don't use plastic wrap or baggies that are not marked *safe for microwave use*. They are not designed as containers for food products during heating.
- Don't use an inverted saucer to elevate foods like turkey or chicken, or whenever fat or steam could create a vacuum underneath the dish. The dish could be so difficult to remove, it could break.

UTENSILS

Nothing has grown so quickly as has the microwave accessory industry in the past 5 years. Some is welcome new equipment, indispensable for good microwave cookery, while some is really (if I may indulge for a moment) off the wall. But before shopping for any of this new equipment, you might check to see what you already have.

Most people can find good microwave utensils just by looking around their kitchen. It is remarkable how useful a dinner plate can be, both as a cooking utensil and as a cover. If you begin to think microwave, a whole new world will open up.

First, it is important to know how to test the dishes you already have, to discover what will work and what will not—and also what *not* to test, and why.

What Does *Microwave-Safe* Mean?

The words *microproof* and *microwave-safe* are used by the industry to indicate an item is safe for microwave use. Columnists and magazine articles giving microwave recipes, as well as most recipe books, use the terms to remind their readers to use proper utensils.

Since you should have a microwave care book that gives you all the necessary information on the care and use of your equipment, I have not used *microproof* or *microwave-safe* each time I have suggested a dish or utensil for cooking—I am assuming you will only use those dishes and utensils that are appropriate for microwave use.

How to Test Your Own Dishes for Microwave Use

To find out if a dish is microwave-safe, use this test. Put the dish in the microwave. Place a 1-cup glass measure filled with water next to the dish. Heat on High (600–700 watts) for 60 seconds. If the dish becomes hot, it is absorbing microwave energy and cannot be used. If it is only slightly warm, it is safe for reheating quick items. If it remains completely cool, it can be used for extended cooking.

There are several reasons why a dish can become warm during this test: It can have a metallic glaze which might heat up, or it can be a pottery with a glaze that has not had a high enough firing to prevent moisture absorption. Moisture from washing the dish or from the food can heat the dish and cause crazing in the dish or in the glaze. Dishes that absorb heat can become so hot that they will eventually break.

What Cannot Work in a Microwave

- *Metal pots and pans:* Because microwaves do not pass through metal, but are reflected, it is inefficient if not impossible to cook food in this type of cookware.
- *Dishes with metal trim, like gold, silver, or*

platinum: The trim will arc off the dish in a sizzling action that might pit the walls of the microwave.
- *Melamine and Centura-ware dishes:* These dishes have metalic materials in their construction which make them unacceptable for microwave use. They should not be used even for reheating.

Dish Shapes: What Shapes Work Best?

The ideal shape is round, oval, or doughnut-shaped. Sharp corners should be avoided. Because microwave energy passes from the outside in, the use of a round or oval dish permits even heating toward the center of the food. When a square pan is used, the corners are receiving energy on three sides, which may cause overheating of the corners before the inside of the food can catch up. The suggestion to cover the corners with foil has never appealed to me. I recommend a proper dish.

When a rectangle is used, the same problem occurs in the corners; it also means that much less energy reaches the center of the dish. If a rectangular dish is used, rearranging the food may be necessary so that the food will get equal amounts of cooking power. If an oval or round dish is used, rearranging may not be necessary.

The appearance of the cooked food and the cooking time can be affected by size and shape of the utensil. Too large a dish results in overcooked edges and an undercooked center; and the juices will run away from the food and absorb much of the microwave energy.

The doughnut shape is excellent because it allows the microwave energy to cook from the outside in and from the inside out. For best results, select a shape that resembles and fits the shape of the food without leaving too much extra dish space.

Cookware Materials

Materials suitable for microwave cookery must be transparent to microwaves in order for the microwaves to reach the food. Quite a few materials will perform well in the microwave; others present problems.

Porcelain

This is an important category for those who wish to cook and serve in the same dish, with perhaps a touch of elegance. It is attractive on the table, and is a sturdy material which will hold up well. It can also be used in a conventional oven.

Pottery

These are attractive to microwave users and can be useful, but should be given the microwave-safe test before using. Depending on the amount of firing the pottery has received, it can be an excellent addition to the microwave kitchen. High firing makes it more resistant to the heat of the food.

Glass

Always an important part of microwave cooking. You should not use expensive glass such as crystal, and certainly not a family treasure. But many glass items are essential, such as the 4- and 8-cup glass measuring cups. No microwave cook should be without them—see-through is a great advantage.

Clay

Used for slow cooking to retain moisture.

Paper

Paper products are invaluable. Many of the paper items we have used in the microwave were not appropriate for heating with food, but were so useful we used them anyway. I am happy to see more and more paper items are now being designed specifically for microwave use.

We shall very shortly see paper towels designed expressly to be used in the microwave. The importance of this cannot be underestimated. With the recycling of paper, it is possible for combustible materials to be part of the paper without our being aware of it. Until paper manufacturers can assure us the paper towels are safe for cooking in the microwave, we should avoid the use of recycled paper.

If a paper towel sticks to the food while cooking bacon, so that it is almost impossible to remove it, switch to another brand—the paper might contain nylon netting or other materials that melt when in contact with hot fat.

Styrofoam

Styrofoam, a rigid plastic foam made from polystyrene, will melt if the food inside is heated hot enough. My feeling is that unless a product is designed for microwave heating, you should not use it.

Styrofoam packaging used to display meats and fish is not microwavable and should not be used. Best to transfer to a plate.

Straw, Wood, and Shells

Utensils made of straw, wood, or shells are suitable for short warm-ups, but not for cooking. Wood and straw will become dry after long use. Wood or straw trays and bowls with a laquered surface are also unsuitable because they may crack or discolor.

Are TV Dinners in Metal Trays Safe to Use?

If your manufacturer says it is all right, you may use these for reheating or defrosting TV dinners. However, they are inefficient. Since the microwaves cannot penetrate metal, the only heating takes place from the top, which slows down the action. If enough food is on the plate, the microwaves are attracted to the food and will not be involved with the metal. However, if only a small amount of food is on the metal with much metal exposed, it can create a problem such as arcing in some microwave units.

Cook-In Pans

Because the frozen food industry needed packaging for both microwave and conventional ovens in a single design, ovenboard was developed. It is what you are seeing more and more instead of metal trays for frozen foods.

Ovenboard is a heavy pressed-paper product with a special polyester coating that goes from freezer to microwave to table. It can also be used in a conventional oven up to 425°F., which makes it an attractive product for frozen food manufacturers.

These ovenboard containers are now available in supermarkets all over the country for consumer purchase. I find them invaluable for home use. They come in sizes from a small tart pan to a large microwave cavity liner that I use for the Dog Biscuits recipe.

Used for cooking, storing, and reheating, you could cook forever in the microwave with ovenboard containers and *never wash a dish*!

Metal in the Microwave?

Now we are told we can place metal in the microwave: the difference is in the metal. The new material has the ability to absorb microwave energy as though it were a food load. Therefore, it is not going to react in the same way as our conventional metal pans.

Unwanted effects can still result from placing metal items into the oven under certain conditions. For example, if metal comes in contact with, or very close to, the wall (which is metal even though it may have a plastic coating), an arc from metal to wall is almost inevitable. Such an arc will tend to alert you because of the popping sound and because the arc flash will be visible through the window. On inspection, you will find the wall will have a slight mark where the arc took place. While this is an aesthetic defect and not a functional one, it is annoying. Any utensil made partially or totally of metal should be placed in the center of the microwave cavity, away from the walls and door.

As long as you use microwave-designed products, no problems will occur. We will be seeing more involvement with metal in the microwave in the future.

Metal Cookware

Metalware designed for microwave use is a fairly new addition to the microwave family of utensils. Designed for an entirely different purpose, this material shields the food from microwave energy and absorbs it. The food is then cooked by the heated metal, much the same as a waffle iron makes waffles. An entire line of these products has been designed for the express purpose of making available to the microwave cook foods that normally would not work in the microwave.

As I view this phenomenon, it appears to me that our future appliances will not require a plug, but will simply be placed into a microwave cavity, and the microwave will become the power source. I find it very exciting. This line features items like a steak maker, hard-boiled egg cooker, pizza crisper, and other interesting designs. It is not unlike the use of ferrite compounds in browning dishes, which create high temperatures for searing.

New Products

Many plastic companies are putting their research departments to work and designing new products for cooking, storing, and reheating for this emerging new giant: the microwave industry. They also appreciate feedback. If you discover a new item which appears to be a useful addition to your microwave kitchen, the manufacturer might enjoy a note from you explaining how you used it and any suggestions you might have for improvement. Consumer comments are always viewed with interest.

On the other hand, we should reject products that cannot be safely used with foods that we cook and consume. If a plastic material melts or deforms in any way through microwave use, it should not be used again, even for reheating. If you notice an odor from the material, it should not be used in the microwave. If plastics melt even slightly, it could mean it is releasing gasses that should not come in contact with our food.

Useful Utensils for the Microwave Cook

It is a new world of cooking utensils, and rather fun when you become innovative. Who would dream that a 4- or 8-cup glass measure could become the most useful cooking utensil in one's kitchen? Now these measures are probably their manufacturer's biggest seller.

Think of microwave dishes in terms of serving. Find the dish that is closest to the size of the contents of the recipe. Then it can go directly to the table; leftovers can be covered, placed in the refrigerator, then reheated in the same dish or right on the dinner plates. That, my fellow cooks, is *living*!

Depending on how you use your microwave, the following equipment might be of value.

• 1-, 2-, 4-, and 8-cup glass measures	All-purpose. For sauces, liquids, vegetables, soups, and candy making.
• All-purpose covers—large and small sizes	Reusable covers for dinner plates and other uses. Should also double as cooking utensils.
• Round Rack	For elevating foods. For baking potatoes and other vegetables in their skins. For bacon, steam puddings, tacos.
• 2-quart casserole with cover (round or oval)	To catch drippings from round rack and separate drippings from the food. For all-purpose cooking: rice, soups, vegetables, casseroles.
• Quiche dish—9″ size	For making quiches, vegetable dishes. For cooking poultry, fish, pies. All-purpose utensil.
• Au gratin dish—pick a size that will suit family needs	Whole chickens, large fish, turkey, whole meals.
• 8″ or 9″ pie plate with handle	Pies, eggs, vegetables, quiches. All-purpose utensil.
• 6-cup ring mold	Vegetable casseroles, meat loaf, quick breads, cakes.
• 10- or 12-cup ring mold	Cake baking.

Thermometers (Probes)

If your microwave does not come equipped with a probe, you may wish to invest in a portable instant-read microwave-designed thermometer. There are several on the market. They can be useful for determining the internal temperature of meat, poultry, casseroles, and candy (however, special microwave candy thermometers are available to go to the higher temperatures needed for candy making).

The thermometer—or probe, as it is called in the microwave—must be placed in the right spot in the food for a proper readout. If you are cooking a 5-pound roast that normally takes 7 minutes a pound for rare, it should be done in about 35 minutes. If the probe doesn't register close to done by that time, it was probably inserted in the wrong spot.

Your recipe guide book should give information on where the probe should be placed in different kinds of food. Here are some additional suggestions:

- Use probe to reheat casseroles to 150°F. by inserting probe into center of casserole and using Medium High (400–500 watts).
- Use probe to judge internal temperature of meat loaf and automatically turn it off at 160°F. Cook meat loaf on High (600–700 watts).
- Use probe to stop cooking on a roast that needs turning over by setting probe at 100°F., then resetting probe temperature to go to a final cooked temperature about 10 degrees below what you want it to be at a done stage. The internal temperature will continue to rise during standing time.
- Use probe to reheat coffee, tea, or soup to the internal temperature you prefer. Start with 120°F. and go up to 150°F.—test to find your favorite temperature. Stirring soup is important to equalize temperature of the liquid; it will be hotter on top.
- Set probe below 220°F. to turn off milk before it reaches boiling point (to avoid boiling over).
- Reheat baby food with probe. Perfect every time, regardless of type of food used.
- Reheat sandwich fillings to avoid overheating.
- Reheat roasts, hams, and turkeys, by using probe and lower power to bring it back to the internal temperature it was when it finished the original cooking.
- Note the internal temperature of finished casseroles and roasts either by checking in your cookbook or by placing a tape on the cooked food. Reheat by probe to that setting.

COVERING

In general, foods that are conventionally cooked covered should also be covered in the microwave. A cover promotes steaming, leaving foods moist and tender, and helps shorten the cooking time by sealing in heat. Main-dish casseroles, fresh or frozen vegetables, poultry, meat, and seafood are almost always cooked covered.

The exceptions would be roasts that are normally dry-roasted to a rare or medium-rare stage. To cover would promote steam, which would not produce the dry crusty exterior this type of roast requires. A paper towel would be more appropriate.

Plastic Covers

Designed for microwave use, plastic wrap and casserole covers (I am rather proud that I designed the first one) are the most frequently used covers, because they provide seals that assure fresh-tasting flavorful results without dehydration. Use them for steaming vegetables that do not require added moisture. Check the package to make sure the brand of plastic wrap is recommended for microwave use. If the plastic wrap stretches and melts into the food, I find this unacceptable—it may not be a material that is compatible with food.

Wax paper and parchment are ideal coverings for foods that do not require trapped steam to make them tender. They form a loose seal that prevents spattering. Parchment has long been a favorite in French cooking and I find it valuable for microwave. Use it for a tent when preparing poultry or seafood dishes for cooking or reheating.

Dinner Plates

Dinner plates can be used as covers for soufflé or other round cooking dishes. Saucers work well for cup or mug coverings or for small bowls. Just be sure the plates are not edged with bands of gold or silver, since microwave action will lift off the metal.

To test your dishes to see if they are microwave-safe, use the test on page 16.

Cooking Bags

Most useful when cooking less tender cuts of meat that need moist cooking. Be sure to discard the metal twist tie, then cut a 1-inch-wide strip from the open end of the bag to use as a tie (newer packages now include a plastic strip for microwave use). Tie loosely to allow some of the steam to escape, rather than punching holes into the bag which will make it impossible to turn the bag to baste the food without juices spilling out. Always place bag inside a shallow baking dish for ease of removing—the bag will get extremely hot.

For your information, the material used for cooking bags is nylon, and not the same as the plastic wrap used for covering. The material is more like the boilable bag made for cooking and sealing foods, designed for use in boiling water or the microwave. These cooking bags can also be safely used in a conventional oven; they do not melt.

White Paper Towels and Napkins

These are invaluable for absorbing spatters and keeping the microwave cavity clean. They do not retain heat or keep in steam, but they do absorb moisture trapped between the food and the floor of the unit. This ability to prevent sogginess makes them ideal for cooking bacon, reheating sandwiches, keeping bread surfaces dry, or as a covering for any food that contains enough moisture to be reheated without becoming dehydrated.

White is recommended because colors contain oil-based ingredients that could ignite if dried out enough. The colors are also not recommended for food contact.

Foil

Contrary to popular belief, foil can be used in the microwave as long as it does not come in contact with the walls of the unit. Lightweight foil is used for shielding rather than covering. When placed over thin or cooked areas of food, it directs microwave energy toward sections that require longer cooking. Foil is also useful for defrosting, it can be placed over thawed sections, allowing the remaining frozen portions to continue defrosting.

TIMING

Timing is probably the most important factor in microwave cooking. It will depend on many variables, including size and shape of food, moisture content, and density.

Some Basic Timing Tips to Remember

- When cooking meat, remember that bones conduct heat, so when a bone is on one side of the meat, that side will cook faster. Boneless cuts take less time and cook more evenly—but you need not be afraid to cook meat with bone in.

- The colder the food is, the longer it will take to cook. Have food at room temperature to speed up cooking action.
- Large amounts of food require a longer cooking time, since energy is dispersed throughout all the food rather than being focused on only one item.
- One distinct plus of microwave cooking in these energy-conscious times is that only the energy needed to cook the food is used. No energy is wasted in preheating, as is done in a conventional oven.
- Standing time is important. After removing food from the microwave, the internal heat of the food will allow it to finish cooking and will avoid the overcooking that toughens food.
- A temperature or sensing probe is a distinct asset. It reads the internal temperature of the food and prevents overcooking by automatically turning off the microwave when the preset temperature is reached. Because of this, there is no need to set a cooking time.

   Insert the probe at least one inch into thawed food (it could break if inserted into frozen food), positioning it as horizontally as possible regardless of the size or shape of the food. Make sure it is not touching plastic or paper, or the door, walls, or floor of the microwave. Probe handles can get hot during cooking, so use a pot holder if necessary. The probe is not recommended for use with a browning dish.

Some Common Internal Temperatures for Reheating Popular Foods

   Sandwiches: 110°F.
   Soups or beverages: 150°F.–160°F.
   Ice cream toppings or syrups: 120°F.–140°F.
   Hot chocolate: 130°F.–140°F.

Once timing is understood, you will be able to calculate just how long a dish should be precooked before it can be held to finish in a few hours, or frozen for use at a much later time. Precooking bacon is a good example. If you use bacon frequently, it's easy to precook it in large batches (a pound or more) in the microwave, then store it in the freezer for later use (see index for Perfect Bacon). Cooking bacon can be a good introduction to details of timing, texture, and advance preparation. Because bacon cooks so quickly and cleanup is minimal you will find it easy to experiment with many recipes.

REHEATING

Reheating dishes cooked ahead (or heating up leftovers) is one of the biggest advantages of the microwave. Quick, easy, and efficient, reheating carries an extra bonus: There is no loss of quality in taste or texture. Food tastes freshly cooked, not tired and warmed over as is frequently the case with conventional cooking. In fact, main-dish casseroles reheat very well, and at times even improve in flavor, especially if made ahead.

Have a day to yourself? Prepare several main dishes, freeze or refrigerate, and thanks to your microwave you'll be all set to accommodate spur-of-the-moment dinner guests or host an impromptu buffet.

There are a few basic techniques to assure even reheating and the freshly cooked flavor you are after.

- Number one is simply, *Don't overdo it*.
- As a general guideline to reheating, it takes about 2 minutes on High (600–700 watts) to reheat 1 cup of solid food.
- Starting temperature is important. Refrigerated foods will take longer than those at room temperature. If possible remove foods from refrigerator or freezer ahead of time and bring to room temperature.
- Moisture plays a role in timing. Some dishes, such as main-dish casseroles, vegetables, and rice, absorb all the liquid during the first cooking. Add two or three tablespoons of water, stock, or wine, or a pat or two of butter, before reheating. Moisture and fat attract energy, reheating foods more evenly.
- Monitoring the internal temperature of the food is most important. Microwave and cookware manufacturers are doing everything they can to help: Most new microwave systems come equipped with built-in sensing probes that read the temperature of the food, and when it is ready will automatically turn the power off. If you own an older unit, there are "instant read" microwave-safe thermometers that are very useful.
- Another way to avoid overcooking is to take full advantage of the variable cooking power of your appliances. Try *not* to reheat foods at 100% power (High 600–700 watts). Experiment with lower settings, such as 70% (Medium High, 400–500 watts), or 50% (Medium, 300–350 watts). On older models, use the Defrost setting (usually 50% or 30% [200–250 watts]; check the owner's manual). Although it may take a little longer, with microwave cooking it's only seconds or minutes—not hours—and the perfect results are worth it.

Microwave cooking may sometimes seem more like a beginning science class than a culinary art, but after a while it all becomes second nature. Be sure to check your owner's manual for specifics, but here are a few tips to aid in reheating some popular foods.

Meat and Poultry

To keep meat and poultry tender, do *not* reheat on High; lower settings will retain more moisture inside the food. Thin slices of meat will reheat more evenly and quickly than thick or irregular pieces. If there is a bit of leftover gravy or sauce to add to the thinly sliced meat, the meat will retain more flavor and moisture. Always arrange food with largest portions facing the outside of the dish, and the thinner portions toward the center. If possible, overlap thin pieces to make the food more even.

To reheat chops, fillets, or poultry parts, arrange in dishes just large enough to contain the food. Too large a dish allows the moisture to run away from the slices of meat and attract microwave energy, causing uneven heating.

Depending on the wattage of the oven, use 300–450 watts for reheating. Smaller ovens can use a lower wattage because the cavity is smaller, and therefore the microwave activity is faster.

If using a temperature probe for reheating, it can be set at 120°F. for rare roast beef, lamb, veal, or ham.

Main-Dish Casseroles

Always use a cover. If reheating a dish straight from the refrigerator, use Medium (300–350 watts). Room temperature foods can be reheated on Medium High (400–500 watts), but be careful if there is meat in the casserole. Stir through several times to promote even reheating. If it appears to be cooking unevenly, turn dish.

When using a probe for a casserole you can set it between 150°F. and 160°F. Or when you have completed cooking a casserole, note what the finished temperature is on your temperature probe, then reheat to that temperature. Simply insert your probe and set it on a lower control setting like Medium or Medium High, and the temperature you wish it to be when finished.

Stews

Use a baking dish just large enough to accommodate all ingredients. Too large a dish will allow food to spread out too much and microwaves will be absorbed by the run-away liquid, rather than the food itself. Using a baking dish or casserole with its own cover is an advantage for long cooking times, and will promote even reheating. Stirring occasionally will also promote even reheating.

Soups

Reheating soups in tureens or individual mugs is a matter of personal preference, but setting the temperature probe between 150°F. and 160°F. is a good general guide. Stir through at least once.

Vegetables

Sauced or creamed vegetables reheat especially well. Always use a cover. Stir through several times, if possible, just as you would on a cook-top. Use lower power to reheat to avoid overcooking a creamed base sauce. Use Medium High (400–500 watts), or Medium (300–350 watts). If using a temperature probe, set it between 150°F. and 160°F. Fresh vegetables will reheat beautifully at Medium.

Cakes, Pastry, Muffins, and Breads

The trickiest category of all—too much reheating can make the most tender baked goods as hard as a rock. Bread slices, rolls, and muffins take only 10–15 seconds on High if not frozen, 15–25 seconds if frozen. If possible, arrange on a microwave-safe rack, or set on a paper towel to absorb moisture. Sprinkled sugar on cake slices will attract microwave energy. Fruit and sugar-type fillings inside pastry will also heat quickly due to the sugar content, although the crust itself may remain relatively cool. It is important to be aware of this for two reasons—first to avoid overheating the crust, and second to avoid biting into a very hot center.

Small Servings

For the most convenience and very little cleanup, reheat leftovers directly on the serving dish or the dinner plates. For best results, follow a few hints that also usually apply to larger quantities of food:

- When reheating several foods on a plate, they should all be about the same starting temperature.
- Arrange the plate with thick or dense foods toward the outside rim and the more delicate foods at the center.
- To promote uniform heating, spoon casseroles or main dishes onto plates or bowls in a shallow, even layer.

- Cover to retain moisture.
- Use Medium High or Medium power for reheating to get uniform heating throughout. Food is ready when it transfers enough heat to the plate to warm it, and when some moisture is visible on the cover.

BROWNING

Browning is one of the most misunderstood techniques in microwave cookery. There are many simple ways to achieve a rich, brown color in foods cooked in the microwave. Here are the basics, along with a selection of products on the market to assist you—many available long before microwave came along.

Natural Browning

Some foods do brown easily in the microwave without any assist from the cook. Bacon is the best example, because of its high fat and sugar content. Small amounts of browning do take place when foods are cooked on High (600–700 watts) and the fat comes to the surface, caramelizes, and browns.

To achieve natural browning in roasts, remove as much fat as possible to allow the microwave energy to reach the meat, and the marbleized roast will begin to brown. When a layer of fat is permitted to remain, it attracts and absorbs all of the microwave energy, and by the time the roast is done, the fat content is still high. In conventional cooking, we need that layer of fat in order to keep the roast from drying out in the hot, dry environment of the oven. *But not in microwave!*

Chopped fresh mushrooms can be used to coat roasts or other large cuts of meat before cooking. The mushroom juices will impart color and flavor.

Commercial Products

Large foods, such as whole turkeys or roasts, have to be cooked at a lower power setting to ensure tenderness and even cooking. Since the cooking power is not high enough to produce a caramelizing effect, many commercial products—both in liquid and dry form—can be used to enhance the color. These also work particularly well with skinless poultry pieces and Cornish hens, which do not have enough fat to brown naturally. These commercial products can be applied before or during cooking, and for a richer flavor can be mixed with the drippings from the food being prepared. To thin down some of the liquids, you can use fat or butter—or sometimes, just water.

When using the natural juices, cook the food about halfway, then add 1–2 teaspoons of bottled browning sauce, soy sauce, or other browning liquid to the liquid in the baking dish and brush or baste over the food. Brush or baste the food several times during the remaining cooking time as well. If preparing poultry, be sure to dry it thoroughly before cooking.

There are also many dry seasoning mixes that can be used to promote browning, including some excellent products developed exclusively for microwave use. Dr. Ghazi Taki, a longtime pioneer in this field, developed a very popular line of products called Micro Shake Foods. Early in the pioneering days of microwave, this talented chemist made it possible for even a novice cook to prepare attractive meat and poultry with just a slight shake of the wrist.

Don't be afraid to experiment on your own. You can try dried herbs, which can be mixed together according to taste and rubbed into meat or poultry before cooking.

Here are some popular commercial products that can be used to promote the browning of meat, poultry, lamb, fish, pork, and hamburger.

- Microwave shake products
- Bottled browning sauce
- Soy or teriyaki sauce (to decrease salt, dilute with oil or melted, unsalted butter, and restrict amount of salt in recipe)
- Melted butter and paprika
- Worcestershire or steak sauce
- Taco seasoning mix
- All dry package mixes
- Dry onion soup mix (to decrease salt, mix with dehydrated onion flakes or minced, canned french-fried onion rings)
- Dry spaghetti sauce mix

Try these suggestions for foods other than meat, fish, or poultry:

- Mix bread crumbs—plain, toasted, or combined with Parmesan cheese—with melted butter and sprinkle over main-dish casseroles just after final stirring.
- Use fruit preserves, jelly, or a favorite glaze to enliven ham, or brush on poultry about halfway through cooking.
- Mix brown sugar, chopped nuts, raisins, and cinnamon and sprinkle over cakes, cupcakes, or breads before cooking to achieve a sweet, brown finish.

BROWNING DISHES

Designed especially for microwave use, these special dishes sear and brown foods in much the same way a skillet does in conventional cooking. Browning dishes have a special coating—a tin oxide—which is applied to the bottom of the dish that absorbs microwave energy in the same way the food does. When the browning dish is placed into the microwave, all energy is absorbed by the coating. The dish can have a maximum absorption of 500°F., depending on its size. Many browning dishes will have a slight yellow glow in the center when they reach their maximum absorption.

Browning dishes are available in a number of sizes, shapes, and designs. Some of the larger dishes have a well around the side to catch drippings and drain accumulated fat. Some even have ridges so the cooked food will look grilled.

Think about how you will use the dish before you make your selection. If you are absolutely against the use of fat, the design that has the well will appeal to you. When I used it for the first time, I was rather shocked to discover that when I placed olive oil and fresh garlic on the preheated grill to brown the garlic slightly before adding veal, the oil ran into the well, and left the garlic to burn—there was no way to keep any liquid in the center of that dish. However, it is great for hamburgers, because the drippings run down.

My students have enjoyed the use of a browning dish, and this book includes my most successful recipes. It is cleaner than using a frying pan, requires much less fat to cook the food, and is faster.

Here is an option, if you decide against purchasing a browning dish. You can sear your food on your cook-top, using a glass ceramic baking dish, then place it in the microwave to finish cooking. This would be similar to the browning dish technique, but you will need to use more fat to keep the pan from burning on the cook-top.

Browning dishes should always be preheated on High (600–700 watts). If you have a turntable-type microwave, you may need to place the dish at the edge of the turntable for preheating rather than the center, since less microwave energy hits the center in this type of microwave.

MICROWAVE BROWNING DISH PREHEAT CHART

Use the times specified below to preheat your empty browning dish (without cover) in your microwave. Then cook food according to recipe (see note below).

Food Group		Small Browning Dish (will hold 1 bread slice)	Medium Browning Dish (will hold 2 bread slices)	Large Browning Dish (will hold 4 bread slices)	Pizza Crisper Browning Dish
Meat	Fish Poultry Beef Veal Lamb	3–4 minutes	4–5 minutes	5–6 minutes	6–8 minutes
Breads	Grilled Sandwiches French Toast	3–4 minutes	4–5 minutes	5–6 minutes	6–8 minutes
Vegetables	Sautéed Stir-Fried	1–2 minutes	2–3 minutes	3–4 minutes	not recommended
Eggs	Omelette Scrambled Fried	1–2 minutes	2–3 minutes	3–4 minutes	not recommended
Convenience Foods	Waffles Pizza Fish Sticks	½–1½ minutes	1½–2½ minutes	3–4 minutes	4–7 minutes

Please note: Times shown are *preheat times* only; consult recipe for appropriate cooking times. Preheat times are approximate and are designed for ovens having a High power of 600–700 watts. Increase preheat times if your oven is of lower wattage. Use butter or oil as you would for conventional frying or sautéeing, after browning dish is preheated.

Preheating time will vary with the recipe: The browning dish should absorb the maximum amount of energy before cooking chops, hamburgers, and fish, but less energy is required for egg dishes and more delicate foods. Once the dish is preheated, simply add the food you want to cook, sear it by microwaving it briefly, turn it over, and if necessary continue cooking. There is no need to wipe out the dish and preheat it again after turning the food over, since it will be served seared side up.

Once the food is added, the microwave energy is attracted to the food and will no longer heat the dish, so the searing occurs only at the beginning.

For best results, do not remove the browning dish to add the food—it cools off too fast. A large brush with an extended handle (made specifically for the microwave) has been designed for spreading melted fat evenly in the dish before adding food, or for basting later if necessary.

Recommendation:

As an alternative to using the browning dish directly on a glass shelf, create a false shelf by inverting a glass ceramic cookware dish that is larger than the browning dish. (The inverted dish must be glass ceramic for maximum heat tolerance.) The browning dish is then placed on this false shelf. The cooking results are usually improved by elevating the browning dish in this way because the bottom receives more reflected microwaves from various angles.

TIME-SAVING TIPS FOR FOOD PREPARATION

There is one aspect of cooking upon which all cooks can agree: preparing dishes ahead—either partially or completely—is the world's biggest time-saver. Luckily for the microwave owner, advance preparation is one of the things this appliance does best. And the microwave is so versatile that even foods that have to be finished in a conventional oven can be partially cooked in a microwave and then held until it's time to finish them up.

Microwave cooking, either alone or in combination with conventional cook-top or oven cooking, reduces the time spent in the kitchen—but not at the expense of nutritious meals.

Time-Saving Tips

- To soften ice cream, heat in container on High (600–700 watts) for just a few seconds. Touch container for warm spots. Start with 30 seconds.
- To soften tortillas, wrap several at a time in a paper towel or cloth napkin and heat on High for a few seconds. For 12 tortillas, use about 45–60 seconds. Timing will depend on how fresh the tortillas are.

- To heat baby food in the jar, remove lid and heat on High 1 minute, stirring after 30 seconds.
- To soften an 8-ounce package of cream cheese, remove wrapper and place in dish. Heat on Low (65–200 watts) for 30–45 seconds or until soft.
- To melt ½ cup butter or margarine, remove wrapper, place on dish, and heat on High 45–60 seconds.
- To melt caramels or marshmallows, add liquid recommended in recipe and place in a bowl. Melt on High about 1 minute per cup.
- To make dry bread crumbs or croutons, cut bread slices into ½-inch cubes. Place on a paper plate. Heat on High about 1 minute per bread slice, or until dry to the touch. Stir once or twice during heating. If using for crumbs, crush in food processor or blender.
- To melt cheese on casseroles or hamburgers, heat on High just until you can see the cheese begin to bubble. Timing will depend upon the amount of cheese. Use about 1 minute per cup of shredded cheese—less cheese will take less time.
- To dissolve gelatin, combine 1 envelope unflavored gelatin and ½ cup water and allow to stand 1 minute. Stir. Heat on High about 45 seconds, stirring after 30 seconds.
- To make instant coffee or tea, heat water first, then stir in coffee granules or add tea bag. Timing depends upon your personal taste. If you prefer boiling liquid, it will take about 2–3 minutes on High (600–700 watts), depending upon the size of your cup. In a glass measure, 8 ounces will take between 2½–3 minutes.
- To freshen stale popcorn, heat on High in an uncovered bowl until crisp.
- To heat a wet compress or to make hot finger towels, place moist towels on plate, heat on High until steaming.
- To scald milk, heat uncovered on High 2½–3 minutes.
- To heat bread or rolls, place in napkin-lined wicker basket (without metal) and heat on High about 15 seconds per roll or slice of bread. Feel bread or rolls to avoid overheating. Start with a minimum of time.
- To heat nuts, place ½ cup on a shallow plate. Heat on High 2–3 minutes, stirring once. Or place nuts in a glass measure with 1 tablespoon butter and heat on High 2–3 minutes, stirring once or twice.
- To make bacon bits, cut bacon into pieces, place into a glass measure, cover with paper towel to avoid splatter, and cook on High about 45–60 seconds per slice of bacon. Remove crisp bacon bits with a slotted spoon and reserve bacon

drippings for another use. (Or reheat frozen crisp bacon prepared in Perfect Bacon recipe—see index.)

- Save leftover pancakes, freeze and reheat on Medium (300–350 watts) about 45 seconds per pancake.
- To reheat pancake syrup in bottle, remove metal cap and heat on High for about 45 seconds–1 minute for ½–1 cup.
- To get more juice from a lemon, heat on High 45 seconds. Pierce center with wooden skewer, squeeze what you need, and refrigerate until more is needed.
- To remove odors in the cavity, combine water and a slice of lemon or 1 teaspoon of vinegar, and bring to a boil. Let stand a few minutes until cooled slightly. Wipe interior with cloth dipped in water solution.
- Fresh coffee taste with leftover coffee? Refrigerate leftovers and reheat in your own coffee cup. Timing will depend on the size of your cup—about 1–2 minutes on High, depending also on your personal preference.
- Separate cold bacon slices by heating package on High for about 30 seconds.
- Toast sesame seeds by placing in small container and heating ½ cup on High for 2–3 minutes, stirring twice.
- Toast coconut by placing ½ cup in small container and heating on High for 1–2 minutes or until brown, stirring once or twice.
- To soften brown sugar, place 1 cup sugar in bowl with a slice of fresh bread. Cover and heat on High for 30 seconds–1 minute.
- To dry leftover parsley or fresh herbs, place about ½ cup leaves on paper plate. Heat on High for about 2–3 minutes, feeling frequently and stopping the moment they begin to feel dry and crumbly.
- To blanch nuts, place in measuring cup and cover with water. Heat on High until boiling; continue to boil for about 1 minute. Drain and rub nuts between paper towel to remove skins.

BABY FOOD

Making nutritious food for your baby is easy to do with a combination of your microwave and food processor or blender. Not only is it better for your baby, but can save you money, since you can prepare your baby's food right along with dinner.

Nutritionists say most baby foods should not have salt, sugar, or other seasonings. When you prepare vegetables or meat for the family, remove the baby's portion before adding seasonings. If you think about it, most foods that babies enjoy do not need enhancing—for example, a raw carrot or apple is delicious in its natural state.

Select foods for baby that have natural flavor. Wash and rinse the equipment and your hands thoroughly before making the baby food. Cook in a small oval or round casserole that just holds the food. The need for additional water will vary with the pot or the way the food is cut—in most cases water is not needed if the pot has a tight-fitting lid.

You may prepare just enough food for one serving, or freeze some for future meals. Keep in mind the best time to freeze is when the food is at its best: *fresh-frozen* means soon after the food is prepared. Put it directly into the freezer rather than in the refrigerator where the quality will deteriorate.

To freeze, place the baby food in ice cube trays. When the cubes are frozen, store in a plastic bag. They will keep for a month. When you need a serving, remove it a bit ahead of time to allow thawing, then heat the cube and it is ready for your baby.

HERBS AND SPICES

Imaginative use of seasoning alone can do much to add variety and life to everyday foods. Good seasoning acts subtly. Used properly, spices and herbs will enhance the natural flavor of food—not disguise it.

Here are some tried and proven seasoning tips categorized for you by type of dish and type of spice.

Beyond these, you will want to experiment on your own. Add your seasoning in small amounts, then taste before adding any more. Keep in mind, too, that ground spices are more pungent than the whole varieties. Whenever available, you may enjoy experimenting with fresh spices and herbs, which I have noticed are becoming more and more popular throughout the country. You can use more of a fresh variety because it is not as concentrated. The packaged and bottled spices and herbs make it possible to use seasonings year-round, when fresh seasonings cannot be obtained.

Some of my inventive friends and students have begun to grow pots of herbs in their kitchens. Visit your closest nursery and give your favorite herb a spot on your windowsill. Even if it is just a parsley plant, it is great fun and the fresh taste will spoil you forever.

Drying Herbs in the Microwave

To dry fresh herbs, place about ½ cup of fresh leaves on a paper plate. Heat on High (600–700 watts) for about 2–3 minutes, feeling leaves frequently and stopping the moment they feel dry and crumbly.

Store in a small covered jar.

3
APPETIZERS

Chicken Wings Parmesan
Chicken Wings Sabra
Taco Chicken
Crab Canapé
Seafarer Hors D'Oeuvre
Coquilles St. Jacques
Shrimp Cocktail
Shrimp Tree
Tuna Olé
Chicken Liver Pâté
Rumaki
Chopped Chicken Livers
Grebenes (Cracklings)
Chili Con Queso
Sombrero Party Dip
Nachos
Nacho Potato Rounds
Mexican Fondue
Mock Derma (Kishka)
Dilled Spinach Dip for Vegetables
Tex-Mex Meatballs
Cocktail Meatballs
Sausage-Stuffed Mushrooms
Mushrooms Florentine
Mushrooms Stuffed with
    Cheddar Cheese and Herbs
Shrimpy Mushrooms
Mushrooms Escargot
Mushroom Caviar

Use attractive porcelain, ceramic, or glass dishes for your appetizers that can go right from the microwave to the table. If you are not quite certain that your dish is microwave safe, there is an easy way to check (see page 16).

Select a plate that will just contain the recipe. Mushrooms tend to shrink while cooking and you may find yourself with more space on your platter than you intended. It is better to crowd the food slightly.

Arrange chilled or frozen appetizers ahead of time on 8- or 9-inch round or oval plates (rather than large platters) and let them come to room temperature before reheating to save time and energy. Using a smaller plate will ensure that the appetizers will be nice and hot as you serve, while another batch heats in the microwave.

Use heavy-duty paper plates for appetizers for a large crowd; it will simplify the cleanup afterward. After heating, garnish the plates with parsley, vegetables, or leaves from your garden, then place the dish on a silver tray —no one will suspect that the elegant presentation hides a humble paper plate.

CHICKEN WING APPETIZERS

If I were able to invite you to a microwave cooking class, you would be certain to see me prepare one of these recipes. Outside of the prime rib, there are few lessons as informative to the budding microwave cook as this.

Since 1968, I have incorporated this into the first class to show how much better a round dish, rather than a square or rectangle, works in the microwave. When we use a 9-inch round dish for 14 little wing sections, there is no need to turn the dish or rearrange the chicken. Even cooking is promoted by the proper placement of the food, and the final result is an easy dish to make for a large group of guests without turning on an oven and without sacrificing food quality.

When the children were young, chicken wing sections were a family favorite for a wholesome snack food. We would cut them up ourselves. Now, markets have caught on to the idea, and chicken wings are packed separately in the fresh poultry sections. If your market doesn't do this, you may wish to use my old system. When you purchase a whole chicken, cut the wings apart, rinse, and freeze in large plastic bags. Then as they accumulate, you can use them for an appetizer with the seasoned coating that appeals to your taste. For a lower calorie version use an egg white instead of butter.

CHICKEN WINGS PARMESAN
Makes 30 appetizers

There is an easy way to time these appetizers—1 minute per chicken section. If you use that system, it is simple to prepare whatever amount you need.

15 chicken wings
¼ cup butter or margarine
20 Ritz crackers
½ cup grated Parmesan cheese
1 tablespoon minced dried parsley
1 teaspoon garlic powder
¾ teaspoon paprika
⅛ teaspoon pepper

Cut off wing tips (these can be used later for chicken stock). Separate wings into two sections at the joint. Wash and pat dry with paper towels.

Melt butter in a flat round dish (a 9-inch pie plate, dinner plate, or quiche dish works well). Combine all remaining ingredients in processor or blender; blend to the consistency of a coating. Dip chicken pieces first in butter, then into coating. Arrange 15 pieces of chicken in spoke fashion, skin side up, with thicker portion of chicken toward outside of the plate. Cover loosely with paper towel to absorb any splatter.

Cook on High (600–700 watts) 15 minutes. Repeat with second group of 15 wings.

Note: This coating is also excellent for the entire chicken, using the same technique. Cook for 7 minutes per pound of chicken.

CHICKEN WINGS SABRA
Makes 14 appetizers

When I asked Bunny Dell, proprietor of The Look and Cook Store in New Jersey, if I could teach a class there on the new and innovative Sanyo microwave ranges, she was less than enthusiastic—her classic cooking background could not relate to this box that looked like a TV set.

Fortunately, her inherent good manners prevailed, and she allowed me to teach one class.

There is nothing like a convert—she has since made many wonderful contributions to microwave cooking. This recipe is one of her original ideas. She now teaches microwave classes regularly, and she has brought this new technology to her community in a beautiful fashion.

7 **chicken wings**
Honey
Soy sauce
Garlic, crushed

Cut off wing tips. Save the tips to use in chicken stock. Separate wings into two sections at the joint and arrange in a flat dish. Spread with honey, add soy to coat, and sprinkle generously with garlic.

Allow to marinate as long as time permits — overnight in the refrigerator or 15 minutes to one hour at room temperature.

Remove from marinade and arrange on a 9-inch round pie plate, thicker parts toward outside. Cook on High (600–700 watts) 14 minutes, brushing with marinade halfway through cooking time.

Note: I like to sprinkle the wings with sesame seeds before cooking; it is a nice touch you might like to try.

TACO CHICKEN
Makes 14 appetizers

This homemade seasoning can be used for a variety of Mexican-flavored dishes. It stores well in your cupboard in a closed container. Use it for all chicken parts, or as a coating for fish.

7 **chicken wings**
½ **cup butter, melted, or 1 egg white**

Taco Seasoning Mix

2 **cups corn flakes**
2 **teaspoons paprika**
2 **teaspoons chili powder**
1 **teaspoon salt**
1½ **teaspoons cumin**
1 **teaspoon onion powder**
½ **teaspoon garlic powder**
½ **teaspoon dried oregano**

Place all taco seasoning ingredients in food processor or blender. Blend into crumbs.

Cut chicken wings in half, trimming off tips (save for chicken soup stock). Dip each section in melted butter or egg white and coat with seasoning mix.

Place into round 8- or 9-inch pie plate or quiche dish in spoke fashion, with larger part of the chicken toward outside of dish.

Cook on High (600–700 watts) for 14 minutes (or 1 minute per chicken section, if you wish to cook just a few at a time).

CRAB CANAPÉ
Makes 24 appetizers

A crowd-pleaser every time. May be assembled ahead and refrigerated, but to avoid a soggy cracker, don't place mixture on cracker until ready to heat.

1 **6½-ounce can crab meat, drained**
½ **cup celery, finely minced**
4 **teaspoons sweet pickle relish**
2 **green onions, thinly sliced**
2 **teaspoons prepared mustard**
1 **teaspoon lemon juice**
½ **cup mayonnaise**
24 **crisp crackers**

Place crab in bowl and flake with fork. Stir in all ingredients but crackers; blend well. Crab mixture may be refrigerated at this time until ready to serve.

To serve, place 12 crackers on an 8- or 9-inch round plate. Place rounded teaspoonful of crab mixture on top of each cracker. Cook on Medium High (400-500 watts) for 45 seconds, just until heated through. Repeat with remaining 12.

SEAFARER HORS D'OEUVRE
Makes 40 appetizers

Your weight-conscious guests will adore you for providing a sliced vegetable instead of a cracker for this tasty dip.

4 **ounces cream cheese**
1 **6-ounce package frozen crab meat or shrimp, thawed and drained**
2 **tablespoons fresh lemon juice**
1 **tablespoon ranch-style dry salad dressing mix**
1 **tablespoon mayonnaise**
2 **medium zucchini, thinly sliced**
Paprika for garnish

Heat cheese in 1-quart bowl on High (600–700 watts) 30 seconds to 1 minute to soften. Add crab or shrimp, lemon juice, dressing mix, and mayonnaise and blend well.

Arrange zucchini slices in one layer on round 8- or 9-inch serving dish. Top each slice with a teaspoonful of crab or shrimp mixture. Sprinkle with paprika. Cook on High until zucchini is crisp-tender, about 1 to 2 minutes. Repeat with remaining slices. Serve warm or chilled.

COQUILLES ST. JACQUES
6 servings

A classic French appetizer made easy. Although it is listed here as an appetizer, we enjoy it as dinner for two with an assortment of fresh vegetables in a tossed green salad and a light oil and vinegar dressing. Add a crusty bread and fruit for dessert—you will have dined like a king.

2 shallots, finely minced
2 tablespoons (¼ stick) unsalted butter
1 pound Bay scallops
⅓ cup dry white wine
¼ teaspoon salt
⅛ teaspoon white pepper
2 tablespoons all-purpose flour
½ cup whipping cream
Minced fresh parsley
Lemon wedges for garnish

Place shallots and butter into a 9-inch quiche dish or an au gratin oval shallow baking dish. Cook on High (600–700 watts) until shallots are soft, about 2 minutes. Stir in scallops, wine, salt, and pepper. Cover lightly with waxed paper. Cook on Medium (300–500 watts) 6–7 minutes, stirring once or twice to move the center scallops to outside of dish and the outside scallops toward the center. Remove scallops with a slotted spoon; set aside covered. Whisk a few tablespoons scallop liquid into flour to prevent lumps. Whisk in remainder of scallop liquid. Transfer to 2-cup measure. Blend in cream. Cook on High 3 minutes or until thickened, without stirring, then stir through several times to blend and eliminate lumps.

Divide scallops evenly among individual shells or ramekins. Just before serving, spoon sauce over top (whisk sauce first if it has separated on standing). Sprinkle with minced fresh parsley and serve with lemon wedges.

SHRIMP COCKTAIL
Serves 2

A simple but elegant dining experience.

Like all seafood, shrimps are delicate and require just a touch of cooking to be ready to eat, so remove them from the microwave the moment they turn pink.

You may cook shrimp in the shell, but I have always preferred to clean out the sand vein before cooking so that the shrimp is washed, cleaned, and ready to eat when the cooking is completed.

½ **pound large shrimp (fresh or defrosted), cleaned and shelled**
Juice of ½ lemon
3 **tablespoons mayonnaise**
2 **tablespoons chili sauce**
1 **hard-cooked egg, grated**
1 **rib celery (tender inside rib), chopped fine**
2 **lemon wedges**
Touch of finely chopped parsley for garnish (optional)

To cook shrimp, arrange shrimp on a heavy-duty paper plate, or use two thin paper plates. (Moisture from the cooking shrimp makes the plate rather soft and a single thin plate might be difficult to remove from microwave.)

Place shrimp with larger part facing outside and the tails inside. Sprinkle with lemon juice. Cover with waxed paper or parchment. Cook on High (600–700 watts) for 1½–2 minutes, checking after 1½ minutes to remove any shrimp that have turned pink. Allow remaining shrimp to finish cooking. Refrigerate covered until ready to serve.

To prepare cocktail sauce, combine mayonnaise, chili sauce, grated egg, and chopped celery. Blend well. Reserve in a covered container in refrigerator until ready to serve.

To serve, divide shrimp between two stemware glasses or small dessert bowls. Place a leaf of lettuce in bottom, then add the shrimp and spoon sauce over top. Serve with a wedge of lemon and a touch of parsley on top.

Note: This is a thousand-island type of sauce. You may prefer to simply purchase the red cocktail sauce available at your supermarket.

SHRIMP TREE
Makes 1½-foot centerpiece—serves 15–20

This is an attractive Christmas holiday centerpiece and an easy way to prepare shrimp.

Remember that shrimp, like all seafood, requires a minimum of cooking—overcooking makes it tough. Remove each shrimp the moment it turns pink.

2 **pounds medium shrimp, peeled and deveined (leave tails intact)**
1 **1½-foot-high polystyrene cone**
2–3 **bunches curly endive or leafy lettuce**
Toothpicks

Cocktail Sauce

1½ **cups catsup**
2 **tablespoons horseradish (or to taste)**
1 **tablespoon fresh lemon juice**
1 **tablespoon Worcestershire sauce**
Dash hot pepper sauce

Arrange shrimp on paper plates with tail end toward center. Cook in batches on High (600–700 watts) until shrimp just turns pink, about 2 minutes per pound. Set aside. Repeat with remaining shrimp.

Combine all cocktail sauce ingredients in small serving bowl. Chill before serving.

To assemble tree: Starting at base of polystyrene cone, cover cone completely with overlapping leaves of endive, securing with toothpicks (cut toothpicks in half and push in firmly so they are completely hidden). Spear each shrimp with a toothpick. Again starting at base, attach shrimp to cone in continuous spiral. Decorate top with bow or other Christmas ornament. Place cocktail sauce alongside tree.

TUNA OLÉ

Makes 2½–3 cups dip

Nutritious, fun, and easy to prepare, Tuna Olé with its Tex-Mex flavor is a nice change for entertaining. Serve with crackers, corn chips, or fried corn tortilla strips. Dieting friends might appreciate zucchini rounds or other fresh vegetable slices instead of a cracker.

2 **tablespoons butter or margarine**
1 **medium onion, chopped**
3 **cloves garlic, minced**
2 **tablespoons flour**
1 **cup milk**
12 **ounces medium-sharp cheddar cheese, shredded**
1 **4-ounce can diced mild green chilies**

¼ **teaspoon liquid hot pepper sauce (like Tabasco)**
1 **6½- to 7-ounce can tuna, drained**

Place butter and onion in a 2-quart bowl. Cook on High (600–700 watts) for 4–5 minutes until well cooked, stirring once. Stir in garlic. Blend in flour and stir until dissolved. Add milk slowly. Continue to cook on High 3½–4 minutes, stirring once or twice, until thick. Gradually stir in cheese; stir until melted. Stir in chilies, hot pepper sauce, and tuna.

Serve warm or at room temperature. To reheat, use Medium (300–350 watts) to avoid overheating the cheese.

CHICKEN LIVER PÂTÉ

Makes about 1¾ cups

For that special occasion, this can be made ahead of time, placed into an attractive mold or bowl, and brought out of the refrigerator just before your guests arrive. Perfect recipe for your food processor as well.

½ **pound chicken livers, rinsed and well-drained**
3 **tablespoons butter**
2 **medium scallions, chopped fine**
2 **tablespoons brandy or liqueur**
Salt, pepper, and nutmeg to taste
Lettuce leaves
Touch of parsley or fresh vegetable for garnish

With a scissors, cut membranes away from livers and discard. Cut livers into pieces. Place livers and butter into a 1-quart glass measure. Cover with a lid or dish that is firm. Cook on Medium (300–350 watts) for 3 minutes. Stir in the scallions, cover, and continue to cook an additional 1–2 minutes, until just barely cooked. The livers should still be slightly pink; overcooking makes them hard to process as well as bitter. Set aside, covered, to cool slightly.

Using a food processor or blender, empty liver mixture into the container. Add liqueur and seasonings and process until smooth.

Press mixture into lightly oiled 1-cup mold or small bowl. Cover and refrigerate several hours. Just before serving, loosen pâté from mold with a small metal spatula. Invert on serving dish, lined with lettuce leaves. Garnish with a touch of parsley or a fresh vegetable.

RUMAKI
Makes about 36 appetizers

An updated old favorite.

½ **pound chicken livers, rinsed and drained**
¼ **cup soy sauce**
½ **teaspoon garlic powder**
18 **thin slices bacon, cut in half**
1 **8-ounce can sliced water chestnuts, drained**
Toothpicks

With a scissors, cut chicken livers into about 36 1-inch pieces. Discard membranes; set aside.

Combine soy sauce and garlic powder; blend well. Place 1 piece liver on 1 piece bacon, and top with 1 slice water chestnut. Roll up and fasten with toothpick. Dip in sauce. Repeat with remaining liver pieces. Place 18 rumaki in a circle on a round roasting rack. Cover with paper towel. Cook on High (600–700 watts) for 4 minutes. Turn rumaki over, cook 3 minutes or until bacon is crisp.

Repeat with remaining 18 rumaki.

CHOPPED CHICKEN LIVERS
Serves 6–8 plain, or 10–15 if served with crackers

This is the way it was before it was turned into a pâté. In the old tradition it was prepared with rendered chicken fat, and "grebenes," or crisp-skin cracklins, were added.

In my early cooking experiments, I discovered many problems with cooking chicken livers in the microwave. Like the membrane on eggs, livers have a tight covering which tends to build up steam inside. This steam forces its way out with explosive power, knocking off the cover and making quite a mess inside the range. The method of cooking used in this recipe eliminates this problem.

Although I have prepared this dish with chicken fat, you may substitute oil—the recipe will be delicious either way. It does make a difference if the onions are cooked separately. The livers have a "juice" of their own which could dilute the rich flavor of the livers and the sautéed onions. That is why the onions are always cooked separately, and why the livers are drained and the liquid from cooking them discarded.

1 **pound chicken livers**
4 **tablespoons rendered chicken fat or salad oil**

2 **small onions, diced**
1 **teaspoon salt**
¼ **teaspoon pepper**
Pinch garlic powder (optional)
2 **hard-cooked eggs**

Wash livers; drain well. With a scissors, cut away the membranes and cut livers into chunks. Place 2 tablespoons fat or oil into a 1-quart oval or round casserole; add the livers. Cover with lid. Cook on Medium (300–350 watts) for 3 minutes; stir to combine with drippings. Cover, continue to cook on Medium 3–4 minutes, or until livers are just barely cooked. They should still be slightly pink. Set aside, covered, to cool slightly.

In a 1-quart glass measure, place remaining fat or oil and onions. Cook on High (600–700 watts) until they begin to appear slightly brown, about 7–9 minutes, stirring once or twice.

With a slotted spoon, remove livers to either a food processor or blender. Add cooked onion with all remaining liquid, salt, pepper, and garlic powder. Process carefully until barely blended. Break up one hard-cooked egg and add to mixture; continue to blend until just barely smooth. Taste and adjust seasonings; remove and place in bowl. Cover and refrigerate until ready to serve. When serving, grate remaining egg over top.

Note: When I purchase a whole chicken I remove the liver, rinse it, and place it into a storage container in my freezer marked *livers.* When I have enough, I prepare a liver dish. They defrost quickly and can adapt to many types of quick-meal recipes as well as the liver pâté.

GREBENES (CRACKLINS) AND RENDERED CHICKEN OR GOOSE FAT
Makes ¼ cup grebenes and about ¾ cup fat

Grebenes are often enjoyed as a snack food by those not concerned with dieting. Children usually adore them. They can also be served on top of rye or egg bread, which is first covered lightly with chicken fat and sprinkled with salt—not very low calorie, but to some, "viva la calories!"

1 **cup pieces of chicken or goose fat and fatty skin**
2 **onions, chopped**

Wash fat and drain well. Place into a 1-quart heat-resistant glass measure. Cover with a heavy-duty paper plate or a glass heat-resistant cover. Cook on High (600–700 watts) until the fat is melted and the skin portions become crisp (about 10–12 minutes). Remove crisp skin (grebenes) with slotted spoon. Add onions and continue to cook until onions become slightly brown. Remove onions from fat and set aside.

These onions may be used for the Chopped Chicken Liver recipe in place of the ones listed in the recipe.

Fat should be allowed to cool slightly, then poured into a glass jar, covered, and kept in the refrigerator for future use.

If desired, grebenes may be processed into the Chicken Liver Pâté by adding them to the livers before processing.

CHILI CON QUESO (CHILI WITH CHEESE)
Makes about 3–4 cups dip

The green chili in this form is mild and is very popular in the west. Combined with cheese, it becomes a thick, delectable dip. If you have leftover dip, it can be used over cooked noodles.

1 **7-ounce can diced green chilies**
½ **pound shredded Monterey Jack cheese**
½ **pound shredded cheddar cheese**
1 **large, firm tomato, chopped fine and drained**
1 **small onion, chopped fine**
Tortilla chips and fresh vegetable sticks
White wine (optional)

Combine all ingredients except tortilla chips, fresh vegetable sticks, and wine in a 2-quart bowl. Heat on Medium High (400–500 watts) for 4–6 minutes, until cheese is melted. Stir to blend well.

For a large group, serve from a chafing dish. Surround dish with tortilla chips and fresh vegetables like celery, zucchini, and carrots.

If mixture becomes too thick, it may be thinned with a bit of white wine.

Note: Always reheat cheese on Medium power (300–350 watts) to avoid "cooking" the cheese—you just want it melted to eating temperature.

The heat level of chilies varies from mild to hot. The label on the can should inform you. All recipes in this book use the mild form. If you select the "hot" be prepared.

SOMBRERO PARTY DIP
Makes 5–6 cups dip

We felt deserted when old friends decided to move far away to Huntington Beach, California—that is, until we were invited to join them there on their boat, to watch the Christmas boat parade at Huntington Harbor. The yachts are dressed to the teeth; music pours from the boats and the lights and decorations are outstanding, since they are competing for awards.

As old friends do, each couple brought a "dish." When this dish was placed on the table, more turbulence took place at the table than in the water. It had been made from a recipe on a seasoning mix package; by reading the ingredient list and experimenting with amounts, this was my final result. Please feel free to make it your own by adding to or subtracting from the seasonings.

I also use it to fill taco shells, which I heat in the microwave—and it can be made into a tostada salad: place dip in the center of a bed of nacho chips and heat for a minute or two on High (600–700 watts). Sprinkle with cheese and add shredded lettuce, tomato, cucumbers, radishes, avocado, and green onions. Delicious!

1 **pound lean ground chuck (have butcher grind lean stew meat)**
1 **large onion, chopped**
1 **teaspoon garlic powder**
½ **teaspoon salt**
1 **tablespoon chili powder**
1 **teaspoon cumin**
1 **teaspoon oregano leaves, crushed**
½ **cup catsup**
3 **drops Tabasco sauce**
1 **24-ounce can red kidney beans, with liquid**
8 **ounces shredded cheddar cheese**
1 **2-ounce jar stuffed green olives, sliced**
4 **green onions, sliced thin, for garnish**
Taco or nacho-flavored chips for dipping

In a 2-quart casserole, cook beef and onion on High (600–700 watts) for 5 minutes, stirring once to keep meat crumbly. Add all seasonings, blend well.

Place beans and liquid into a food processor or blender, and mash. Add to beef. Cook on High, covered, 10 minutes, stirring after 5 minutes and when done. Sprinkle cheese over top, and garnish with olives and green onions. Serve immediately, surrounded by plenty of chips.

Note: Dish can be made ahead of time by leaving out cheese, olives, and green onions until after it is reheated.

NACHOS
Makes about 40 appetizers

Recipes for this popular treat have been published in many books and magazines. In case you have not tried this version, consider this: We could not make them fast enough for our children's party—in fact, the children ended up helping, and then took over completely.

It is a good, wholesome snack for children or adults—the beans are simply seasoned beans that have been mashed.

1 **5-ounce can tortilla chips (or similar round flavored cracker)**
1 **14-ounce can refried beans**
½ **cup shredded Monterey Jack cheese**
½ **cup shredded cheddar cheese**

Fill each cracker with beans. Sprinkle with cheese. Arrange about 10 crackers in a circle on round platter. Cook on High (600–700 watts) until cheese begins to melt, about 45 seconds. (Timing will depend on how many appetizers you heat at once.) Serve immediately.

Note: For variety, you can add a 4-ounce can of chopped green chilies. Sprinkle a few on top of the cheese before heating.

NACHO POTATO ROUNDS
Makes about 20 appetizers

Instead of a cracker, try a potato—a nice snack for adults and youngsters alike. Don't use the taco sauce unless you enjoy a "hot" flavor. Great fun for the vegetable crowd!

1 **large potato, washed; do not peel (choose one that is long and thin)**
2 **tablespoons taco sauce**
¾ **cup shredded cheddar cheese**
1 **4-ounce can green chilies, chopped**

Cut potato across the top into 20 circle slices as evenly as possible. Place half the slices in a circle in a round plate. Brush lightly with taco sauce. Cover; cook on High (600–700 watts) 5 minutes, or until the potatoes are just fork tender.

Sprinkle with cheese and chilies. Cook on High uncovered 2 minutes, or until the cheese is

completely melted. Allow to set a few minutes before serving. Repeat with remaining slices.

Note: This can be done all in one step without precooking the potato. However, we found in testing that the potato was sure to be cooked through by using the first method. You may wish to try both ways: Cook the first 10 circles covered for 5 minutes, add the cheese and chilies, and continue cooking for 2 minutes. Cook the second group uncovered with all ingredients placed on the potato rounds at once. Timing would be the same—about 7 minutes total.

MEXICAN FONDUE
Serves about 20

Use mild chilies, or hot, hot chilies, depending on your taste. For first-time tasters, you might like to try the green chilies. I adore them. They are mild, and add just the right touch for those of us who are not quite ready to go all the way.

¾ **pound cheddar cheese**
2 **7-ounce cans Acapulco hots or chopped mild green chilies**
Tabasco sauce, to taste
1 **loaf French bread, cubed, or 1 box nacho chips**

Cut cheese into 1-inch cubes. Combine cheese, chilies, and a touch of Tabasco in a 2-quart bowl. Heat on Medium (300–350 watts) for 5–7 minutes, or until cheese is melted.

May be transferred to a fondue pot over a burner, or served immediately to your guests.

MOCK DERMA (KISHKA)
Makes about 36 appetizers

A fun appetizer with a taste that will surprise your guests. Children will love it—a nice change of pace for after-school snacking. Easy to prepare in your food processor, and it freezes well. No need to defrost—by the time you have sliced the rolls, they will be just the right temperature for cooking.

1 **12-ounce box Ritz crackers or Tam-Tams**
2 **large ribs celery, cut into 1½-inch slices**

2 **large carrots, cut into 1½-inch pieces**
1 **medium onion, quartered**
1 **stick (¼ pound) butter or margarine, melted**
½ **teaspoon paprika**
½ **teaspoon garlic powder**
½ **teaspoon salt**
¼ **teaspoon pepper**

Use steel blade in food processor bowl. Pour entire box of crackers into bowl; process until fine crumbs are formed. Transfer crumbs to a large bowl. In same food processor bowl, use steel blade to finely chop celery, carrots, and onions (you may wish to do each vegetable separately).

Add chopped vegetables to crumbs. Stir in butter and seasonings and mix until well blended. Shape mixture into three 2″ x 6″ cylinders. Wrap in foil and freeze until firm.

To cook, remove cylinder from foil and slice into ½-inch rounds. Place 12 slices in a circle on a 9-inch round dish. Cook on High (600–700 watts) for 3–4 minutes or until heated through. Serve immediately.

DILLED SPINACH DIP FOR FRESH VEGETABLES
Makes about 3 cups dip

Although not a true microwave recipe, this is such a hit at parties that I felt I should include it. This recipe was given to me years ago by Shirley Hart, who has a natural talent for entertaining — she collects only the finest recipes, and then improves on them!

It is best when made the night before serving. It can also be used for leftover cooked vegetables, especially the crisp ones from your microwave.

1 **10-ounce package frozen chopped spinach**
1 **cup sour cream**
½ **cup mayonnaise**
½ **cup parsley, freshly minced**
½ **cup green onion, finely chopped (all of it)**
1 **teaspoon fine herbs**
½ **teaspoon dill weed**
Juice of ½ lemon
Salt and pepper to taste
Fresh vegetable sticks and slices, such as carrots, celery, cucumbers, radishes, tomatoes, zucchini, squashs, mushrooms

Place unopened package of frozen spinach on a plate to catch drippings. Defrost on High (600–700 watts) for 5 minutes. Allow spinach to remain in unopened package an additional 5 minutes to complete defrosting.

Drain spinach thoroughly; place in mixing bowl. Stir in sour cream, mayonnaise, parsley, onion, herbs, dill, lemon juice, salt, and pepper and blend well. Place in serving bowl or au gratin dish. Garnish with touch of fresh dill or parsley. Keep covered until ready to serve; serve with vegetable sticks and slices.

TEX-MEX MEATBALLS
Makes about 20–30 meatballs

This is a mild version of a Mexican dish, because the green chilies are not hot and it uses only a small amount of chili powder. It is a nice way to treat a meatball.

1 **pound lean ground beef**
1 **slice firm-textured bread, rinsed in water and squeezed dry**
1 **egg, lightly beaten**
¼ **cup fresh parsley, chopped**
¼ **cup onion, minced**
1 **clove garlic, minced**
1 **teaspoon salt**
⅛ **teaspoon freshly ground pepper**
1 **4-ounce can diced mild green chilies**

Sauce

1 **cup tomato puree**
¼ **cup onion, minced**
½ **teaspoon chili powder**
3 **tablespoons fresh cilantro or parsley, chopped**

Combine the beef, bread, egg, parsley, onion, garlic, salt, and pepper with half of the green chilies. Gently shape into small meatballs. Arrange in a circle on a round microwave-safe rack set in a shallow baking dish. Cook on High (600–700 watts) for 7 minutes.

Drain off the fat. Transfer the meatballs to a chafing dish or shallow serving dish and keep warm.

Combine the remaining chilies with the sauce ingredients in a large measuring cup. Cover and cook on High for 5 minutes. Spoon over meatballs. Sprinkle with chopped cilantro or parsley and serve immediately.

COCKTAIL MEATBALLS
Makes about 40–50 meatballs

This recipe has been around as long as I can remember. I find it easier to prepare in my microwave than conventionally—especially since we now have fondue pots designed for cooking in the microwave, that can then transfer to a holder with a heating system to keep your food warm at the table.

Meatballs

1 pound lean ground beef (preferably beef stew or chuck ground to order)
½ cup fresh bread crumbs
½ cup chopped onions
¼ cup catsup
1 egg
½ teaspoon salt
⅛ teaspoon pepper
Few drops Worcestershire sauce

Sauce

1 12-ounce bottle chili sauce
1 10-ounce jar grape jelly

Mix all meatball ingredients together, and shape into ½-inch balls. Arrange about 20 meatballs on a round rack which permits drainage (or place on a 9-inch plate with paper towels underneath).

Cook on High (600–700 watts) for 3 minutes. Turn meatballs over and continue to cook for 2–3 minutes, until meatballs are just cooked through. Continue as above with remaining meatballs. If splatter occurs, cover with paper towel.

To make sauce, place chili sauce and jelly into large glass measure; stir. Cover with paper towel or wax paper. Heat on High 6–7 minutes, stirring once, until mixture comes to a boil. Stir in meatballs until they are well coated. Continue to heat for about 1 minute until meatballs are heated through. Serve hot.

Meatballs may be frozen in the sauce. If time permits, remove from freezer several hours before serving to allow them to come to room temperature before reheating. Reheat on Medium (300–350 watts) and stir through several times to ensure even reheating.

SAUSAGE-STUFFED MUSHROOMS
Makes 24 appetizers

I used this fragrant and delicious stuffing as a filling for crescent dinner rolls in a microwave/convection cookbook. Since dinner rolls belong in a hot dry environment (not a microwave), I put the same filling into a mushroom—equally enjoyable, easy to prepare, and the ideal "holder" for appetizers. It is low in calories and does not need to be sautéed in fat, so it is easy to cook.

24 medium mushrooms
1 medium onion, chopped
1 teaspoon oil
½ pound lean sausage meat
2 tablespoons freshly chopped parsley
1 tablespoon catsup or tomato sauce
1 teaspoon lemon juice
Paprika

Gently rinse mushrooms, remove stems, and set aside.

Combine onion and oil in a 1-quart glass measure. Cook on High (600–700 watts) for 4–5 minutes, until onion is well cooked. Stir, then add crumbled sausage meat. Cook on High 5–7 minutes, stirring once or twice to keep meat crumbly. Drain off fat. Stir in parsley, catsup or tomato sauce, and lemon juice.

Divide mushrooms. Place 12 on a round or oval shallow plate. Fill centers with about 1 teaspoon of filling and sprinkle with paprika. Equally fill remaining mushrooms. Heat 12 at a time on High for 2–3 minutes, until filing is steaming hot.

Note: The mushrooms may be stuffed ahead of time, placed on a serving dish, and stored in the refrigerator until ready to heat and serve. Remember, if you have your appetizers at room temperature, the reheat time will be much faster.

STUFFED MUSHROOMS FLORENTINE
Makes 24 appetizers

At my son Paul's engagement party, the appetizer everyone clamored for was a fila pastry stuffed with feta cheese and spinach.

I wanted to share that taste with my students, and since I would never cook fila pastry in a microwave, I decided to use a mushroom cap instead. It is probably my best appetizer—and will be yours, I am sure. It is low in calories, because mushrooms do not need to be coated in butter to stay moist.

If I have a special dinner party, I try to find huge mushrooms, then fill them with this filling and use it for my vegetable. Great fun.

This recipe inspired one of my students to develop a unique way to have a few of these appetizers available at all times.

She rolls the filling as you would a miniature meat ball, and places the balls on a cookie sheet in the freezer until they are firm. She then transfers them to a plastic bag. As needed she removes a few, puts them inside mushrooms and by the time the mushrooms are cooked, the filling is hot!

24 large fresh mushrooms
1 10-ounce package frozen chopped spinach
4 ounces Greek feta cheese, crumbled
½ cup green onion, finely chopped (all of it)
½ cup fresh parsley, finely chopped
½ cup grated Parmesan cheese

Wipe mushrooms with moist paper towel. (To get the maximum flavor from a mushroom, they should not be soaked in water.) Remove caps (use stems for a salad or sauté for Mushrooms Escargot — see index. Place 12 mushroom caps in a 9-inch shallow round baking dish, quiche dish, or pie plate.

Place unopened package of frozen spinach in a dish. Defrost on High (600–700 watts) for 3 minutes. Allow spinach to remain in the box for an additional 5 minutes to soften. Then drain spinach well, removing all the moisture you can.

Place feta cheese in a bowl; crumble it with a firm fork until it resembles small beads. Add the drained spinach, onion, parsley, and Parmesan. (The cheese is crumbled first because once you add the other ingredients, it is difficult to break up the cheese.) Mix well and stuff mushroom caps, mounding high in the center. If some is left over, roll the mixture into small balls and freeze.

Cook 12 mushrooms on High for about 3 minutes, just until filling is beginning to steam. Serve immediately while you heat the second batch.

Note: Don't buy feta cheese in a can; it is not the Greek variety. Greek feta is dry goat's milk cheese. It is quite salty, and crumbles. It is also low in fat and calories.

Your book may tell you to use the Defrost setting on a 10-ounce package of frozen vegetables — but it takes forever. This makes no sense to me at all. Besides, you don't want to cook the spinach; you just want to defrost it enough so that it can be used in the mixture. (It is never necessary to puncture the box or open the side.)

MUSHROOMS STUFFED WITH CHEDDAR CHEESE AND HERBS
Makes 24 appetizers

The Los Angeles County Fair is, I am told, one of the largest in our country — if not the largest. The Home Arts Building, thanks to Coordinator Nadine Lawrey, has emerged as one of the highlights of the Fair and attracts thousands of people year after year. So you can imagine my delight when she agreed to include a microwave division in their annual cooking contest.

An optimist by nature, I was shocked to discover that after months of advertising, only 30 microwave entries had been mailed into the Pomona Fair Association. (Since this was 1975, I should not have been so surprised — after all, we were just beginning to learn about the microwave, let alone expect the consumer to be creative.)

However, this recipe was one of the winners — everyone loves the taste. I usually stuff the mushrooms ahead of time and place them on a paper plate. When ready to serve, I heat them and place the paper plate on a silver platter. I garnish to hide the paper plate, thus eliminating plate washing. If your help in the kitchen is you, try this for easy entertaining.

24 large mushrooms
2 green onions, finely chopped
⅓ cup fine, fresh bread crumbs
½ cup shredded cheddar cheese
½ teaspoon salt
¼ teaspoon pepper
½ teaspoon mixed Italian herbs, crumbled with
**   your fingers**
¼ teaspoon garlic powder
½ teaspoon Worcestershire sauce
¼ cup butter, melted
Dash Tabasco
Dash paprika

Wipe mushrooms with damp paper towel; remove stems. (Just move the stem back and forth — it pops right out of the mushroom cap.) Set caps aside. Chop stems fine.

Place all ingredients except mushroom caps and paprika in a bowl, and mix until well blended. Stuff the caps with mixture and sprinkle with paprika.

To heat, place 12 mushrooms on a 9-inch round plate. Cook on High (600–700 watts) for 2–3 minutes, until mushrooms feel slightly soft to the touch. Repeat with remaining mushrooms.

SHRIMPY MUSHROOMS
Makes 24 appetizers

When entertaining, the microwave can be the most useful tool in the kitchen. Most people adore mushrooms, and at the price of a box of crackers, you can enjoy the flavor of fresh mushrooms with an innovative filling.

I saw this prepared by a young girl at a recent seafood microwave contest. It was a winner—and is!

24 large mushrooms, stems removed
1 8-ounce package cream cheese, at room temperature
½ pound small-size shrimp
2 tablespoons freshly chopped parsley
1 teaspoon garlic salt
1 can french-fried onion rings
2 tablespoons butter, melted

Wipe mushrooms clean with a damp paper towel or mushroom brush. Combine cream cheese, shrimp, parsley, and garlic salt and stir until smooth.

Stuff mushroom caps with mixture. Top each mushroom with some onion rings (you may need to crumble them a little).

Place butter in a 9- or 10-inch shallow round platter. Melt on High (600–700 watts) for 1 minute. Place mushrooms in plate. Heat on High about 4 minutes, until mushrooms are heated through. Serve immediately.

Note: If entertaining a small group, you may wish to heat a few mushrooms at a time so that hot appetizers are available throughout the cocktail hour, rather than allowing them to become cold on a table. Timing will be less, and a smaller plate should be used for a more attractive presentation.

MUSHROOMS ESCARGOT
Makes about 40 appetizers

When dining with friends who adore escargots, I always have bread handy for dunking—I adore the sauce but can't handle the snails. Here is my version, sans snails, which I developed for the California Mushroom Growers' Association.

During an appearance at a TV studio in San Francisco before an audience of about 50, I attempted to serve just a few—but ended up with the entire audience demanding a taste. I was told that two months later the studio crew could still smell the garlic, and kept asking when I was coming back!

½ cup butter
3–4 large cloves garlic, finely chopped
1½ pounds whole small mushrooms
1 cup fresh parsley, finely chopped
1 cup grated Parmesan cheese

Melt the butter with the garlic on High (600–700 watts) and cook until the garlic is soft, about 1½–2 minutes. Stir in the mushrooms and continue stirring until they are well-coated. Cook on High for 3 minutes, or until slightly tender. Do not overcook.

Stir, add the parsley and Parmesan cheese. Cook on High for 1 minute. Stir and serve immediately.

Note: For best results, don't soak the mushrooms. Simply wipe them clean with a damp paper towel.

MUSHROOM CAVIAR
Makes about 1½ cups

We adapted this recipe from *Inside Your Food Processor Cookbook*. Combining food processor and microwave makes this a breeze to prepare.

Nice to serve with sesame crackers.

1 clove garlic
2 shallots
½ pound fresh mushrooms
3 tablespoons butter
1 tablespoon dry white wine
2 tablespoons sour cream
Salt and pepper to taste
2 tablespoons pignolia nuts, toasted

Using steel blade in your food processor, add garlic and shallots to work bowl. Process until minced and set aside.

Insert shredding disk. Load feed tube with mushrooms and shred, using medium pressure.

Place butter, garlic, shallots, and mushrooms in a 1-quart bowl. Sauté vegetables about 3 minutes on High (600–700 watts), stirring once. Add wine and continue to cook 45 seconds. Remove and set aside until cool.

Stir in sour cream and season to taste. If texture is too coarse, return to work bowl and pulse several times.

Place pignolia nuts in a 1-cup glass measure; put 1 teaspoon butter on top. Cook on High 1–2 minutes, stirring once, until nuts just begin to appear toasted. Do not overcook.

Mix toasted nuts into mushroom mixture. Serve cold.

4

SOUPS

Black Bean Hearty Soup
Broccoli Soup
Cream of Mushroom Soup
Cream of Potato Soup
French Onion Soup
Fresh Spinach Soup
Cauliflower Soup
Cioppino
Lentil Soup
Ham Hock and Lentil Soup
Manhattan Clam Chowder
Nice and Easy Split Pea Soup
Fresh Vegetable Soup with Meat
Oriental Soup Mix
Velvet Cream of Corn Soup
Chili Con Queso Soup
Short Rib Country Soup
   with Fresh Garden Vegetables
Old World Chicken in the Pot
Oyster Soup

Cooking soups in the microwave is becoming more popular with the advent of variable controls, which make it possible to slow down cooking, and to cook denser foods that need longer simmering to become tender.

It is also important to remember that when you are using a large amount of liquid, that very volume is slowing down the cooking process. That is why all soups are started on High power (600–700 watts) in the microwave. When you cook soup on a gas or electric cook-top, you start with a high flame or high setting, then cut down to a simmer setting when the liquid reaches boiling. You now do the same in the microwave.

Since microwave cooking does not dissipate the liquid as conventional methods do, it is seldom necessary to add more liquid as you do on a cook-top. If you should decide to convert a family recipe, try cooking for half the time of the original recipe, then increase your time as needed to finish the cooking. Cooking time will vary with the quantity of the ingredients and liquid.

The use of lower power settings helps to tenderize and bring moisture back into dried vegetables such as lentils and beans. It is also a good idea in dried lentil or bean recipes to allow a standing time, covered, of about 15–30 minutes after cooking to enhance the blend of flavors, and to give all the ingredients time to finish tenderizing and absorbing moisture.

When using dried beans that call for soaking overnight, simply bring the beans and liquid to a full boil in the microwave, then remove and set aside, covered, for 1 hour. You can then cook as the recipe specifies.

Because the liquid absorbs so much of the microwave energy, I add fresh vegetables from the beginning of the cooking time to make certain they are cooked through. If the vegetables are added near the end as in conventional methods, they stay too firm, since they do not get enough cooking action.

With the microwave, the best bonus of all for me is that I do not have to be there to constantly stir the beans to prevent them from burning on the bottom of the pot—and my cook-top is not full of splatter.

BLACK BEAN HEARTY SOUP
Serves 8–10

This soup is different in appearance, so be prepared for the finished product to be as black as the bean itself. Ethnic recipes can be found right on the bean package—you can adapt the seasonings by using the technique used in this recipe. Do not reduce the water if using the entire pound of beans. If you prefer a thick soup, after the soup is cooked you may place ¼ of the beans and some broth in a blender and puree the mixture, then return it to the soup and reheat for about 10 minutes. Even if the package recommends soaking beans overnight, by precooking for 15 minutes and allowing beans to soak for just 1 hour, you will get the same results.

1 **1-pound package black beans, washed**
7 **cups water**
1 **large onion, chopped**
3 **large cloves garlic, minced**
4 **teaspoons bouillon granules**
1 **cup dry white wine**
1 **cup sour cream**
Parsley (optional)

In a 5-quart casserole, combine beans and water. Cover with lid, not plastic wrap. Cook on High (600–700 watts) for 15 minutes. Set aside and allow to remain covered for at least one hour. Add onion, garlic, and soup granules. Cover and cook on High 10–15 minutes to bring the liquid to boil. Reduce setting to Medium Low (200–250 watts) and cook 90 minutes, or until beans are fork tender. Stir in wine. Taste and adjust seasonings. To serve, reheat on High, either entire pot or individual servings in bowls. Place a heaping mound of sour cream in the center of each bowl after heating. For a nice touch, place a sprig of parsley in the center of sour cream.

BROCCOLI SOUP
Serves 4–6

A low-calorie version of creamed soup. Any vegetable may be substituted.

3 **tablespoons butter or margarine**
1 **medium onion, chopped**
4 **cups hot chicken stock or bouillon**
1½ **pounds broccoli, stems peeled**
½ **cup low-fat milk**
1 **egg yolk**
½ **teaspoon salt**
⅛ **teaspoon white pepper**
Minced fresh parsley, or chopped green onion, or both, for garnish

Combine butter and onion in 3-quart casserole. Cover and cook on High (600–700 watts) 5 minutes, stirring once. Stir in heated stock.

Slice broccoli stems into rounds; cut florets into sections. Stir into stock. Cover and continue to cook on High 15 minutes, or until broccoli is fork tender.

Whisk milk and egg yolk in small bowl. Blend a bit of hot soup into milk mixture, then add it to the soup, blending well. Cover and continue cooking on High 2 minutes. Let stand covered 5 minutes. Taste and add salt and pepper as needed. (Always make certain the stock is not salty before adding more salt.)

Transfer soup to blender in batches and puree. Pour into casserole or tureen. Sprinkle with parsley or green onion and serve immediately.

Soup may be prepared ahead. To reheat, stir through several times, cover, and cook on Medium High (400–500 watts), stirring once or twice, until heated through.

CREAM OF MUSHROOM SOUP

Serves 6–8

A favorite traditional French recipe.

¼ **cup onion, finely chopped**
3 **tablespoons unsalted butter**
3 **tablespoons flour**
4 **cups boiling water mixed with 4 teaspoons concentrated chicken granules, or 4 cups chicken stock (preferably homemade) heated to boiling**
2 **pounds fresh mushrooms, stems finely minced, caps thinly sliced**
1 **teaspoon fresh lemon juice**
1 **bay leaf**
⅛ **teaspoon dried thyme**
½ **cup whipping cream**
2 **egg yolks**
1 **tablespoon dry white wine**
Minced fresh parsley or chervil for garnish

Combine onion and butter in 4-cup measure. Cover and cook on High (600–700 watts) 3 minutes. Stir in flour, blending well. Cook on High for 1 minute.

Combine hot chicken stock and mushroom stems in 2-quart bowl or casserole. Cover and cook on High 15 minutes, stirring once. Strain stock into bowl.

Place stems in processor or blender. Add 1 cup

stock and puree. Return to remaining stock, blending well.

Lightly butter large bowl. Add sliced mushroom caps and lemon juice. Cover and cook on High 3 minutes; stir and let stand 2 minutes; stir again. Add to soup with bay leaf and thyme. Cover and cook on High 9 minutes, stirring once halfway through cooking time.

Beat cream with egg yolks in small bowl. Add a little warm soup and blend well. Beat a little at a time into remaining soup, blending well. Stir in wine. Cook uncovered on Medium Low (200–250 watts) until just heated through; do not boil. Sprinkle with parsley or chervil and serve immediately.

CREAM OF POTATO SOUP

Serves 4

A delightful, light soup that will complement any meal. For lower calories, you can use milk instead of cream. In testing with low-fat milk as well as regular milk, the flavors remained intact, since the potato acts as a natural thickener.

1 **small potato (about 6 ounces)**
½ **onion**
1 **carrot**
1 **cup chicken stock, or 1 cup water plus 1 teaspoon chicken granules**
2 **cups chicken stock, or 2 cups water plus 2 teaspoons chicken granules**
1 **cup milk**
½ **teaspoon salt (if needed)**
Dash white pepper
Chopped parsley for garnish

Peel potato and cut potato, onion, and carrot into 1-inch cubes. Place in 2-quart casserole with 1 cup of chicken stock. Cover; cook on High (600–700 watts) 15 minutes or until vegetables are fork tender. Allow to cool covered.

Puree mixture in a blender or food processor. Pour back into 2-quart casserole. Add 2 cups chicken stock, cover, and cook on High 10 minutes. Stir in 1 cup milk, cover, and cook 4 minutes. Taste and adjust seasonings, adding salt and pepper as needed.

After serving, garnish each bowl with chopped parsley.

FRENCH ONION SOUP
Serves 6-8

This recipe is an adaptation of a Julia Childs recipe. The traditional thick onion soup requires long, slow cooking of the onions before adding the broth and wine. Using a microwave cuts down on time; eliminates the possibility of scorching; and reduces calories, because you use less butter.

4   pounds onions, thinly sliced
4   tablespoons unsalted butter
1   tablespoon vegetable oil
¼ teaspoon sugar
3   tablespoons flour
8   cups beef broth, homemade or canned—if using canned, use 3 cans soup plus 3 cans water
½ cup dry white wine
1½-2 cups freshly grated Parmesan cheese
1   cup freshly grated Swiss or Monterey Jack cheese

Garlic Toast

1   long loaf French bread
Oil
1   clove garlic, or 1 teaspoon garlic powder

In a 6-quart bowl combine onions, butter, and oil. Cover and cook on High (600-700 watts) for 10 minutes. Stir in sugar. Continue cooking on High for 20-30 minutes until onions begin to brown slightly. Sprinkle with flour and blend well. Cook on High for 1 minute.

Bring broth to a boil on cook-top. Add to onion mixture, and stir in wine. Cover and cook on High for about 10 minutes, until soup has thickened. Stir in ½ cup of Parmesan. Sprinkle with ½ cup Swiss or Monterey Jack cheese.

Cut bread into ½-inch thick rounds. Brush with oil and rub with cut clove of garlic or sprinkle with garlic powder. Place the rounds on a rack and cook on High until dried and lightly browned, 2-3 minutes.

There are two methods for serving the soup:
1. Float slices of garlic toast on top of the soup. Sprinkle with some of the remaining cheese (pass the rest separately). Place in the microwave and cook on High 1-2 minutes to melt the cheese.
2. Ladle the soup into individual bowls; float the toast rounds on the soup, cover with the remaining cheese, and cook on High for 1-2 minutes until the cheeses melt.

FRESH SPINACH SOUP
Serves 4

Quick to prepare when you take advantage of frozen chopped spinach. The original recipe uses cream, but in the interest of lower calories, I use milk. The flavor from the onion and chicken stock makes it rich in taste.

1   10-ounce package frozen chopped spinach; or 1 bunch fresh spinach, washed and chopped, with stems removed
1-1½ cups milk
1   cup chicken stock, or 1 cup water plus 1 teaspoon chicken granules
1   thin slice onion
3   tablespoons flour
Salt and pepper to taste
¼ cup chopped scallion

To prepare frozen spinach, place unopened box of spinach on a plate in microwave. Cook on High (600-700 watts) 3 minutes. Set aside in closed box an additional 5 minutes to complete defrosting.

To prepare fresh spinach, place in casserole, add ¼ cup water. Cover; cook on High 3-4 minutes, stirring once. Allow to cool covered. Use remaining liquid when blending spinach.

Place spinach, milk, chicken stock, onion slice, and flour into a blender. Puree several seconds. Pour into a 2-quart bowl. Cook covered on Medium (300-350 watts) 8-10 minutes, stirring once or twice. Taste and adjust seasonings.

Sprinkle each bowl with chopped scallion, and serve hot.

CAULIFLOWER SOUP
Serves 4

This is the original version of a soup I first used in a Sanyo tempura cooker. It is a most pleasing combination of flavors and is beautiful as a presentation.

Because everyone enjoys it, I have also included the creamed version, which I did for low-calorie classes. I used skimmed milk in the adaptation, but because the cauliflower was pureed, it tasted rich and creamy.

3 tablespoons butter
¼ cup all-purpose flour
⅛ teaspoon freshly grated nutmeg
4 cups chicken stock heated to boiling, or 4 cups
    boiling water mixed with 4 teaspoons
    concentrated chicken granules
1 large head cauliflower, broken into florets
¼ cup whipping cream, evaporated milk, or
    regular milk
1 egg yolk
1 sliced green onion for garnish
Minced fresh parsley for garnish (optional)

Melt butter in a 2-quart casserole. Stir in flour and nutmeg and mix until smooth. Blend in heated stock. Add cauliflower, cover, and cook on High (600–700 watts) until cauliflower is fork tender, about 12–15 minutes.

Beat cream and yolk in small bowl. Add a little hot soup and blend. Beat mixture a little at a time into soup, blending well. Sprinkle with green onion and serve immediately.

CREAMED CAULIFLOWER SOUP

The fashion of pureeing a cooked vegetable to thicken a soup base is known as *nouvelle cuisine*. The creamed version of cauliflower soup gives you the option of using that technique. If you substitute skim milk for the cream you may never be able to tell the difference. Reserve a few cauliflower florets to float on top of the soup when serving.

To prepare a creamy cauliflower soup, follow the instructions above through the first paragraph. Then set soup aside, covered, until slightly cool.

Puree in batches in blender, making certain you reserve some small florets. Return to bowl and reheat on High 2–3 minutes.

Whisk cream (or skim milk) and egg yolk in small bowl. Add a little warm soup and blend. Stir remaining mixture a little at a time into soup, blending well. Serve in individual bowls, garnished with small florets, onion, and parsley.

CIOPPINO

Serves 6

Legend has it that years ago in San Francisco, after the daily catch was sold, the fishermen would "chip in" any remaining fish and cook it together on the pier in a dish known as *cioppino*.

Some time ago, while waiting to be next on a cooking presentation at the Los Angeles County Fair, I first saw this magnificent recipe being prepared conventionally by Doris Robinson, Home Economist from the Department of Fish and Game. It seemed as though it would be so easy to do in the microwave.

By the next time Doris was scheduled to go on, she was making it in my microwave—and I had picked up a great recipe and a great friend. Isn't food a remarkable opener?

2 cloves garlic, finely chopped
1 large onion, finely chopped
¼ cup olive oil
3 cups hot water
1 28-ounce can peeled plum tomatoes, with
    liquid
2 8-ounce cans tomato sauce
1 3-ounce package dry spaghetti sauce mix
    (preferably extra rich and thick, Italian style)
¼ teaspoon freshly ground pepper
1 cup dry white wine
1½–2 pounds rockfish, sea bass, or cod, cut into
    chunks
12 sea scallops, halved if large
8–10 large shrimp, cleaned and deveined, tails
    left on
8 clams (optional)

Combine the garlic, onion, and oil in a 4-quart casserole. Cover and cook on High (600–700 watts) for 4 minutes. Add the water, tomatoes, tomato sauce, spaghetti sauce mix, and pepper; cover, and cook on High for about 10 minutes, until the mixture comes to a full boil.

Stir in the wine and add the fish, scallops, and shrimp. Cover and cook on High until the fish turns opaque, about 7–10 minutes. Do not overcook—the fish will continue to cook for several minutes after dish is removed from the oven. Let stand covered.

If using clams, place washed clams in a circle on a plate. Cook on High, watching constantly, and remove the clams the moment they open. Do not allow them to cook longer than a few minutes. Discard any that do not open. Add cooked clams to soup, and stir through, allowing them to float on top.

Other cooked seafood can be added, such as crab legs cut into chunks, or lobster chunks. These can also be stirred into the soup after the other fish have been cooked through.

LENTIL SOUP

Serves 4–6

If you have cravings for a hearty soup, rich in color and filled with wholesome nourishment, choose a soup with beans. Lentils, in the same food family as beans, are popular with people who enjoy grains. If the word *lentil* is still a mystery, buy a bag and try it—then experiment with flavorings until it is the way you like it. By itself, lentil soup is rather bland; it accepts seasonings quite well.

5 cups water
1 large onion, chopped
1 cup dried lentils, rinsed and drained
½ cup celery with leaves, chopped
1 large tomato, chopped (peeled if you wish)
1 clove garlic, minced
¼ teaspoon salt
¼ teaspoon pepper
Minced fresh parsley for garnish

Place water, onion, and lentils in a 4-quart casserole. Cover and cook on High (600–700 watts) 20 minutes. Remove and allow it to stand 20 minutes. Stir in all remaining ingredients but parsley. Continue cooking on High, covered, for 35 minutes. Remove cover; stir. Cook uncovered on High 10 minutes. Garnish with parsley and serve hot.

If not serving immediately, allow to remain covered until it cools, then refrigerate.

HAM HOCK AND LENTIL SOUP

Serves 8–10

This is a hearty soup, with a rich broth from the bones, lentils, and fresh vegetables. So easy to prepare and so filling. Serve with fresh crusty bread with butter, or perhaps with garlic butter and Parmesan cheese placed into the microwave and heated (see page 143). Freeze leftover soup in servings for one, right in the soup bowls. Great for that pick-me-up on a cool evening.

8 cups water
2½ pounds ham hocks, trimmed of fat
2 cups lentils, soaked overnight in water to cover, and drained
4 carrots, thinly sliced

4 celery stalks, thinly sliced
1 large onion, chopped
3 tablespoons chopped fresh parsley
1 teaspoon dried basil, crumbled, or 3 tablespoons fresh basil, chopped
1 bay leaf
Salt and freshly ground pepper

Combine all ingredients except salt and pepper in large bowl or baking dish. Cover and cook on High (600–700 watts) until lentils are tender, about 1½ hours. Remove ham hocks. Shred meat, return to soup, and stir through. Season to taste with salt and pepper. Serve hot.

Note: After washing and sorting lentils, they may be placed in 5-quart casserole with 8 cups water. Cover. Cook on High for 25 minutes. Set aside covered for 1 hour. Then continue with recipe. This will eliminate the need for overnight soaking.

MANHATTAN CLAM CHOWDER

Serves 4–6

You may use fresh clams if you wish, but I find the flavor of the canned variety quite good. If you enjoy this type of clam chowder, the results should please you. The clams are added toward the end of the cooking time to avoid overheating them.

2 medium potatoes, pared and diced
1 16-ounce can whole tomatoes, with liquid
1 cup water
¼ cup chopped onion
2 tablespoons flour
½ teaspoon thyme
Salt and pepper to taste (amount depends on saltiness of clams)
1 10-ounce can whole baby clams, with juice

In a 2-quart casserole, place potatoes, tomatoes with liquid, water, and onion. Cover; cook on High (600–700 watts) for 15–20 minutes, stirring once or twice, until potatoes are fork tender. Blend flour and seasonings with ¼ cup of hot liquid from casserole. Add to casserole; blend well. Stir in clams and clam juice. Cover; cook on High just until chowder comes to a boil, about 4–5 minutes.

To reheat, use Medium power (300–350 watts).

NICE AND EASY SPLIT PEA SOUP

Serves 4–6

The can of soup is your flavor base. By adding fresh vegetables, you can create a soup to complement any meal. You can use this technique with the soup base of your choice.

It's great for that emergency dinner, or when you eat out of the cupboard.

Serve with crusty French bread.

1 tablespoon butter
½ cup chopped celery, with leaves
2 11½-ounce cans condensed green pea soup, undiluted
2 cups water
1 cup grated carrots
1 bay leaf
Salt and pepper to taste

Combine butter and celery in a 2-quart bowl. Cook on High (600–700 watts) for about 2 minutes, until celery is slightly soft. Stir in the remaining ingredients. Cover and cook on Medium High (400–500 watts) 10 minutes or until the carrots are tender. Stir once or twice during cooking. Taste and add salt and pepper if needed.

FRESH VEGETABLE SOUP WITH MEAT

Serves 6–8

Debbie Krieger is a protégé of mine who combines her artistic skills with her talent for teaching and cooking. She is in the unique position of having her husband Bernie, an engineer who specializes in advanced microwave technology, as her own personal research scientist.

Bernie early recognized the need for quality instruction to consumers on microwave technology—and Debbie used her teaching skills to help fill this need. It was exciting for me to be asked by Debbie to work with her. Debbie is enjoying pioneering in microwave cooking with consumers in the East, and I think Stamford, Connecticut is fortunate to have her.

I asked Debbie to send me a favorite recipe of her students' to share with you.

1 small head cauliflower, coarsely chopped
2 medium red peppers, coarsely chopped
2 medium green peppers, coarsely chopped
3 medium yellow squash, coarsely chopped
3 medium leeks, coarsely chopped
4 cups chicken broth
3 medium tomatoes, quartered
¼ pound small mushrooms, thinly sliced
½ teaspoon salt
¼ teaspoon freshly ground pepper
2 teaspoons fines herbes (a combination of parsley, chervil, chives, and tarragon)
1½ cups cooked meat, finely chopped (chicken, turkey, lamb, beef, or pork)
Freshly grated Parmesan cheese (optional)

In a 4-quart covered casserole, combine cauliflower, red and green peppers, squash, leeks, and ½ cup broth. Cook on High (600–700 watts) 15–18 minutes until vegetables are tender. Add tomatoes. Cook on High 3 minutes.

Puree vegetables in two batches in food processor. Pour into large bowl.

Return pureed vegetables to casserole. Add mushrooms, the rest of the broth, salt, pepper, fines herbes, and cooked meat. Stir well. Cook on High 7–10 minutes until piping hot.

When serving, sprinkle with freshly grated Parmesan cheese.

ORIENTAL SOUP MIX

Makes 4 small servings or 2 large adult servings

A can of soup plus frozen vegetables can make a delicious snack or meal; you can use the idea in a variety of ways. Look in the freezer section of the market for these new and interesting combinations of vegetables. Some have seasoning packs to go with the vegetables, or you can use frozen vegetables without the seasoning pack and add your own. Remember, you will have the seasoning flavors that are in the can of soup as well.

1 10¾-ounce can chicken with rice soup
1 10-ounce package frozen stir-fry vegetables with seasoning pack
1 can water

Place all ingredients in a 4-cup bowl. Cover. Cook on High (600–700 watts) for 8–10 minutes until it is just the right serving temperature. For more even cooking, stir it once after 5 minutes, just as you would stir soup you were heating on a cook-top.

VELVET CREAM OF CORN SOUP
Serves 4

Some years ago while visiting Hong Kong, we were adopted by a charming young Chinese who insisted on taking us to a place to eat not frequented by tourists. We were the only Occidentals there. It was an experience: no menus—we just chose whatever appealed to us from carts that were brought to our table.

The food was outstanding. One of my favorites was a corn soup, which was thick and creamy. I became so interested in it that our friend left the table and came back with the head chef. He insisted on showing me his kitchen and led me right to the soup pot!

With the help of my interpreter, I wrote down some ingredients. After several tries, I arrived at this combination. I hope all of you corn soup lovers will find this a wonderful addition to your winter menus.

1   10¾-ounce can chicken broth
⅔ cup water
1   17-ounce can cream-style corn, undrained
1   tablespoon cornstarch
2   tablespoons water
2   eggs
1   green onion, finely sliced

Combine broth, water, and cream-style corn in a 2-quart casserole. Cover. Cook on High (600–700 watts) 10 minutes. Dissolve cornstarch in the 2 tablespoons water; stir until smooth. Stir into soup and blend well.

Cook uncovered on High 5 minutes. Beat eggs lightly with a fork. Add to hot soup in thin stream, stirring briskly.

Serve immediately. Garnish each bowl with green onion.

CHILI CON QUESO SOUP (CHILI WITH CHEESE SOUP)
Serves 4–6

A thick robust soup, colorful and mild in flavor—almost a meal in itself. It will please those who already enjoy Tex-Mex seasoning; or make a good

introduction to Mexican cooking. Serve it with tacos and fresh fruit.

2   tablespoons butter
1   large onion, minced
1   28-ounce can peeled tomatoes, with liquid
1   4-ounce can diced green mild chilies
1   2-ounce jar diced pimientos
½ pound Monterey Jack cheese, shredded
½ pound cheddar cheese, shredded
Salt and freshly ground pepper to taste
Cilantro or parsley for garnish

Combine butter and onion in a 2-quart casserole. Cook on High (600–700 watts) for 7 minutes, stirring once. With a scissors, snip the tomatoes into pieces. Add tomatoes with liquid, chilies, and pimientos; blend well. Cover; continue to cook on High until soup comes to a full boil (about 9–10 minutes).

Stir in cheeses; continue to cook uncovered on High until cheeses are melted, about 1 minute. Taste, and add salt and pepper to taste.

Serve hot with a sprinkle of cilantro or parsley.

Note: To reheat soup, use Medium power (300–350 watts) to avoid cooking cheese.

SHORT RIB COUNTRY SOUP WITH FRESH GARDEN VEGETABLES
Serves 6

Many wonderful recipes originated with peasants in farm communities or cold climates, where men came home after putting in many hours at hard labor. Now these recipes are seldom used—probably because the need for stick-to-the-ribs meat and vegetables does not apply to the lifestyle of many of us.

However, this is a healthy way to enjoy meat and potatoes in a fat-free broth filled with a nutritious blend of flavors. I always prepare this to leave at home for my family when traveling. All it needs is a touch of horseradish on the side and fresh fruit for dessert—it has it all. It also freezes well.

I like to prepare it the day before serving, so that all the fat will rise to the top and harden. It can easily be removed with a spoon and discarded.

It is also important to select the right beef. This calls for short ribs (also known as cross ribs). These are tender enough to barbecue. If you select English cut or Boston cut they are not quite as tender, and may require about 30 minutes longer cooking time.

1–1½ **pounds beef short ribs**
1 **6-ounce package dry vegetable soup mix with mushrooms**
1 **teaspoon salt**
⅛ **teaspoon pepper**
1 **teaspoon basil, crumbled**
4 **small potatoes, peeled and cut into chunks**
3 **slender carrots, peeled and cut into chunks**
1 **small onion, diced**
1 **medium parsnip, peeled and cut into chunks**
2 **slender celery stalks, cut into chunks, plus celery leaves**
1 **bay leaf**
8 **cups boiling water**
Chopped fresh parsley for garnish

Trim all visible fat from short ribs. You won't be able to get between the bones, but do not worry; this will be skimmed off the top after cooking. Rinse ribs under hot running water and drain.

Combine all ingredients except parsley in a 5-quart casserole. Cover. Cook on High (600–700 watts) for 20 minutes. Stir ingredients. Continue cooking on Medium (300–350 watts) for 60 minutes.

Check ribs with a fork to see if tender. If not, continue to cook on Medium an additional 30 minutes, or until ribs and soup ingredients are fork tender. To heighten flavor and make meat more tender, allow to stand covered 30 minutes after cooking.

Discard bay leaf before serving. Sprinkle with freshly chopped parsley.

OLD WORLD CHICKEN IN THE POT (SOUP)
Serves 4–6

You do not often see this soup on menus, yet I still find it a favorite of many people. When served in a restaurant, it is customarily brought to the table in a small pot with serving spoon. The pot usually contains whole pieces of succulent chicken, carrots, celery, and parsnip—a touch of home for many.

It never would have occurred to me to adapt this recipe (which takes the same amount of time on a cook-top), if I had not been asked by a young student with a new baby, "How does one make chicken soup?" She had never seen it done and felt she wanted her baby to taste the fresh flavor she had enjoyed as a child.

The recipe works beautifully in the microwave. Since there is little evaporation of moisture, it is seldom necessary to add liquid, which makes the soup extremely rich in flavor. Even if you do not care for boiled chicken, this recipe makes a delicious chicken soup, and also provides chicken stock that can be frozen and used later in other recipes. The boiled chicken makes excellent sandwiches, or can be used for chicken salad or in a variety of Oriental recipes.

1 **4- to 5-pound frying or roasting chicken (*not* a stewing hen), disjointed**
Giblets from chicken (not liver or kidney)
4 **slender carrots, cut diagonally into 3 sections**
3 **celery stalks, with tops cut diagonally into 3 sections (separate tops from stalks)**
1 **large parsnip, cut in half, then into 3 pieces each half**
1 **medium size onion, left whole**
1 **teaspoon salt**
⅛ **teaspoon white pepper**
6 **cups water**
Fresh chopped parsley for garnish

Pour boiling water over chicken and clean well. Rinse with hot water.

Place chicken and giblets into a 5-quart casserole. Add remaining ingredients, except celery tops and parsley. Cover chicken with about 5 cups water, making sure water completely covers the ingredients. Place celery tops on top. Cover; cook on High (600–700 watts) 1 hour. Let rest 15 minutes. Remove celery tops and onion. You may strain the broth if you wish.

Garnish with parsley when served. Accompany the chicken with crackers, catsup, and horseradish to add a bit of flavor. Use Chopped Chicken Livers as an appetizer, and add a light dessert such as a mixed fruit compote with cookies to complete the meal.

If prepared ahead of time, soup may be cooled and the layer of fat that forms on the top can be easily removed with a spoon.

Note: This recipe calls for cleaning the chicken with boiling water. This is done because it is not convenient to skim the top of the soup while it is cooking inside the microwave cavity, and cleaning with boiling water eliminates this.

OYSTER SOUP
Serves 4

Rich and creamy, this will satisfy the most discriminating palate. Since there is no direct heat underneath the pot, the delicate ingredients are safe from burning on the bottom and the pot does not require the cook's constant attention. Serve with crisp cracker assortment.

2 **8-ounce cans òysters, drained and coarsely chopped (reserve liquid), or 1 pound fresh oysters if available in your area**
1 **tablespoon butter**
3 **green onions, thinly sliced**
3 **cups chicken stock**
4 **egg yolks, beaten**
1 **cup light cream (half and half), or substitute regular (not low-fat) milk**
Dash cayenne pepper
Salt and white pepper to taste
1 **green onion, thinly sliced**

3 **tablespoons fresh parsley, chopped**

If using canned oysters, drain and reserve liquid.

If using fresh oysters, season oysters with a bit of white pepper. Place in a 2-quart casserole. Cook on High (600–700 watts) for 2–3 minutes, just until their edges are slightly curled. Set aside, reserving ½ cup oyster liquid.

Place butter and 3 sliced green onions into 2-quart glass measure. Cook on High (600–700 watts) 2 minutes. Stir in the chicken broth and oyster liquid. Heat on High 7 minutes. Stir in oysters. Heat on High 2 minutes.

Combine egg yolks and cream in a glass measure. Whip together and slowly add some of the hot soup mixture to the yolks and cream. Add to oysters. Add cayenne pepper; taste for seasoning. Depending on how salty the oysters are, add salt and pepper to taste.

Heat on Medium (300–350 watts) about 5 minutes, stirring twice. Just heat until steaming; do not allow to boil.

Serve in bowls; garnish with sprinkle of green onion and parsley.

5

EGGS AND QUICHES

Hard-Cooked Egg

Eggs Sunnyside Up

Fluffy Scrambled Eggs

Poached Egg

Lox and Eggs

Salami and Eggs

Thelma's Diet Eggs

Peppered Shrimp and Eggs

Puffy Cheese Omelet

California Omelet

Fluffy Eggs and Bacon

Eggs Benedict

Cheese Soufflé

Chiles Rellenos

California Quiche

Quiche aux Oignons

Spinach Quiche

Spinach and Feta Cheese Quiche

Quiche Florentine

Quiche Lorraine

Italian Sausage Quiche

Salmon Quiche

Mushroom Quiche

EGG COOKERY

How do you cook eggs in a microwave? You cook them to your liking by "looking," as you would prepare eggs in a frying pan. No expert in microwave timing can give you an exact formula, even though microwave experts are supposed to come up with the exact time, to the second. However, no two eggs are exactly alike, you may not be using the exact bowl that I used in testing, and the other ingredients may be a different starting temperature. Also, microwaves vary, as do conventional ovens, cook-tops, and frying pans. So recognize that there are variables.

The problems that occur in cooking eggs in the microwave are easily remedied: If your eggs turn to rubber, you have simply cooked them too long. If they are runny, they have not cooked enough. If they are soft in the center and overdone on the outside, they were not stirred frequently enough.

What is the advantage to cooking eggs in the microwave? Well, they do turn out so well, they are cooked directly in the serving dish, and they leave no frying pan or cook-top to clean up afterwards.

Cooking Techniques

As every cook knows, cooking eggs demands close attention to time and temperature. Although the microwave has always done an excellent job of scrambling and poaching eggs, the early models were not equipped with the range of controls necessary for the more delicate types of egg cookery—such as soufflés, quiches, and custards—that require fairly long, slow cooking. But the lower power settings made available through advances in microwave technology have brought these hitherto difficult dishes within reach.

There are still some cautions to observe. For instance, don't try to microwave an egg in its shell. The tight membrane surrounding the yolk collects microwave energy, which causes steam to build up inside the shell (much as steam builds up inside the skin of a conventionally baked potato), and the result can be a small explosion, with a not-so-small mess to clean up. Keep this membrane in mind when poaching eggs, too, or anytime you want to keep the yolk intact—lightly puncturing the yolk with a skewer or the tine of a fork will eliminate a burst yolk and will not cause the egg to run (surprising, but true).

Another thing to remember about eggs in the microwave is that the yolk, with its high protein content, absorbs microwave energy faster than the white; so it cooks faster. If you have ever tried to cook an egg sunnyside up without using a browning dish, you have learned this the hard way. For those who just can't start the day without eggs fried sunnyside up, there are two solutions. The first is the browning dish, which cooks the white with direct heat while the microwaves are cooking the yolk. The second solution is to cook the eggs in a custard cup, or an attractive egg cup designed for microwave. The white of the egg is forced up around the sides of the cup so that the microwaves must pass through the white en route to the yolk. It produces a compact egg, ready to serve in the dish in which it was cooked (and don't forget to puncture the yolk!).

A useful tool for stirring eggs is a pair of wooden chopsticks. I always told my students that before they made Mexican Eggs in their microwave, to go to an Oriental place for dinner and steal the chopsticks! I use the chopsticks to stir the eggs from the outside in. Then I simply rest the sticks across the dish. Then when stirring is needed, I use the same chopsticks, without using a fork, which then requires a dish to rest it on. A true microwave cook does not dirty additional dishes unless absolutely necessary!

HARD-COOKED EGG
Serves 1

1 egg

Break egg into a small glass measuring cup. Pierce yolk with fork. Cover cup with a saucer, and cook on Medium (300–350 watts) until egg just begins to firm, about 1–2 minutes. Remove from microwave and let stand a few minutes—egg will continue to cook as it stands.

If you are using the egg in a recipe that calls for a grated egg, immediately begin mashing with fork upon removal from microwave, and continue blending until egg is completely hard-cooked and grated.

EGGS SUNNYSIDE UP
Serves 1

I was never again going to prepare eggs sunnyside up in the microwave after my first attempt, because they did not turn out well. The white refused to cook, the yolk absorbed the microwave energy faster and was done before the white even got started.

When browning dishes were introduced a few years later, eggs sunnyside up became an excellent microwave recipe. Preheating the browning dish to the proper temperature for eggs will depend upon the size of your browning dish; the larger it is, the more preheating time is required. Check the instructions that came with your dish. Use the glass cover, if your browning dish came with one.

1 **tablespoon butter or margarine**
2 **eggs**
Salt and freshly ground pepper

Preheat browning dish on High (600–700 watts) for appropriate time. (The inside of the dish should glow yellow.) Add butter and allow it to melt completely. Break eggs onto dish and pierce yolks. (I find that most often the yolks do not pop with a browning dish, but I recommend piercing for insurance.) Season to taste with salt and pepper.

Cover (if dish has no cover, leave uncovered) and continue to cook on High 45–60 seconds or until yolk has the degree of firmness you prefer.

FLUFFY SCRAMBLED EGGS

Serves 1

There are many ways to enjoy scrambled eggs in your microwave. I use leftover vegetables, bits of cheese, and spices that I enjoy—and even make eggs for two at the same time, in separate bowls, with different ingredients.

2 **eggs**
2 **tablespoons milk or water**
Salt and pepper to taste
1 **teaspoon butter**

Whip together the eggs, milk, and seasonings. In a deep cup or bowl, with handle, melt butter on High (600–700 watts) for 45 seconds. Add the egg mixture.

Cook on High 1½–2 minutes, stirring twice. Outside edges will cook first, as they do in a fry pan, making it necessary to stir the uncooked eggs toward the edges. Leave eggs a bit on the underdone side when you stop cooking, since they will continue to set after removing.

For a nice touch, add any of the following to the egg mixture, or design your own additions. The cooking time will be slightly longer.

2 **tablespoons cheddar, Monterey Jack, or any cheese of your choice**
1 **tablespoon chopped green onion**
1 **tablespoon fresh or dehydrated onion**
1 **tablespoon chopped green chilies**
Sprinkle of fresh chopped parsley

POACHED EGG

Serves 1

Attempting to poach an egg in the microwave can be a harrowing experience. But not to worry, or to give up on acquiring the timing and technique. It is easy to learn.

There is a tight membrane surrounding the yolk of the egg, which builds up pressure inside when heated. Unless the membrane is punctured, it will pop with a loud noise. (The membrane does not run, which surprised me, too, when I first did it.)

If you do not have a cup with a handle that gives you good results, you may use a small custard cup. Place it on a saucer, since the cup gets too hot to handle; the saucer will stay cool and make it easy to remove. I also use a saucer as a cover.

Should your effort produce an egg not to your liking, continue to cook it until it is hard-cooked, and use it for salads.

1 **egg**
2 **tablespoons water**
Salt and pepper to taste

Place water in cup; heat 45 seconds. Break egg into water. Pierce yolk several times with a toothpick. Cover; cook on Medium (300–350 watts) for 1–1½ minutes. Timing depends on how firm you like your egg. It is best to experiment with different times, until you discover the best time for your individual taste.

Remove egg with a slotted spoon, or carefully pour off liquid before eating.

For 2 or more eggs, increase size of bowl, amount of water, and cooking time. It will take about 1 minute per egg (on Medium).

LOX AND EGGS
Serves 4

Lox, also known as smoked salmon, goes well with eggs, especially when served with bagels and cream cheese.

2 tablespoons butter or margarine
1 small onion, finely diced
3 ounces lox, diced
6 eggs
6 tablespoons milk
Minced fresh parsley (garnish)

Melt butter on High (600–700 watts) in an 8-inch microwave fry pan or pie plate. Tilt dish to coat. Sprinkle onion over butter. Continue to cook on High until onion is soft and beginning to crisp slightly, about 2–3 minutes, depending on the size of your small onion. Stir in the salmon and continue to cook for 1 minute.

Whisk together the eggs and milk. Add to the dish and continue to cook on High until eggs are set, stirring from outside to center as often as every minute. Timing is about 30 seconds per egg, plus the other ingredients, so your total timing would be 3–4 minutes.

Undercook slightly to keep eggs moist, since they will continue to cook before they cool down enough for you to taste them. Sprinkle with parsley before serving.

SALAMI AND EGGS
Serves 3–4

A deli special in your own kitchen. No need to add fat—just cook it out of the salami before adding the eggs.

This is cooked on a lower power to produce a pancake-style egg. If you wish to speed up the action you may cook it on High (600–700 watts), stirring every few minutes to bring the egg mixture from the outside of the dish to the center where there is less cooking action. If you use a lower power, the eggs will set more slowly.

6 slices of salami, about ¼″ thick
6 eggs
6 tablespoons water
Salt and pepper to taste

Place slices of salami in an 8-inch round deep dish pie plate or quiche dish. Cook on High (600–700 watts) 2 minutes. Turn pieces over and cook an additional 1–2 minutes until salami is fairly crisp, or to your liking.

Beat eggs and water together, adding seasoning to your taste. Pour over heated salami. Cook on Medium (300–350 watts) 3–5 minutes, lifting egg mixture with a spatula to allow liquid part of mixture to run underneath the cooked egg portion.

When bottom of mixture becomes firm and slightly brown, turn it over with spatula and cook an additional minute.

THELMA'S DIET EGGS
Serves 1

Every Monday morning I start faithfully on my diet. You who identify with that can smile, but I assure you I have every intention of following through. I do have obstacles, however: My test kitchen is in constant use, my refrigerator and freezers are bursting at the seams, and I adore food. Besides, I recently woke up to the fact that when I do go on a specific diet, I not only eat all the diet foods, but also taste (and taste and taste) all the recipes being tested that day.

I remember sitting in a restaurant one day with my young children and some of their friends, when one observant child remarked, "Cottage cheese must be fattening because only fat people eat it!"

That was when I finally became aware that it was not *what* I was eating, but the *amounts* I was consuming. So on to my Monday diet! And I will start with my eggs, because, first I enjoy eating them; second, they are high in protein and give me a good burst of energy; and third, in my microwave, I do not need fat to cook delicious eggs—all good reasons to include them in dieting.

2 eggs
3 heaping tablespoons low-fat cottage cheese
3 tablespoons shredded Monterey Jack cheese
1 green onion, chopped (optional)

Combine all ingredients in a small bowl or cup, with just enough room to be able to whisk all ingredients and leave room for eggs to puff up on top.

Briskly whisk until ingredients are well blended. If using a cup, it will have a handle for easy removal; if using a bowl without handles, place it on a saucer (which will remain cool during cooking).

Cook on High (600–700 watts) 2–3 minutes, stirring briskly once or twice to keep mixture fluffy. Just cook until it begins to appear cooked through. This mixture is puffy and soft, rather like a soufflé. If you prefer your eggs quite dry, this is not the recipe for you.

PEPPERED SHRIMP AND EGGS
Serves 3–4 generously

Nice Sunday brunch idea, along with crisp toast and fresh fruit.

The first time I prepared this recipe was in Bodega Bay above San Francisco, when the Department of Fisheries had a workshop on seafood for the University Extension home economists. I was invited to present an update on microwave cooking. It was my first experience in a prop plane where the pilot landed in a field of grass, and rolled his window down to see how to land. They had to carry me into the plane!

When we arrived, I was taken to the one and only local store to shop. Fortunately I was able to find all the ingredients for a recipe in one of the Department of Commerce's new cookbooks. Although none were yet being done in microwave, they were easy to adapt. This was a perfect choice, and since we started early in the morning, it became a lovely breakfast treat for those attending the workshop. I used bulk shrimp, but it is available in a can. It can also be done with crab or a seafood of your choice.

½ **pound baby shrimp (fresh or frozen), cooked and cleaned, or 2 4½-ounce cans baby shrimp**
1 **cup chopped green pepper**
1 **cup chopped onion**
2 **tablespoons butter**
6 **eggs**
¼ **cup milk or cream**
½ **teaspoon Worcestershire sauce**
¼ **teaspoon salt**
⅛ **teaspoon cayenne pepper**
3 **slices bacon, cooked crisp and crumbled**
Freshly chopped parsley for garnish

If using frozen shrimp, thaw before using; if using canned shrimp, drain and rinse with cold water. If baby shrimp are not available, cut large shrimp in half.

In an 8- or 9-inch pie plate or quiche dish, place green pepper, onion, and butter. Cook on High (600–700 watts) for 3–4 minutes until soft, stirring once

Stir in shrimp. Cook on High 1 minute; stir again. Whisk together eggs, milk, and seasonings. Pour over shrimp mixture. Cook on High 4–5 minutes, stirring every minute to bring cooked outside egg mixture to center of pan. Wooden chopsticks are perfect to use—they can rest on the top of the dish while cooking continues.

When eggs are almost firm, stir in the bacon. Stop cooking eggs a bit before they are completely set, since they continue to cook for a while after removed from the microwave and may become overdone if allowed to cook too long.

For a nice touch, sprinkle top with freshly chopped parsley.

PUFFY CHEESE OMELET
Serves 2

This dish is cooked more slowly to allow the separated eggs to firm as they puff. It is most attractive and makes a delicious Sunday breakfast or even a light evening meal with hot rolls and sliced tomatoes.

3 **eggs, separated**
⅓ **cup mayonnaise**
2 **tablespoons water**
2 **tablespoons butter**
1 **cup shredded cheddar cheese**
Fresh parsley, minced for garnish

Using electric mixer, beat egg whites in large bowl until soft peaks form. In separate bowl, without washing beaters, beat yolks with mayonnaise and water. Gently fold yolks into whites, blending carefully. (Don't use electric mixer; it will deflate the egg whites.)

Melt butter on High (600–700 watts) in a 9-inch pie plate. Tilt dish to coat completely. Pour egg mixture into dish and cook on Medium (300–350 watts) 7–8 minutes, rotating dish if eggs appear to be cooking unevenly.

When eggs are set but still a bit moist on top, sprinkle with cheese. Continue to cook on Medium until cheese is melted, about 1 minute. Gently fold omelet in half and slide onto serving plate. Sprinkle with parsley and serve immediately.

CALIFORNIA OMELET
Serves 3 – 4

My Mother always used sour cream in scrambled eggs when we were children. And the eggs were always light and fluffy with marvelous flavor and texture.

This is a good brunch or late supper dish. It can be placed into a chafing dish after cooking to keep it hot, since the flavor and consistency will not be affected. If you wish to increase the amount of the recipe, simply add about 30 seconds more for each egg and increase your stirring time. Eggs cook exactly the same way they cook in your frying pan, from the outside in; you must stir the cooked portion toward the center so the uncooked portion is moved to the outside.

6 **eggs**
½ **cup dairy sour cream**
½ **cup shredded cheddar cheese**
1 **large, firm tomato, peeled and chopped, drained of juice**
2 **green onions, chopped**
2 **tablespoons butter**
Salt and pepper to taste

Whip eggs with sour cream, then add the cheese, tomatoes, and onions.

Place butter in an 8- or 9-inch microwave fry pan, or a 9-inch pie plate. Melt on High (600 – 700 watts) for 1 minute, moving dish around to coat bottom with butter. Pour mixture into plate; sprinkle with salt and pepper. Cook on High 5 – 6½ minutes, stirring every minute. Remember, eggs continue to cook so remove from microwave while still slightly soft; by the time you can eat them, they will be perfect.

Serve with fresh toast or crusty French bread.

FLUFFY EGGS AND BACON
Serves 1

The butter and onion are cooked before the eggs are added—the same technique used in a frying pan on a cook-top. Time will vary, depending on how you enjoy your eggs. If you do not have sour cream on hand, substitute milk.

2 **slices bacon, cooked crisp and cut into pieces (see page 98)**
2 **teaspoons butter**
¼ **cup onion, thinly sliced**
2 **eggs**
2 **tablespoons sour cream**

Combine butter and onion in small au gratin dish (about 4″ x 7″). Cook on High (600 – 700 watts) until onion is softened, about 3 minutes. Stir through several times. Beat eggs with sour cream in small bowl. Pour over onion. Cook on High, stirring several times, until eggs are soft, about 1½ minutes. Sprinkle bacon along rim. Cook on High 30 seconds.

EGGS BENEDICT
Serves 4

In my travels I am amazed at how many people order this for breakfast. It is always a temptation to share this easy microwave adaptation with them. It sounds so exotic, yet it is simply muffins, bacon, some poached eggs, and a simple sauce made with eggs, butter, and lemon.

Never try, never learn.

4 **English muffin halves, toasted**
4 **teaspoons butter, room temperature**
4 **thin slices Canadian bacon**
4 **Poached Eggs (see index)**
Perfect Hollandaise Sauce (see index)

Spread each muffin with butter. Arrange on individual plates. Top with bacon and egg. Spoon hollandaise sauce over just before serving.

CHEESE SOUFFLÉ
Serves 4 – 6

Another hurdle of microwave cooking conquered! When lower powers were introduced, it became possible to slowly cook more delicate recipes, such as soufflés. The combination of evaporated milk with other ingredients produce a lovely soft texture. A bit different than oven baked, but no less tasty.

Soufflés are meant to be cooked and eaten with no delay. They are slightly soft in the center, almost like a pudding. So when you serve, use a large serving spoon and go directly to the bottom, so that each serving has some of the firmer outside soufflé and the pudding in the center and bottom.

¼ **cup all-purpose flour**
¾ **teaspoon salt**
½ **teaspoon dry mustard**
⅛ **teaspoon paprika**
1 **13-ounce can evaporated milk**
2½ **cups shredded sharp cheddar cheese**
6 **eggs, separated (whites at room temperature)**
1 **teaspoon cream of tartar**

Combine first 4 ingredients in 8-cup glass measure and blend well. Stir in milk. Cook on High (600–700 watts) until thickened, 4 to 5 minutes. Remove and whisk until smooth. Blend in cheese and cook on High until cheese is melted, about 1 minute.

In large mixing bowl beat egg whites until foamy. Add cream of tartar and continue beating until stiff and glossy. Set aside. Without washing beaters, beat yolks in smaller mixing bowl until thick and lemon colored. Add cheese mixture to yolks and whisk until well blended.

Gently fold yolk mixture into whites, blending thoroughly. Pour into 2-quart soufflé dish. Cook on Medium Low (200–250 watts) until edges of soufflé begin to appear a bit dry and look set, about 17-23 minutes. Turn dish as necessary if soufflé appears to be cooking unevenly. Serve immediately.

CHILIES RELLENOS
Serves 4

Tex-Mex cooking, California style. You can't miss with cheese, eggs, and a touch of Mexico in the form of chilies. More like a custard pie, the dish can be served almost anytime of day or evening. I like to prepare it in a quiche dish, because it is so attractive. If you use a pie plate, it is best to use one with higher sides to hold the ingredients.

5 **eggs**
2 **cups shredded Monterey Jack cheese**
1 **cup cottage cheese, very well-drained**
¼ **cup all-purpose flour**
1 **4-ounce can mild green chilies, chopped**
½ **teaspoon baking powder**
½ **teaspoon cornstarch**

Place eggs in mixing bowl, whisk until frothy. Whisk in remaining ingredients until well blended. Pour into 10-inch quiche dish. Cook on Medium High (400–450 watts) until set, about 12–15 minutes, turning dish if eggs appear to be cooking unevenly.

THE QUICHE

The simplicity of cooking quiches in the microwave is turning the American kitchen into instant gourmet food service! Even children who cannot pronounce the word are doing it. Once you discover that your local market carries a variety of preformed crusts waiting to be filled, you are on your way.

A quiche can have many different fillings. It is simply a custard pie, originally made with eggs and cheese and whatever the French farm wife had left over in her kitchen. In the microwave, the pie shell must always be cooked first, then the filling is added and the quiche is cooked. The reason for this is that microwave power enters the food from the top and is absorbed by the liquid in the filling; the pie shell therefore receives little energy during the time the quiche is cooking, and will remain uncooked.

Even some conventional recipes call for a precooked pie shell to ensure a nice, brown, crisp texture. Although a microwave crust is not as brown, the egg-wash technique described in Pie Shell Technique ensures an attractive glaze that also makes the crust crisp.

If you prefer to make your own (especially with a food processor to speed up the procedure) use the recipe on page 148—or try your own family favorite.

The only problem I have encountered is in the use of an all-butter crust. It appears that melting the butter so quickly dissolves the pastry—although it tastes delicious, it slips down the sides of the baking dish before it has time to cook. If you prefer a butter crust, do it conventionally in a ceramic, glass, or porcelain quiche or pie plate, then finish the recipe in your microwave.

CALIFORNIA QUICHE
Serves 6

9 strips bacon, crisply cooked and crumbled (see Perfect Bacon recipe)
2 cups grated Monterey Jack cheese
1 4-ounce can diced mild green chilies
3 green onions, thinly sliced
1 baked 9-inch deep-dish pie shell
1 13-ounce can evaporated milk (regular or skim)
4 eggs

Combine first 4 ingredients in small bowl and toss lightly. Sprinkle about ¾ of the mixture over pie shell.

Heat milk in measuring cup on High (600–700 watts) for 2½ minutes. Beat eggs in separate bowl. Add hot milk and beat again. Pour evenly into pie shell. Sprinkle with remaining bacon mixture. Cook on Medium High (400–500 watts) until center is barely set, about 12–15 minutes. Let stand 5 minutes before cutting into wedges and serving.

Note: Quiches tend to stay soft in the center. By adding about ¼ cup additional cheese to the center of the quiche just before baking, it will "fill" the liquid and help it set up.

QUICHE AUX OIGNONS (ONION QUICHE)
Serves 6-8

Cooking onions in the microwave is easy—simply cover to get a soft texture. There is no need to stir constantly as in conventional cooking, since there is no possibility of scorching.

The taste of this quiche is surprisingly sweet. I have seen onion-haters take three helpings! And no aftertaste.

2 pounds onions, chopped
3 tablespoons butter
3 tablespoons oil
1½ tablespoons all-purpose flour
1 cup sour cream
¼ cup whipping cream
2 eggs, beaten
6 tablespoons Swiss cheese, grated
1 teaspoon salt
⅛ teaspoon freshly grated white pepper
1 baked 9-inch deep-dish pie shell
½ teaspoon nutmeg
Minced fresh parsley

Combine onion, butter, and oil in large bowl. Cover and cook on High (600–700 watts) until golden, about 20 minutes, stirring once or twice. Stir in flour. Cover and cook on High an additional 3 minutes.

Combine sour cream and whipping cream and blend well. Mix in eggs, 4 tablespoons cheese, salt, and pepper. Add to onion mixture, blending well. Pour into pie shell and sprinkle with remaining cheese and nutmeg. Cook on Medium High (400–500 watts) until center is barely set, about 12–14 minutes. Let stand 5 minutes. Sprinkle with minced fresh parsley before serving.

SPINACH QUICHE
Serves 6

2 tablespoons (¼ stick) butter
1 medium onion, minced
1 garlic clove, minced
¾ cup whipping cream (may substitute milk)
½ cup sour cream
¼ cup fresh parsley, chopped
4 eggs
3 tablespoons green onion, chopped
2 cups Swiss cheese, shredded
1 10-ounce package frozen chopped spinach, thawed and squeezed dry
1 teaspoon salt
⅛ teaspoon nutmeg
⅛ teaspoon freshly ground pepper
1 baked 9-inch deep-dish pie shell

Cook first 3 ingredients on High (600–700 watts) until onion is soft, about 3–4 minutes.

Combine next 5 ingredients in bowl and beat until well blended. Add cheese, spinach, and seasoning and mix thoroughly. Pour into pie shell. Cook on Medium High (400–500 watts) until center is barely set, about 15 to 20 minutes. Let stand 5 minutes before serving.

SPINACH AND FETA CHEESE QUICHE

Serves 6–8

4   ounces Greek feta cheese, well rinsed, patted
     dry, and crumbled
½   cup Parmesan cheese
½   cup green onion, chopped
½   cup fresh parsley, minced
¼   cup fresh bread crumbs
1   10-ounce package frozen chopped spinach,
     thawed, squeezed dry
1½ cups shredded Monterey Jack cheese
1   baked 9-inch deep-dish pie shell
1   cup whipping cream
4   eggs
Parmesan cheese
Minced green onion
Minced fresh parsley

Combine first 6 ingredients in mixing bowl and
blend well. Sprinkle Monterey Jack cheese on pie
shell. Spoon spinach mixture over top. Heat cream in
measuring cup on High (600–700 watts) 1½
minutes. Beat eggs in separate bowl; add hot cream
and beat again. Slowly pour over spinach mixture,
allowing spinach to absorb cream before adding
more. Sprinkle top with Parmesan, onion, and
parsley. Cook on Medium High (400–500 watts)
about 12 minutes until center is barely set, turning if
necessary to promote even cooking. Let stand 5
minutes before serving.

QUICHE FLORENTINE

Serves 6

Roberta took my quiche recipe and simplified it. It has
been said that every mother wishes for her children to
be better than she—but a daughter-in-law?
However, in the interest of good microwave cooking
(which is what this book is all about), here is
Roberta's version. I recommend it!

1   10-ounce package frozen chopped spinach
½   cup chopped green scallion
2   cups shredded cheddar, Swiss, or Monterey
     Jack cheese

4   eggs, beaten
1   9-inch prebaked pie shell (see index)
½   cup grated Parmesan cheese
1   tablespoon butter
Paprika

Place spinach on plate. Defrost on High (600–700
watts) for 3 minutes. *Do not* drain. Set aside.
Combine scallion, cheese, and beaten eggs.
Break up spinach package with your fingers to
soften. Open box and add to mixture. Blend well.
Pour into pie shell. Sprinkle with Parmesan to form a
crust. Dot with butter and sprinkle with paprika.
Cook on Medium (300–350 watts) for 14–16
minutes until just beginning to set. It will firm as it
cools.

QUICHE LORRAINE

Serves 6

The classic quiche.

9   strips bacon, crisply cooked and crumbled
     (see Perfect Bacon recipe)
2   cups shredded Swiss or Monterey Jack
     cheese
½   cup green onion, thinly sliced
1   baked 9-inch deep-dish pie shell
1   13-ounce can evaporated milk (regular or
     skim)
4   eggs
2   teaspoons Dijon mustard
¼   teaspoon nutmeg
Dash of cayenne pepper

Combine first 3 ingredients in small bowl and toss
lightly. Sprinkle about ¾ of mixture over pie shell.
Heat milk in measuring cup on High (600–700
watts) for 2½ minutes. Beat eggs with mustard,
nutmeg, and cayenne pepper in a separate bowl.
Add hot milk and beat again. Pour into pie shell and
sprinkle remaining bacon mixture over top. Cook on
Medium High (400–500 watts) until center is barely
set, about 12-15 minutes. Let stand 5 minutes before
serving.

Note: For a more firm center in the quiche, add an
additional ¼ cup cheese to center before baking.

ITALIAN SAUSAGE QUICHE
Serves 6

⅔ **pound sweet Italian bulk sausage**
½ **cup onion, chopped**
2 **tablespoons all-purpose flour**
1 **13-ounce can evaporated milk**
4 **eggs**
2 **cups sharp cheddar cheese, shredded**
1 **baked 9-inch deep-dish pie shell**
2 **teaspoons fresh parsley, minced**

Cook sausage and onion uncovered on High (600–700 watts) until crumbly, stirring once (about 4 minutes). Drain off fat. Stir in flour and cook on High another minute.

Heat milk in measuring cup on High 2½ minutes. Beat eggs in separate bowl. Add hot milk and beat again.

Add cheese to sausage mixture and toss lightly. Spoon into pie shell. Pour milk and egg mixture over top. Sprinkle with parsley. Cook on Medium High (400–500 watts) until center is barely set, about 12-15 minutes. Let stand 5–10 minutes before serving.

SALMON QUICHE
Serves 6

1 **1-pound can red salmon, drained and flaked**
   (tuna may be substituted)
½ **cup green onion, minced**
¼ **cup fresh parsley, minced**
¼ **cup fresh bread crumbs**
1 **3-ounce package cream cheese, softened**
2 **teaspoons lemon juice**
1 **tablespoon red prepared horseradish**
⅛ **teaspoon each salt and pepper**
1 **13-ounce can evaporated milk**
   (regular or skim)
4 **eggs**
1 **baked 9-inch deep-dish pie shell**
Paprika

Place salmon, onion, parsley, bread crumbs, cream cheese, lemon juice, horseradish, salt, and pepper in a mixing bowl. Reserve a little onion and parsley for topping.

Heat milk in a 4-cup glass measuring cup for 2 minutes on High (600–700 watts). Whip eggs; add hot milk. Combine with salmon mixture. Pour carefully into pie shell. Sprinkle with paprika and a bit of green onion and parsley.

Cook on Medium High (400–500 watts) 12–15 minutes or until it begins to appear set. Turn if necessary for even cooking. Allow to rest about 10 minutes to set before serving.

MUSHROOM QUICHE
Serves 6

3 **tablespoons butter**
2 **tablespoons shallot, chopped**
1 **pound mushrooms, sliced**
2 **tablespoons Madeira wine**
1 **teaspoon fresh lemon juice**
1 **teaspoon salt**
3 **eggs**
¾ **cup sour cream**
¼ **cup whipping cream**
1 **baked 9-inch deep-dish pie shell**
¼ **cup shredded Swiss cheese**
Nutmeg

Combine butter and shallot in large bowl and cook on High (600–700 watts) for 2 minutes. Add mushrooms, wine, lemon juice, and salt and toss lightly. Cook on High until liquid is evaporated, about 15-20 minutes, stirring once or twice.

Beat eggs with whisk. Add sour cream and whipping cream and blend well. Add mushroom mixture and mix thoroughly. Pour into pie shell and sprinkle with cheese and nutmeg. Cook on Medium High (400–500 watts) until center is barely set, about 8–11 minutes. Let stand 5 minutes before serving.

6
SANDWICHES AND SNACKS

HEATING SANDWICHES

Think about this: Microwaves cook from the outside in, heating the top layer before they move down to penetrate the center of the sandwich. Bread then will first become soggy, then tough, if overcooked—and this is what happens when an entire sandwich is heated at once.

Placing a sandwich in the microwave to heat certainly improves the flavor of many sandwiches, especially ones with meat or cheese. A simple way to heat the sandwich is to remove the top piece of bread or roll, heat the filling 45 seconds–1 minute, then add the top bread for about 15 seconds.

If you are reheating a sandwich with slices of chicken or with meat in a gravy sauce, reheat the filling first, then add the bread for 15–20 seconds to bring out the best in the filling and the bread.

If you brought a hamburger to the office for lunch, it will taste much better if it is removed from the bun entirely, reheated for about 30 seconds, then heated in the bun for an additional 15–20 seconds. Timing will always depend upon the temperature of the food you are heating. Refrigerated food takes longer than food at room temperature.

Check the Kid's Corner for heating information on hot dogs. (They deserve better treatment than they usually receive in the microwave.)

TUNA MELT
Serves 4

This is delicious on either English muffins or toasted bread and takes almost no time to prepare. You can even mix the tuna salad in advance and refrigerate until you're ready to make a snack.

1   6½-ounce can of tuna
½ cup chopped celery
¼ cup chopped onion
1   hard-cooked egg, finely chopped (see Index)
1   green scallion, minced
1   tablespoon relish
¼ cup mayonnaise
Salt and pepper to taste
4   English muffin halves or 4 slices of bread
¼ cup shredded cheddar or Monterey Jack cheese

Combine all ingredients except muffins and cheese and mix well. Place equal amount of tuna salad on all four muffins or slices of bread. Sprinkle cheese on top. Place on a round plate in a circle. Heat on High (600–700 watts) for one minute or until heated through.

CHILI DOG
Serves 4

This old favorite is delicious when cooked in the microwave.

4   hot dog buns
1   16-ounce can of chili
4   knockwurst dogs, sliced halfway through on a diagonal
½ cup onion, finely chopped
Mustard and relish to taste

Place the chili into a small bowl, covered, and heat on High (600–700 watts) for 2–3 minutes until heated through. Set aside. Place the hot dogs on a paper plate and heat on High for one minute per hot dog. Place hot dogs in buns, and continue to heat for 15 seconds per bun. Spoon hot chili over dogs, adding onion, mustard, and relish to taste.

RICH-BOY SANDWICH
Serves about 8

We all have heard about "poor boy" sandwiches. When first I shopped for this recipe, I realized a poor boy could never afford it, because the best place to shop for the ingredients is your finest Italian grocery store, where they will cut the meat and cheese to order, right in front of you—and where they also have outstanding marinated artichoke hearts in bulk.

I first began to buy poor boy sandwiches for my ball-playing sons to avoid the dinner-time stampede. I purchased the sandwiches at a takeout which prepared them to order, and they would wolf them down in the car between coming home from school and running to practice.

I had always wanted to try my own poor boy sandwich, and looked forward to experimenting with it in the microwave. My opportunity came at a social gathering of old friends from the EWRT (Electrical Woman's Round Table). I volunteered my home for the pre-Christmas event. Since all of us worked and no one had time to cook, I offered to pick up some sandwich makings on the way home.

I purchased the longest bread they had, and several of us assembled the long sandwich. To serve, I placed the entire loaf on a large breadboard with a sharp bread knife alongside. I put this sign on top of the microwave:

Cut a slice off the loaf—be generous. Place on napkin on paper plate. Remove top crust so that the meat will heat without overheating the bread. Heat on High (600–700 watts) as follows:

Heating Time

2″	3″	4″	5″
		1 min.,	1 min.,
45 sec.	1 min.	30 sec.	45 sec.

Halve bread horizontally through center and place halves cut side up on work surface. Spread mayonnaise on top half and mustard on bottom. On the bottom side, arrange drained artichoke pieces to stretch across loaf (use the liquid from the jar for your salad dressing).

Sprinkle with capers. Place onion slices across loaf. Layer overlapping slices of meat and cheese, draping meat slightly over edge. Close sandwich. (At this point, if you are not serving immediately, wrap tightly and refrigerate until ready to serve.)

To serve, cut into serving pieces, remove top section of sandwich, and heat on high power according to chart; replace top and heat an additional 15 seconds, just to warm the top of the bread. If it is a crusty loaf, too much microwave energy will soften the crust.

Note: You may notice I seem to prefer Monterey Jack cheese to mozzarella. That is not altogether true—it is just that I have been spoiled by the Sonoma and Monterey Jack cheese available to us here—it melts so beautifully in the microwave, and I find it retains more moisture. Do experiment with both, and mix them.

Along with the sandwich I served a large, freshly tossed salad with an Italian dressing; a large bowl of fresh fruit; and for fun, a chocolate mousse in a large champagne glass.

It was easy, and fun—I have used this idea for New Year's Eve parties, children's parties, and whenever good friends arrive unexpectedly. Everyone heats their own and it is all done on paper plates. How much easier can things get?

1 1- to 1½-pound loaf Italian or French bread
2 tablespoons mayonnaise
2 tablespoons prepared mustard
1 6-ounce jar marinated artichoke hearts, cut into pieces
1–2 tablespoons capers, drained
1 large bermuda onion (or regular onion if purple onion is not available), sliced into thin rings
1½ pounds assorted sliced Italian meats (mortadella, salami, prosciutto, roast beef, etc.)
½ pound sliced provolone or mozzarella cheese
½ pound sliced Monterey Jack cheese

REUBEN SANDWICH
Serves 1

To avoid a soggy sandwich, heat the meat on the bottom slice of bread first, then add the second slice. Remember: microwaves travel from the outside in. By the time the meat is heated through, the bread would be overcooked.

2 slices rye bread, toasted or plain
Cooked corned beef, thinly sliced
2 tablespoons sauerkraut, well drained
1 slice Swiss cheese
1 tablespoon thousand island dressing

Place corned beef on one slice of bread, then add sauerkraut and Swiss cheese. Spread second piece of bread with dressing and set aside. Heat bottom half of sandwich on paper towel on rack or plate on High (600–700 watts) for 45 seconds. Place second slice on top. Heat for 15 seconds.

HEARTY ITALIAN MEATBALL SANDWICH
Serves about 4

Man does not live by ham and cheese alone. For a little investment in time, you can enjoy a robust man-sized sandwich.

Make meatballs ahead of time, freeze them on a cookie sheet, then transfer to a plastic bag and remove as needed. You can prepare them in small crusty rolls that can also be frozen, so that this recipe does duty as a last-minute freezer-to-table dish. Just remove the amount of meatballs you need, and the rolls (which should be sliced before freezing). Defrost the meatballs on High (600–700 watts) about 30 seconds per meatball. Use the rolls frozen to make certain they are not overheated—the meatballs can take more heating than the rolls, and should be hot before they are added to the roll.

1 **pound lean ground beef**
1 **small onion, chopped**
1 **egg**
1 **tablespoon Italian herb seasoning**
1 **15-ounce jar spaghetti sauce, or 2 cups homemade (see index)**
1 **1-pound loaf French or Italian bread, halved lengthwise**
Grated Parmesan cheese
Sliced purple onion, tomatoes, and lettuce (optional)

Combine beef, onion, egg, and seasoning and shape into 8 meatballs. Place in a circle on a rack. Cover with waxed paper. Cook on High (600–700 watts) 3 minutes. Turn meatballs over, and continue to cook 2–3 minutes, just until meat loses its pink color. Place in casserole; stir in the spaghetti sauce. Cover; cook on High until meatballs are hot. If heating the bread, place bottom side of bread on rack or a long platter. Spoon meatballs and sauce on the bread; sprinkle with Parmesan. Cover with top of bread. You may serve at this point, or if you would like to freshen the bread. heat on High about 30–45 seconds, just until bread is warm.

Sliced purple onion, tomatoes, and lettuce can be added after heating. It is not usually served this way in Italian delis but is a nice way to eat a bit of salad in your sandwich.

Note: If meatballs are made ahead, reheat them in the casserole before placing on the bread; otherwise the bread will be overcooked and will turn hard before the meat is heated through.

TAKE A TOASTED ENGLISH MUFFIN...

For a quick snack, a toasted muffin can become almost any ethnic adaptation you might dream up. Because it is first toasted in your toaster, it stays nice and crisp and lends itself to a variety of toppings. Here are a few suggestions. I am sure you will have many of your own to experiment with as you go along.

PIZZA MUFFIN
Serves 2

1 **English muffin, split and toasted**
2 **tablespoons pizza sauce**
6 **slices pepperoni**
¼ **cup shredded Monterey Jack or mozzarella cheese**

Spread each muffin half with 1 tablespoon pizza sauce. Arrange 3 slices of pepperoni on top and sprinkle with cheese. Place on paper plate. Heat on Medium High (400–500 watts) for 1 minute, or just until cheese begins to melt. Do not overheat.

MUFFIN GARLIC BREAD
Serves 2

1 **English muffin, split and toasted (preferably sourdough variety)**
1 **teaspoon garlic powder**
2 **teaspoons butter**
Parmesan cheese

Place muffins on paper plate. Sprinkle with garlic powder and spread butter over top. Sprinkle with Parmesan. Heat on Medium High (400–500 watts) for 1 minute, or just until butter begins to bubble.

CHEESY MUFFINS
Serves 2

1 **English muffin, split and toasted**
2 **teaspoons butter (optional)**
¼ **cup shredded cheddar or Monterey Jack cheese**
1 **chopped scallion, or chopped salami, or leftover meat, etc.**

Place muffins on paper plate; brush with butter. Sprinkle cheese and scallions (or any topping of your choice) over top. Heat on Medium High (400–500 watts) for 1 minute, just until cheese begins to melt.

EASY POTATO SALAD FOR ONE
Serves 1

1 medium potato (about 7 ounces), rinsed and patted dry
2 to 3 tablespoons mayonnaise
1 hard-cooked egg, grated (see index)
1 small stalk celery, finely chopped
1 small green onion, finely chopped
¼ teaspoon salt
⅛ teaspoon freshly ground pepper
1 large Bibb or Boston lettuce leaf
Minced fresh parsley (for garnish)
Pimiento for garnish (optional)

Cook potato on rack on High (600–700 watts) until just done, but still firm (about 6 minutes). Let cool 5 minutes. Peel and cut into ½-inch squares.

Transfer potato to bowl. Add mayonnaise, egg, celery, onion, salt, and pepper and blend well. Spoon into large double lettuce leaf and sprinkle with parsley. (You can add a bit of pimiento for color.) Place leaf inside a plastic bag; tie opening. Place in refrigerator until ready to leave for school or office.

POPCORN

In the early days of microwave, we all did popcorn in paper bags—until the reports began to come in. Many people discovered that under the right conditions, the bag can ignite. Because popcorn is a dry food with no moisture to absorb microwave energy, there is an intense heat buildup on the paper. It is the same principle as starting a fire by rubbing two sticks together until the heat builds up and the wood ignites. (By the same principle, the wood would *not* burn if it were moist.)

So, please, no bags. If you have been doing it with no problems so far you have been fortunate. Should a fire ever occur inside the cavity, simply turn off the unit; the fire will go out with the door closed.

Popping corn in the microwave is great fun, and many popcorn poppers have been designed in plastic for microwave. However, if your manufacturer states you should not do popcorn, don't.

Plastic poppers for microwave use do not absorb microwave energy. Only use a properly designed popper. Glass and ceramic do not perform as well, because these materials get extremely hot and breakage may occur.

Only use ½ cup of unpopped corn for each batch. It will make about 1 quart of popped corn. You will not get as much popped corn from the microwave as you will from your cook-top; but do not attempt to continue to pop the unpopped corn because it will burn.

I find High power (600–700 watts) works best—the lower wattages do not do as well. Most manufacturers of popcorn poppers recommend a limit of 4½ minutes for ½ cup of unpopped corn.

BUTTERY CARAMEL CORN
Makes about 4 quarts

Although this makes use of a paper bag, *do not pop corn in the paper bag, as bag could start a fire*.

Betty Sullivan shared this excellent technique for making caramel corn. Serve it to TV watchers, or take it as a hostess gift during holiday visits. For fun, place bag of caramel corn inside a larger bag and use a bright ribbon to tie it closed. If you take a copy of the recipe with you, be sure to explain why they should not use a paper bag, except as described for this technique (see previous recipe on popping popcorn).

1 cup brown sugar
¼ cup light corn syrup (like Karo)
¼ pound (1 stick) butter or margarine
½ teaspoon salt
1 teaspoon vanilla
½ teaspoon baking soda
16 cups popped popcorn (using a microwave popcorn popper)

Combine sugar, syrup, butter, and salt in 2-quart glass measure. Cook on High (600–700 watts) 2 minutes. Stir well. Continue cooking for 3 minutes, stirring once or twice to help dissolve the sugar. Stir in vanilla and baking soda.

Place popcorn in a paper bag (*not* recycled paper). Pour heated mixture over popcorn, and fold bag ends together. Shake well. Cook on High in the following sequence, keeping the bag closed:

1 minute—then shake bag
1 minute—shake bag
30 seconds—shake bag
30 seconds—shake bag

Pour out caramel corn onto a piece of foil and let cool. Store in airtight container.

BAKED APPLE
Serves 1

When you eat an apple, you don't pour sugar on it, so why add sugar when nature already provided it all? For the microwave, I prefer the Rome Beauty apple. When it is not in season, I try to select a large baking apple variety, but it is never quite as good.

For those who prefer the added sweetness, here are some delicious alternatives to the natural one. If there is someone in your family who must be on a sugar free diet he will greatly appreciate your thoughtful preparation of a Rome apple, with a bit of cinnamon or perhaps prepared with walnuts, golden raisins, and a touch of apple juice instead of water.

1 **Rome Beauty apple**
Sprinkle of cinnamon

Remove core from apple. Cut into apple at angles. Place into a small bowl, stemware safe for microwave, or a saucer. Sprinkle with cinnamon. Cover with a bowl, or plastic wrap. Cook on High (600–700 watts) 3–4 minutes, until just cooked. Timing will depend upon the size of the apple.

For several apples, you may place in individual bowls arranged in the microwave in a circle, or in a round baking dish just large enough to contain apples. Cook on High about 3 minutes per apple, then add time if needed.

VARIATIONS

Here are several suggestions to experiment with until you come up with your own favorite. All recipes are for one; use the guide for cooking additional apples.

1 **large apple, preferably Rome Beauty**
3 **tablespoons water or apple juice (unsweetened)**
2 **teaspoons brown sugar**
1 **teaspoon chopped walnuts**
¼ **teaspoon cinnamon**

Follow directions for preparing apple. Add water to bowl. Place remaining ingredients into center of apple. Follow directions for cooking.

1 **large apple, preferably Rome Beauty**
1 **teaspoon butter**
2 **teaspoons brown sugar**
¼ **teaspoon cinnamon**
2 **teaspoons golden raisins**
2 **tablespoons water or apple juice**

Follow directions for preparing apple. Set aside. In small glass measure, combine butter, sugar, cinnamon, raisins, and water or apple juice. Heat on High (600–700 watts) 45–60 seconds. Stir and fill center of apple with filling. Cover apple with bowl or plastic wrap. Cook on High 3–4 minutes, just until apple becomes tender.

OLD FASHIONED COCOA
Serves 1

The timing on liquid always depends on how much liquid is being heated. For example, an 8-ounce glass measuring cup with tap water may take from 2½–3 minutes. When you are heating water, it will not matter if you go over the heating time for drinking temperature and the water begins to boil. But if you are heating milk, when the boiling starts, the milk will boil over the cup. So we always use less time than we need and add more time by 15 or 20 seconds at a time to avoid a spillover.

In this recipe, we are using water to dissolve the cocoa. You may use all milk if you prefer, but remember to watch closely to avoid a boilover.

If you decide to prepare more than 1 serving at a time, just put the other cups in at the same time and add 1 minute of time for each cup you are adding, to dissolve the chocolate, then add 1 minute of time for each cup after you add the milk.

¼ **cup water**
2 **tablespoons sugar**
1 **tablespoon unsweetened cocoa powder**
¾ **cup milk**
1 **marshmallow (optional)**

Place water, sugar, and cocoa in a large mug or cup. Stir well. Heat on Medium (300–350 watts) for 2 minutes. Stir in the milk and continue cooking on Medium until cocoa is hot, about 50–70 seconds. Top with marshmallows.

7
SEAFOOD

Fish Julius
Fish Creole
Waldorf Layered Fillets
Grilled Swordfish
Pescale Con Tomaté
Fillet of Sole with Almonds and Wine
Fish Fillets in a Crumb Coating
Mountain Trout
Halibut Steaks
Fish Poached in Vegetables and Wine
Poached Whole Fish with
  Spinach Tarragon Stuffing
The Saucy Fish Caper
Poached Salmon
Grilled Salmon Steaks
Scampi
Shrimp Veracruz
Shrimp and Artichokes
Lobster Tails Supreme
Clams Casino
Steamed Clams with Garlic Butter and Parsley
Crab Divan

One of the most exciting things about microwave cooking is its role in preserving the natural flavors of foods. We cook fish to develop its flavor, to soften its small amount of connective tissue, and to make the protein easier to digest. This is accomplished beautifully in the microwave. In addition, fish is more moist than when cooked conventionally, simply because the conventional oven uses hot, dry air which automatically removes much of the moisture.

The most important point about cooking fish, by microwave, or any other method, is to stop cooking the fish the minute it loses its translucence. (At this stage the juices become milky, giving the flesh an opaque, whitish color.)

If you plan to delay serving the fish for a short time after removing it from the microwave, be sure to undercook it slightly, then keep it covered so it can continue to cook during the holding time. If serving immediately, cook only until it turns opaque.

Fish is at its best when barely cooked and served immediately. Most people who do not enjoy fish have tried to eat fish that was not properly prepared. "Gifts from the sea," as some fishes are called, are truly nature's gift to our table. Do take the time to learn some new recipes and techniques—it is worth the effort.

THE INS AND OUTS OF FROZEN FISH

There are many remarkable stories associated with foods. The frozen food industry, for example, owes its beginning to a lucky coincidence which occurred a little over 70 years ago.

In 1912 Clarence Birdseye, a young American biologist, was attracted to a fur-farming venture in Labrador. While there, he saw Eskimos catching fish in 50-degree-below-zero weather. These fish froze stiff almost as soon as they were taken from the water. Months later, when thawed and eaten, they tasted as if they had been freshly caught.

Birdseye had stumbled onto one of nature's secrets. Foods such as fish and game, when frozen rapidly at a low temperature and held constantly at a low temperature until time of use, are much more juicy and delicious than those frozen slowly and stored at a temperature only slightly below their freezing point.

Spurred by the dream of providing consumers with fresh foods out of season, he experimented with a number of quick-freezing methods and succeeded in developing a system of freezing foods in consumer-size packages. The first commercial product to which he successfully applied his quick-freezing technique was fish. By 1926 he was turning out packaged frozen fish fillets for the American market.

So much for the discovery. But the story does not end there. Birdseye and other packers of frozen foods in the late '20s and '30s were faced with a food distribution system devoid of suitable cold storage. The result was that when their products reached the consumers, many were of such notoriously poor quality they were rejected. Public acceptance of frozen fish fillets, and frozen foods generally, did not occur until deep-freeze cabinets in retail stores were commonplace, and home refrigerators were available with adequate freezing compartments.

Today a wide variety of ocean and lake fish are filleted, packaged, and frozen. Some of this activity even takes place on the high seas, right on the fishing boats.

Quick freezing at a low temperature is important to flesh foods such as fish fillets that contain a percentage of water which, on freezing, is changed to ice crystals. When freezing is slow, large crystals are formed which rupture the tiny cells. When freezing takes place quickly at a temperature of minus 20°F. or colder, the crystals formed are very small and do not rupture the cell walls. As a result, on thawing there is less loss of flavor and nutrients in drippings.

All frozen foods, fish fillets included, gradually lose quality in the freezer. Chemical and physical changes occur in the food. In the case of fish fillets, there is a gradual toughening of the flesh, fading of the characteristic good flavor, and possible development of off-flavors.

How quickly frozen foods lose quality depends on the cold storage temperature. A higher temperature speeds quality loss, while a low one slows it. To keep the quality high, some foods need a lower cold storage temperature than others, and frozen fish is one of the foods which needs a *very* low storage temperature. Provided fish fillets are well protected from drying with a snug-fitting, moisture- and vapor-proof covering, a steady temperature of minus 15°F. will preserve initial good quality for six months or longer. At a steady temperature of minus 5°F. to 0°F., quality loss is much faster.

Here are four home freezing guidelines:

- For best retention of quality, keep fish solidly frozen in the unopened package until ready to use.
- Store no longer than one week in the freezer compartment of a home refrigerator where the temperature is likely to be 10°F. to 25°F.
- Store no longer than three months in a home freezer where the temperature is 0°F. Even when you can provide zero storage or lower, the fish

will be tastier if used within a few weeks of purchase.

- If there are still a few ice crystals left in the package of fish that is slightly defrosted, they can safely be refrozen. However, refreezing will cause quality damage. For optimum eating enjoyment, do not refreeze. Cook and serve within a day.

Guide to Better Buying

- Buy in a food market where the frozen fish chest is clean, orderly, free from frost and ice, and—most important—the visible temperature indicator reads 0°F. or lower (the colder the better).
- There is a line on the inner side of most freezer cabinets above which food should not be stacked. Avoid packages stacked above this load-limit line.
- Buy only packages which are hard-frozen.
- Avoid damaged packages, as breaks in the wrapping can adversely affect the contents.
- Avoid packages coated inside or out with frost or ice.
- When the fillets can be seen through clear cello-wrap, avoid any which show white patches (indicating freezer burn) or other discoloration.
- Avoid packages having a strong odor.
- Pick up fish just before going to the check-out counter, place them in an insulated freezer bag (if available), and take directly home. Store in the freezer or freezing compartment.
- *Do not buy* fish from a fish counter display that is marked *fresh frozen defrosted*! You don't know how long it has been defrosting. If you cannot buy the fish fresh, buy it completely frozen according to the guidelines given.

When to Thaw

- Partial thawing of fillet blocks is required to ease cutting into portions or chunks.
- Complete thawing of fillet blocks is required in order to separate individual fillets for such procedures as rolling, stuffing, or skinning.
- Schedule thawing so that the fillets will be cooked soon after they are thawed. Drip or loss of flavorful, nutritious juices continues even after thawing is complete. Do not hold thawed fish longer than a day.

How to Defrost

- Remove foil, metal rings, or wire twist ties from

packaging. You may remove fish from its original wrapper—or, if you prefer, start defrosting in the package, then remove when thawing begins.

- Place package of fish on shallow dish to catch any drippings.

FISH COOKING TECHNIQUES

Poaching

This is probably the most frequently used method for cooking fish in the microwave. For best results when poaching seafood, always arrange it with the thickest portion facing the rim of the dish and the thinner portions toward the center. Cover loosely with wax paper or parchment to promote even cooking. As a general guide, allow 4 minutes per pound on High (600–700 watts) for thick fish steaks and 2–3 minutes per pound for thinner cuts. If the fish is quite thin—such as sole and other fillets—there is no need to turn it during cooking. Just turn off the power and let it stand in the hot liquid to finish. Vary the poaching liquid to enhance flavor: use white wine, clam juice, chicken broth, or even tomato juice.

Grilling

A browning dish is ideal for grilling in the microwave, especially for thick cuts of fish such as halibut, salmon, or swordfish steaks. Cover loosely with wax paper or parchment when cooking, or with the glass cover if one came with your browning dish. For maximum surface crisping, always turn fish over as soon as juices begin to appear on top—otherwise it will begin to steam and the fish will lose its crisp outside texture. For 1 pound of fish steaks, grill the first side about 2 minutes on High (600–700 watts), then turn over and add 1 minute.

Steaming

Use a casserole with cover to promote as much moisture as possible. Use 4 minutes per pound on High (600–700 watts) as a guide, but less time if using thin fillets. You can always judge the timing by appearance—the fish is done when it turns opaque.

Oven-Fried

You can produce a delectable flavored fish by making your own coating, first dipping the fish in melted butter, egg, or egg white.

However, if you purchase a coated frozen fish and try to make it work in the microwave—it won't. Why not? First, the moisture that collects in frozen foods generates moisture during cooking that you cannot control, as you can when you prepare it yourself. Second, the coatings have not been designed for microwave use, but rather for a conventional oven.

The coating can be a combination of cornflakes, Parmesan cheese, ground almonds, or interesting crackers, blended with seasonings into crumbs. For the diet-conscious, use your favorite diet bread toasted, made into crumbs and seasoned with herbs and spices.

Do not cover the coated fish with an airtight wrapping: this will cause steam and the coating will become soggy. However, you can cover with a paper towel to prevent splattering. For 1 pound of coated fillets, cook on High (600–700 watts) for 3–4 minutes, just until fish turns opaque.

DEFROSTING GUIDE: SEAFOOD

All defrosting is done on a power setting of Medium Low (200–250 watts)

Food	Amount	Power Setting	Time (in minutes)	Standing Time (in minutes)	Comments
Fish Fillets	1 lb.	Defrost (200–250 watts)	4–6	5	Defrost in package on dish. Turn once. Carefully separate fillets under cold water.
	2 lb.	Defrost (200–250 watts)	5–7	5	
Fish Steaks	1 lb.	Defrost (200–250 watts)	4–6	5	Defrost in package on dish. Separate steaks under cold running water.
Whole Fish	8–10 oz.	Defrost (200–250 watts)	4–6	5	Defrost on shallow dish. Turn once. Should be icy when removed. Complete defrosting at room temperature.
	1½–2 lb.	Defrost (200–250 watts)	5–7	5	
Lobster Tail	8 oz.	Defrost (200–250 watts)	5–7	5	Defrost on shallow dish.
Crab Legs	8–10 oz.	Defrost (200–250 watts)	5–7	5	Defrost on shallow dish. Break apart; turn once.
Crab Meat	6 oz.	Defrost (200–250 watts)	4–5	5	Defrost in package on shallow dish. Break apart; turn once.
Shrimp	1 lb.	Defrost (200–250 watts)	3–4	5	Defrost in package. If in block, spread out on baking dish. Turn over and rearrange during defrosting as necessary. Rinse under cold running water.
Scallops	1 lb.	Defrost (200–250 watts)	8–10	5	
Oysters	12 oz.	Defrost (200–250 watts)	3–4	5	Defrost on shallow dish. Turn over and rearrange during defrosting as necessary.

FISH JULIUS
Serves 4

To get the entire meal on the table at once, cook rice ahead of time (see index). 1 cup raw rice will give you 3 cups cooked. Stir in the butter and peanuts, and set aside, covered, until fish is cooked.

1 pound fresh fish fillets (such as halibut, cod, haddock)
¼ cup brown sugar
¼ cup bottled chili sauce
1 tablespoon prepared mustard
1 tablespoon bourbon
1 clove garlic, crushed
1 tablespoon butter
½ cup peanuts
3 cups hot cooked rice

Cut fish into 4 serving pieces; place in shallow baking/serving dish. Combine sugar, chili sauce, mustard, bourbon, and garlic. Spread over fish pieces. Cover and cook on High (600–700 watts) for 6 minutes, or just until fish flakes easily.

Add the butter and peanuts to hot rice. Arrange rice on serving platter with cooked fish. Serve at once.

Note: If using rice that was prepared ahead, add the butter and a few tablespoons of water to the rice, and reheat it covered about 4 minutes on High. Timing will vary with the starting temperature of the rice and the container—for example, if the rice has come right from the refrigerator, timing is longer than at room temperature.

FISH CREOLE
Serves 4

Mushrooms may be added to this low calorie recipe (only about 150 calories per serving). There is enough sauce to serve it over rice.

2 cups tomato juice
1 small green pepper, cut into chunks
1 small onion, cut into thin slices and separated into rings
1 tablespoon parsley, chopped
¼ teaspoon Italian seasoning
¼ teaspoon pepper

Salt to taste (optional)
1 pound fish (cod, turbot, or halibut)

Combine all ingredients except fish in shallow au gratin dish. Cook covered on High (600–700 watts) 7 minutes, or until pepper and onion are fork tender.

Add the fish, spoon sauce over top. Cook covered on High 6–7 minutes, or until fish is opaque. Timing will depend on thickness of fish; take care not to overcook it.

WALDORF LAYERED FILLETS
Serves 4

Contests are always exciting, particularly when they combine seafood and microwave. We had a cook-off, and the winner was Margauerite Balbach, who has distinguished herself in contests many times. Her originality has never been displayed more than in this spectacular dish.

1 16-ounce package frozen cod or other fish fillets, partially thawed
¼ cup butter or margarine
½ cup thinly sliced celery
1 cup apples, unpeeled and chopped
½ cup mayonnaise
1 cup herb-seasoned stuffing mix
¼ cup chopped walnuts (reserve 2 tablespoons for topping)
2 tablespoons lemon juice
Parsley for garnish
Cranberry sauce wedges (optional)

Slice fish block in half horizontally.

Set aside 2 tablespoons butter for topping. Place remaining butter, celery, and apple in a 1-quart bowl. Cook on High (600–700 watts) for 3 minutes, just until celery is tender. Blend in mayonnaise and toss with stuffing mix and walnuts.

Place half of fish in oval baking dish. Spoon waldorf mixture over fish. Top with second half of fish. Combine reserved butter and lemon juice. Heat until butter is melted. Pour over top of fish. Cover with wax paper or dish cover. Cook on High 4 minutes; turn dish around. Continue to cook 3–4 minutes, until fish turns opaque. Let stand 2 minutes. Sprinkle with reserved nuts. Garnish with parsley and ¼ slice cranberry sauce wedges, if desired.

GRILLED SWORDFISH
Serves 2

The use of a browning dish makes this fish taste as though grilled, and the soy sauce gives the fish a robust color. The good blending of flavors in the marinade enhances this thick slice of fish. Easy to prepare, but fit for a king.

2 swordfish steaks cut 1 inch thick (may substitute salmon)
Lemon wedges
Freshly chopped parsley for garnish

Marinade

¼ cup salad oil
2 tablespoons soy sauce
2 teaspoons Dijon mustard
1 teaspoon lemon rind

Combine marinade ingredients in a shallow container which will hold the fish steaks side by side. Pierce fish with fork to absorb marinade. Refrigerate and marinate about 3 hours, turning fish a few times.

Preheat browning dish to its maximum absorption (see manufacturer's instructions). Place fish steaks on preheated dish. Cook uncovered on High (600–700 watts) for 2 minutes, or just until tiny juices begin to appear on top of fish. Turn fish over with large spatula. Cook only 1 minute, just until fish turns opaque. For best results do not overcook.

Serve garnished with lemon wedges and sprinkle with parsley.

PESCALE CON TOMATÉ (FISH IN TOMATO SAUCE)
Serves 3–4

While watching a friend from the Isle of Rhodes, Greece prepare dinner for his family one evening, I could visualize it becoming a great microwave recipe. It worked the first time. Not a bit of fat—perfect for calorie watchers. Some of my best microwave adaptations have come from the Rugetti family and their rich heritage in cooking. Interesting to me (but not to my husband) was the fact that he did all of the marketing and cooking.

1 1-pound fish steak (whitefish or halibut)
1 14-ounce can whole peeled tomatoes

1 lemon, sliced
1 tablespoon olive oil (may substitute your favorite cooking oil)
1 clove garlic
3 tablespoons fresh parsley, chopped

Place fish in shallow oval baking dish, just large enough to hold fish and sauce. Set aside.

Place all other ingredients in a 4-cup glass measure or bowl. Cook on High (600–700 watts) for 2 minutes. Pour over fish; cover with parchment or waxed paper. Cook on High 4–5 minutes per pound of fish, adding 1 minute for the sauce. If fish is thin rather than a thick fillet, timing may be less.

For best quality, do not overcook. Fish is done the moment it turns opaque.

FILLET OF SOLE WITH ALMONDS AND WINE
Serves 2–4

Sauté the almonds first, because after you add the fish, the almonds do not get enough microwave energy to become brown and crisp.

⅓ cup slivered or sliced almonds
⅓ cup butter or margarine
2 tablespoons lemon juice
2 tablespoons white wine or sherry
½ teaspoon dill weed
Salt and pepper to taste
1 pound fresh or frozen halibut, perch, or sole fillets, thawed
Lemon slices for garnish
Chopped parsley for garnish

Use shallow oval or round dish, just large enough to contain recipe.

Combine almonds and butter. Cook uncovered on High (600–700 watts) about 5 minutes or until butter and almonds are golden brown, stirring once or twice.

Stir in lemon juice, wine, dill, and salt and pepper to taste. Arrange fish in butter mixture, with thickest sections facing outside. Spoon sauce over fillets; cover with waxed paper. Cook on High 4–5 minutes or until fish is no longer transparent.

Allow to rest about 2 minutes, covered, before serving. Garnish with lemon slices and parsley.

Fish will be most tender if just cooked until it is opaque. Overcooking toughens.

FISH FILLETS IN A CRUMB COATING

Serves 4

For those who prefer a dry fish with a nice, almost-crisp coating, this will be appealing. The egg white acts as a barrier between the fish and the coating to keep it fairly crisp. Great for calorie watchers—no fatty frying, and the egg white is "free."

4–5 fish fillets (about ¾ pound)
¼ cup grated Parmesan cheese
⅓ cup Italian seasoned bread crumbs
½ teaspoon garlic powder
1 egg white
Chopped fresh parsley
Lemon slices for garnish

Rinse fish and pat dry. Place on paper towels. Combine Parmesan, bread crumbs, and garlic powder in a flat dish. Dip fillets in egg white, then into crumb coating, taking care to cover the fish well.

Place in oval or round shallow baking dish, with thickest portion of fish facing outside. Cover with paper towel. Cook on High (600–700 watts) 3–4 minutes per pound, just until fish turns opaque.

To serve, sprinkle fresh parsley over top and garnish with lemon slices.

Note: If you wish to avoid bread crumbs, use a diet bread that has been toasted; use your blender or food processor to process it into fine crumbs, then add the seasonings of your choice.

MOUNTAIN TROUT

Serves 2

Mountain trout is a national treasure, and we now have trout farms which produce fresh trout in abundance. Over the years I have included cooking trout in class. When I cannot get 2 8-ounce trout, I purchase a 1-pound trout and use the same technique.

The recipe used here can adapt to any fillet of fish.

2 fresh 8-ounce trout
2 tablespoons lemon juice
¼ cup butter, melted
¼ cup dehydrated onion

2 teaspoons toasted slivered almonds
4 teaspoons chopped parsley
Salt and pepper to taste

Wash fish and pat dry. Place in an au gratin baking dish just large enough to contain recipe. Sprinkle inside and out with lemon juice.

Heat butter in 2-cup glass measure on High (600–700 watts) about 30 seconds, until completely melted. Pour 1 tablespoon melted butter inside each trout. Place half the onion, almonds, and parsley inside each cavity. Season to taste. Pour remaining butter over fish. Cover with wax paper.

Cook on High (600–700 watts), or until fish can be flaked with a fork. (The fish will turn opaque.) Do not overcook.

Garnish with lemon wedges and serve.

HALIBUT STEAKS

Serves 2

This marinade can be used for other fish as well. We always enjoy it with whatever fish is fresh and in season.

Timing on this recipe is for fish steaks about 1-inch thick. If you substitute thinner fillets, be sure to cut your time down by about 2 minutes: you can always add more time.

1 tablespoon lemon juice
1 tablespoon olive oil
2 tablespoons white wine
¼ cup water
¼ teaspoon salt
⅛ teaspoon white pepper
Lemon slices and fresh parsley sprigs for
**   garnish**

Combine all ingredients but fish in a shallow baking dish, just large enough to contain the fish. Add fish, turning it several times to coat. Cover and marinate in refrigerator 1–2 hours, turning once. (If your fish is frozen, allow it to defrost in the marinade overnight.)

To cook, allow the dish to return to room temperature. Cover with parchment or wax paper. Cook on High (600–700 watts) 5 minutes or just until fish turns opaque. Allow it to stand covered for 3–4 minutes before serving. Garnish with lemon slices and fresh parsley.

FISH POACHED IN VEGETABLES AND WINE
Serves 2–4

If you enjoy poached fish, you may enjoy experimenting with poaching liquids...here we have added carrots and wine, a good marriage of flavors. I like to cook this long enough for the carrots to become tender, so I can serve them with the fish.

1 cup dry white wine
6 lemon slices
3 celery stalks with leaves, cut into pieces
2 carrots, sliced at an angle with entire eye showing
1 medium onion, sliced into thin rings
6 peppercorns
1 parsley sprig
1 teaspoon salt
¼ teaspoon crumbled dried thyme (optional)

Combine all ingredients except fish in a 2-quart round or oval casserole. Cover and cook on High (600–700 watts) for 15 minutes. Strain poaching liquid (this is optional; it is the correct way to poach) and return liquid to casserole.

Add fish, spooning liquid over top. Cover and continue to cook on High just until fish turns opaque, about 3–4 minutes. Let stand covered several minutes to finish cooking.

POACHED WHOLE FISH WITH SPINACH TARRAGON STUFFING
Serves 6–8

Served hot and stuffed with spinach and mushrooms, a whole poached fish makes a truly elegant presentation. But even without the stuffing you'll have a delightful appetizer or entrée that can be served either hot or cold.

Select a cooking dish approximately the same size as the fish, preferably a bit shorter. An oval au gratin dish with ears on each end is a good choice. Position fish so the tail extends out the end of the dish; then place in the microwave with the tail resting against one side of the oven wall. This keeps the thinner portion of the fish from being overcooked and also forces the tail to remain in an upright position for an unusual, dramatic presentation.

1 10-ounce package frozen chopped spinach
12 large mushrooms, minced
2 shallots, minced, or 1 garlic clove, minced, mixed with 1 tablespoon minced onion
1 tablespoon butter
1 3-ounce package cream cheese, room temperature
2 tablespoons fresh parsley, chopped
1 teaspoon dried tarragon
½ teaspoon allspice
Dash nutmeg
Salt and freshly ground white pepper
1 whole 4–5 pound fish (preferably coho, silver salmon, striped bass, or trout)
Dry vermouth
1–2 lemons, thinly sliced
Minced fresh parsley
Lemon wedges and parsley sprigs for garnish

Place unopened package of frozen spinach on plate. Place in microwave and cook on High (600–700 watts) until barely defrosted, about 3–4 minutes. Allow to remain in box 5 minutes to complete defrosting. Transfer spinach to colander and drain well. Set aside.

Place mushrooms in one corner of towel and press out as much moisture as possible (this will reduce cooking time). Transfer to large mixing bowl and add shallots and butter. Cook on High until all moisture has evaporated, about 10–15 minutes (cooking time will vary with size and amount of mushrooms). Add spinach, cream cheese, 2 tablespoons parsley, tarragon, allspice, nutmeg, salt, and pepper and mix well. Taste and adjust seasonings if necessary.

Rinse fish under cool running water and pat dry with paper towels. Place in cooking dish with tail extending up and fill cavity with stuffing. Add vermouth, using just enough to barely cover bottom of dish. Pour vermouth over top of fish. Arrange lemon slices along top of fish, overlapping slightly. Sprinkle with minced parsley and additional tarragon, if desired.

Place dish in microwave so tail leans up against one wall. Cover with plastic wrap. Cook on High 5 minutes per pound, basting several times. When fish turns opaque, remove from microwave, baste several times, and allow to rest in juices, covered, for 10 minutes.

For easier serving, set lemon slices aside, peel off skin of fish and discard (it comes off easily). Replace lemon slices. Transfer to platter and garnish with lemon wedges and parsley sprigs (or any attractive leaves from your garden). Slice top layer above bone into wedges as you serve; when entire bone is exposed, remove it by simply lifting and cutting it at the base. The bottom layer is then ready to be sliced and served.

THE SAUCY FISH CAPER
Serves 4

This recipe won a recent seafood contest at the Pomona Fairgrounds. Everyone there loved it. Easy to prepare, and the unusual ingredients do combine extremely well.

1 **pound fresh fish fillets**
¼ **cup apple cider**
1 **clove garlic, minced**
¼ **cup sour cream**
½ **cup cheddar cheese, shredded**
2 **tablespoons mayonnaise**
1 **teaspoon Dijon mustard**
1 **teaspoon horseradish**
1 **tablespoon capers**

Place fish in shallow baking dish. Cover with apple cider and garlic. Cover loosely with waxed paper. Cook on High (600–700 watts) 5 minutes.

Combine all other ingredients; spread over fish. Cover loosely with waxed paper. Cook on Medium (300–350 watts) for 3–4 minutes, just until heated through.

POACHED SALMON
Serves 4

While this recipe calls for fresh salmon, you can substitute any fish that is suitable for poaching. This dish can be served hot or cold and goes well with baked or boiled potatoes and a fresh vegetable in season.

2 **cups water**
3 **tablespoons white vinegar**
1 **lemon, thinly sliced**
1 **small onion, thinly sliced**
1 **celery heart, cut into pieces**
1 **bay leaf**

½ **teaspoon salt**
⅛ **teaspoon white pepper**
Celery tops
Fresh parsley, minced
2 **large or 4 small salmon steaks**
Lemon wedges and parsley sprigs for garnish

Combine all ingredients except fish and garnish in 2-quart oval or round casserole. Cover and cook on High (600–700 watts) for 10 minutes. Add fish, spooning lemon slices, onion, and celery and parsley over tops. Cover and continue to cook on High just until fish begins to turn opaque, about 3–4 minutes. Let stand covered several minutes to finish cooking.

Serve with the poached onion rings and garnish with lemon wedges and parsley.

For serving two, follow the same cooking instructions, but cut the timing to 2–3 minutes.

GRILLED SALMON STEAKS
Serves 2–4

For fish fanciers with a browning dish, this is a winning combination. It "grills" the fish but does not release any of its natural moisture. My husband tells me it is the best salmon recipe he has ever tasted!

2 **salmon steaks, about 8 ounces each;**
  or 1 salmon fillet, about ¾ pound
Oil
Pepper
Paprika
Freshly chopped parsley
Lemon wedges

Preheat browning dish to its highest absorption temperature (use the timing for grilling steaks; that should be the highest). Brush salmon on one side only with oil. Sprinkle with pepper and paprika. Place seasoned side down on preheated browning dish. If your browning dish comes with a cover, use it; otherwise, drape a piece of waxed paper or parchment over top. Cook on High (600–700 watts) for 2 minutes, just until a "milky" substance begins to appear in drops on top of fish. Turn fish carefully with spatula (mine is wooden). Re-cover and allow to heat on second side about 2 minutes.

Serve the browned, seasoned side up. Sprinkle a touch of fresh parsley over the top and garnish with a wedge of lemon.

SCAMPI

Serves 2

If you adore scampi and think it is only possible to enjoy it at a fine restaurant, read on. Preparation is as easy as scrambling an egg. I often serve this as an entree, although it's a popular appetizer. It can be a complete meal when served over a bed of rice, since the garlic and wine sauce will flavor the rice as well. Add a freshly cooked vegetable in season, a crusty French loaf of bread, a bottle of your favorite wine and because it is such a light meal...include a rich chocolate dessert!

2 large garlic cloves, minced
2 tablespoons oil
2 tablespoons dry white wine
3 tablespoons minced fresh parsley
⅛ teaspoon paprika
⅛ teaspoon onion powder
¾ pound large uncooked shrimp, peeled, deveined and washed, leave tails on
Juice of ½ lemon
Salt and freshly ground pepper
Minced fresh parsley (for garnish)

Combine garlic and oil in au gratin-type dish, just large enough to accommodate shrimp. Cook on High (600–700 watts) 2 minutes. Stir in wine, parsley, paprika, and onion powder and continue cooking on High 3 minutes. Add shrimp, lemon juice, salt, and pepper and stir to coat shrimp. Arrange shrimp with thickest part toward the outside of dish. Cover with parchment or wax paper, continue to cook on High until shrimp are just barely cooked, they will be pink. Timing will be about 2–3 minutes. Do not overcook or shrimp will be tough. It is best to stir the shrimp once or twice while cooking and move any shrimp that turn pink before the others to the center.

SHRIMP VERACRUZ

Serves 4

This is a recipe I was asked to adapt from a dish originated to honor the President of Mexico and Mexico's wonderful shellfish. Cooking time given for the onion and green pepper will leave them rather crisp, so if you prefer them less crunchy, cook a bit longer before adding shrimp.

1 large onion, cut into chunks
1 large green pepper, seeded and cut into chunks
2 tablespoons oil
2 garlic cloves, crushed
1 8-ounce can tomato sauce
¼ cup dry white wine
½ teaspoon dried oregano
½ teaspoon salt
¼ teaspoon ground cumin
Dash of hot pepper sauce
1 pound uncooked jumbo shrimp, shelled and deveined
2 tablespoons chopped fresh parsley for garnish
Freshly cooked rice or noodles

Combine onion, pepper, oil, and garlic in shallow baking dish. Cook on High (600–700 watts) 3 minutes. Stir in tomato sauce, wine, oregano, salt, cumin, and hot pepper sauce. Cover with waxed paper and cook on High 5 minutes.

Add shrimp and toss lightly to coat with sauce. Cook on High until shrimp just turn pink, about 3–4 minutes. If you notice several shrimp are done before the others, move them to center of dish, leaving uncooked shrimp on outside.

Garnish with parsley and serve immediately, accompanied by hot rice or noodles.

SHRIMP AND ARTICHOKES

Serves 2–3

Easy but elegant.

Leftovers may be served in a cold pasta salad—just combine with some cooked spaghetti and leftover vegetables, a bit of Parmesan cheese, and whatever else from your refrigerator that seems to fit in—to stretch it into another meal. At the price of shrimp these days, it is practical to think ahead.

1 pound medium to large shrimp, peeled, cleaned, and deveined
1 6-ounce jar marinated artichoke hearts, liquid reserved

¼ **cup lemon juice**
2 **cloves garlic, minced**
½ **teaspoon salt**
½ **teaspoon oregano leaves**
½ **teaspoon dillweed**
⅛ **teaspoon pepper**

Arrange shrimp in a circle in a single layer on a round paper plate with tails facing center and thicker part facing outside area of dish. Cover with wax paper. Cook on High (600–700 watts) for 2–3 minutes, just until shrimp turn slightly pink.

You may wish to do this in two batches if the shrimp are medium-sized. Shrimp should only be cooked briefly since overcooking will make them tough. If the shrimp in the center cook more slowly, remove the ones that are cooked and allow the rest to finish.

Remove 2 tablespoons of the marinated artichoke liquid. (Use the rest for the pasta salad or a regular salad.) Place the 2 tablespoons liquid, the artichoke hearts, and all other ingredients in a bowl. Heat on High 1 minute, just until it is heated through. Stir in shrimp. Serve immediately. For a full meal, serve over a bed of rice.

LOBSTER TAILS SUPREME
Serves 2

Every lobster lover should own a microwave. The results are perfect, succulent lobster tails every time. Many restaurants have discovered the superior quality of the lobster meat, when it is not exposed to a hot dry environment. This method requires less basting because the lobster is not drying out while it cooks.

2 **8-ounce lobster tails**
2 **tablespoons butter or Clarified Butter (see Index)**
½ **teaspoon lemon juice**
Paprika

Split each lobster tail and carefully pull lobster meat through the top shell, leaving small end attached to shell at other end. Place on shallow baking au gratin dish. Melt butter and combine with lemon juice and paprika. Brush over tails.

Cover loosely with parchment or wax paper. Cook on High (600–700 watts) 5–6 minutes, just until lobster meat turns opaque. Do not overcook. Observe lobsters while cooking and turn dish if they do not cook evenly. Additional timing information: Use 1 teaspoon butter and ½ teaspoon lemon juice for each lobster tail. One tail, cook 3 minutes; 2 tails, cook 5–6 minutes; 4 tails, cook 9–10 minutes.

Note: If you are fond of garlic, add 1 large clove, quartered, to the butter while melting. Remove it before brushing lobster with butter. This adds a subtle garlic flavor that is not overpowering.

CLAMS CASINO
Serves 2

Clams are most interesting to watch cook in the microwave. They open their shells a bit at a time. Those that do not open after a few minutes are considered unsuitable for eating and should be discarded. The delicate clam should be removed immediately to prevent overcooking.

12 **clams**
½ **cup butter (room temperature)**
¼ **cup finely chopped onions**
¼ **cup finely chopped green pepper**
¼ **cup finely chopped celery**
¼ **cup finely chopped fresh parsley**
2 **tablespoons lemon juice**
1 **5-ounce jar chopped pimientos**
4 **slices bacon, cooked and crumbled**

Arrange half of the clams in a circle on a shallow plate with hinges facing the outside of the dish. Cook on High (600–700 watts) for 3 minutes, removing each clam as the shells open. Repeat with remaining clams.

In a 1-quart bowl, combine softened butter, onion, green pepper, celery, parsley, and lemon juice. Blend well. Arrange half of the clams in a circle on a shallow round plate. Top each clam with equal portion of the mixture. Sprinkle with some chopped pimientos and bacon. Cook on High 2–3 minutes until heated through. Repeat with remaining clams. Serve immediately.

STEAMED CLAMS WITH GARLIC BUTTER AND PARSLEY

Serves 4

Clams, like all seafood, are at their best if not overcooked. They will steam in their shells, and the moment the shells begin to open, they should be removed from the microwave. Since they will vary in size and moisture, the timing on each clam will be slightly different. Remove each one as it opens to assure tender, succulent clams.

2 dozen clams in the shell, well scrubbed (use a small brush)
½ cup butter or margarine
2 cloves garlic, minced
2 tablespoons fresh parsley, chopped
1 teaspoon lemon juice

Arrange half the clams in a circle on a round serving dish with hinges facing the rim of the dish. Cook on High (600–700 watts) for 3–5 minutes, or until all shells open, removing clams just as they open. Discard any shells that do not open. Repeat with remaining clams.

Combine butter, garlic, parsley, and lemon juice in an attractive serving bowl. If it does not have a handle, place a saucer underneath for ease of handling. Cook on High 1½–2 minutes, until butter is bubbling. Serve clams in serving dish, or arrange on individual serving plates and pass garlic butter separately. Serve immediately. Great with crusty garlic bread (see index).

CRAB DIVAN

Serves 4 as a side dish, or 2–3 as a main dish

I saw this recipe in a beautiful California Sea Food Association cookbook, and the picture immediately said "microwave."

Although the recipe calls for crab, any seafood —or even chicken—could be substituted. I have also prepared it with leftover fish.

The recipe mentions frozen broccoli; however, the fresh tastes and looks much better in this dish. It is very attractive when served in a quiche dish, and I would not hesitate to prepare it for guests as a unique appetizer or for two as a whole meal.

1 pound Dungeness crab meat
**   (fresh, frozen, or canned)**
1 pound fresh broccoli, or
**   2 10-ounce packages frozen broccoli spears**
1 tablespoon butter
2 tablespoons flour
½ teaspoon salt
¼ teaspoon pepper
½ cup milk
¼ cup grated cheddar cheese
1 1-pound can tomatoes, well drained
2 tablespoons crushed corn flakes

If crab meat is frozen, thaw for 1 minute on High (600–700 watts) and drain well. Cut into 1-inch pieces and set aside. If fresh, wash broccoli and cut spears in half lengthwise, splitting stalks slightly. If frozen, place unopened box in microwave and cook on High for 3 minutes. Let stand 5 minutes; remove from box and drain.

Arrange broccoli spears in ring fashion with flowers facing outside, in a 9- or 10-inch quiche dish. If broccoli is fresh, sprinkle with a few tablespoons of water, cover and cook on High for 4 minutes. Set aside, covered.

In large glass measure, heat butter until melted; stir in flour, salt, and pepper until well blended. Add milk slowly, stirring until smooth. Cook on High until thick, about 1–2 minutes. Stir in cheese until melted. Blend in tomatoes.

Drain any remaining liquid from the dish in which the broccoli was cooked. Place cooked crab meat in center of dish. Pour sauce over crab and sprinkle with corn flakes. Cook on High 5 minutes, or until steaming hot.

8
POULTRY

POULTRY: TIPS AND TECHNIQUES

Whole poultry is especially well-suited to microwave cooking because of its empty cavity.

When preparing a whole chicken or turkey, I prefer to start it breast side up and finish breast side down, so that all of the juices flow into the white meat and keep it moist. Whether you choose this method or not, the whole bird should be turned over at least once during cooking to ensure even cooking.

Many books recommend the use of foil on the wings and parts of the leg to avoid overcooking; I do not feel this is necessary, as most people enjoy them crisp. Besides, if the wings and legs are overcooking, you can simply use a lower power level to slow cooking down.

Poultry has always been one of the most popular microwavable foods. It has been widely used from the beginning—in recipes ranging from poached chicken to Cordon Bleu—as microwave cooks made use of its flexibility. And there is seldom a group that does not ask about cooking turkey in the microwave, and if there are any limitations.

Like all cooking, there is a technique to making the food turn out in the best possible fashion. In this chapter I separate the chicken from the turkey. Because chicken can cook on High power and does it so well, there is seldom a reason to slow it down. On the other hand, turkey is thicker, less tender, and needs a lower setting so heat can penetrate the areas around the leg bone and thighs. Of course, both chicken and turkey parts will cook best if arranged on the dish with the thickest portion on the outside, where it will receive the greatest amount of microwave energy.

Whole Chicken

Timing: 7 minutes per pound on High (600–700 watts).

Wash cavity inside and out; remove kidneys with a spoon and rinse cavity well. Pat dry and season with your favorite seasoning (you may salt if you wish). Place in an oval or round shallow baking dish, just large enough to contain chicken.

The use of a rack is optional—with it, the results will be slightly different. If elevated on a rack, the bird will have a slightly crisper skin texture and it will brown a bit better. (You will also need to wash the rack.)

If you cover the bird with parchment or wax paper, the environment close to the bird will equalize and provide more even heating, without the steaming it would experience with plastic wrap.

Cook chicken breast side up for half the cooking time, baste, then turn it breast side down for the remaining time. If the bird is cooking unevenly, turn the dish to a different position. For more flavor and color, baste again.

After the initial cooking time is completed, you can keep the chicken warm and ensure that the areas around the bone are completely cooked by lowering the power to Medium Low (200–250 watts) for about 5–7 minutes. This will also improve flavor and make carving easier.

Chicken Parts

Timing: 7 minutes per pound on High (600–700 watts).

Arrange chicken parts in a shallow baking dish just large enough to contain pieces. Place thickest parts facing outside of dish, and thinnest parts pointing toward the inside.

Use your favorite seasoning or coating. For tender, moist chicken parts, cover with parchment or wax paper. To crisp coated chicken parts, cover with paper towel.

Turning chicken parts over is optional—they will cook evenly without turning. However, some recipes are improved by turning—either to baste chicken in the juices, or to adapt to a specific recipe.

Chicken Breasts

Timing: 5 minutes per pound on High (600–700 watts).

Always the fastest part of the chicken to cook. When boned, it will cook even faster. When using with other parts, place it either in the center or toward the center of the dish.

Allow breasts to remain covered for a few minutes after cooking for juices to redistribute.

Cornish Hens

Timing: 8–9 minutes per pound on High (600–700 watts).

Because they have little fat attached to the skin, they need help with color: follow recipes that give suggestions for stuffing and basting. Although I still recommend starting breast side up and ending breast side down, it improves the appearance of a cornish hen to turn it back to breast side up for an additional 2 minutes on High.

Larger hens (weighing over 1 pound) should be

cooked on Medium High (400–500 watts) for 10–11 minutes per pound to ensure that the areas around the bone are completely cooked.

Poached Chicken

Cook chicken in hot broth, covered, for 5–7 minutes per pound.

Stuffed Chicken

Use your favorite stuffing; or recipes in this book. No change in cooking time is needed.

Coated Chicken

See technique used in Chicken Marengo recipe (see index).

Chicken in a Sauce

Cook chicken with coating until almost done, then add sauce and heat together.

Chicken Soup (from scratch)

All ingredients go into the soup pot at the same time. Cooking time for 4–6 servings is about 1 hour.

DEFROSTING GUIDE: POULTRY

Food	Amount	Power Setting	Time (in minutes per pound)	Standing Time (in minutes)	Comments
Capon	6–8 lb.	Medium High (400–500 watts)	2	60	Turn over once.
Chicken Cut-Up	2–3 lb.	Medium Low (200–250 watts)	5–6	10–15	Turn ½ way through defrost time. Rearrage pieces when partially defrosted.
Chicken Whole	2–3 lb.	Medium Low (200–250 watts)	6–8	30	Turn over once.
Cornish Hen	1–1½ lb. 2–2½ lb.	Medium Low (200–250 watts)	12–13 20–21	20 30	Turn over once.
Duckling	4–5 lb.	Medium High (400–500 watts)	4	30–40	Turn over once.
Turkey Whole	Under 8 lb.	Medium Low (200–250 watts)	3–5	60	Turn over once.
	Over 8 lb.	Medium High (400–500 watts)	3–5	60	
Turkey Breast	4–5 lb.	Medium Low (200–250 watts)	4–5	30	Turn over once.
Turkey Drumsticks	1–1½ lb.	Medium Low (200–250 watts)	5–6	15	Turn and separate ½ way through defrost time.
Turkey Roast Boneless	2–4 lb.	Medium Low (200–250 watts)	3–4		Turn over once.

Whole Turkey

Timing: 7–10 minutes per pound (with or without stuffing).

Use rack to lift turkey away from juices to prevent white meat from overcooking. Use High (600–700 watts) for 20 minutes to get bird started, then slow cooking to Medium High (400–500 watts) so the heat can penetrate the areas around the bone.

Start turkey breast side up and finish breast side down to permit the juices to drain into the white meat in the breast. Since the back of the turkey contains little meat, doing the major portion of the cooking with the breast side down will produce a juicy turkey.

Here's why a rack is recommended for turkey and not for chicken: Chicken cooks rapidly and does not accumulate as much liquid as turkey. The juices the chicken sits in add flavor and moisture. With the turkey, the cooking time is much longer and the drippings are much greater. The turkey does not need this extra moisture to stay moist during the cooking period, since there is a large enough layer of fat in the turkey to baste the turkey as it cooks.

Seasoning and browning techniques for poultry can be found among the recipes in this chapter, or in Chapter 2 under Browning.

Evenly Cooked Turkey

As I was putting the finishing touches on a quiche at the San Francisco Gourmet Products Show last year, I heard an unmistakable southern accent saying "Why, there's Thelma." It was Dinah Shore, who came over immediately to share her turkey microwave technique with me.

Since the white meat cooks faster, it is always possible that it may overcook while you are trying to get the area around the leg and thigh done. What Dinah suggests is to cut the breast away, cover the rest of the bird with wax paper or parchment, and place it back for a few minutes of cooking time until the leg and thigh are done.

I have tried it, and she is right—it is a great idea.

JUST PLAIN CHICKEN
Makes 3–4 cups shredded chicken for salads or chicken recipes, or just plain chicken for 3–4

When I am not in the mood to cook I pick up a fresh plump chicken at the market, or take one from my freezer. I defrost it, season it lightly, place it in a shallow au gratin dish, and cook it, always starting it breast side up and finishing breast side down so that all of the juices drain into the white meat.

We dine on moist, tender chicken and continue to enjoy it as chicken salad or cold sandwiches for the next few days.

1 4- to 5-pound roaster
Salt, pepper, garlic powder, and paprika to taste

Wash chicken; remove giblets and separate the liver. Freeze liver in a separate container to be added to whenever whole chickens are used. Giblets can be cleaned and placed in a container in the freezer to be used for soups or chicken stock. Remove kidneys (they are embedded in the back portion of the chicken), using a spoon to scoop them out. (They make the chicken bitter.) Rinse well.

Season inside and out. Place breast side up in shallow baking dish just large enough to contain chicken. Cover with parchment or wax paper. Cook on High (600–700 watts) for 15 minutes. Turn chicken breast side down, basting with drippings. Continue cooking on High for 15 minutes, or until chicken is tender. If using a probe, set at 180°F. If not, cook chicken for 7 minutes per pound, dividing the cooking time in half to turn chicken over.

POACHED CHICKEN BREAST
Serves 2

When a recipe calls for cooked chicken, this can be an easy way to prepare it. It is also delicious in sandwiches, salads, or on its own as a fine meal, served with a baked potato and green salad.

Although you can remove the skin before poaching, I leave it on because it adds more flavor to the chicken, especially if you are using chicken granules instead of a rich chicken broth. I do not season because the broth is salted (and the chicken granules contain salt).

**1 whole chicken breast, boned and halved
    (about 10 ounces)**
**½ cup chicken broth; or ½ teaspoon chicken
    granules, dissolved in ½ cup hot water**

Arrange the halved chicken breast skin side up in a small casserole, just large enough to contain the recipe. Add the broth. Cover. Cook on High (600–700 watts) for 4–5 minutes, just until chicken is tender. Turn in the broth several times to baste. Allow to cool in the juices if serving cold.

KAHLUA FRUITED CHICKEN ACAPULCO

Serves 4–6

Some time ago I was asked by the producer of a training film on cooking to cook the food for the film. The recipes, though developed for conventional cooking, were excellent. After explaining that my field was microwave (and recommending a professional food stylist), I suggested they include a microwave adaptation of one of the recipes. It was hard to decide which one to use — they all adapted well. However, we felt this recipe would be a good choice, since chicken is such a popular food. To make the recipe work in the microwave, I added kitchen bouquet for color and cornstarch as a thickener.

1 3½- to 4-pound fryer, cut into pieces (skin may be removed—optional)
2 tablespoons liquid browning sauce
1 tablespoon oil
½ teaspoon garlic powder
½ teaspoon salt
½ teaspoon powdered ginger
1 8-ounce can chunk pineapple (unsweetened, in its own juice), drained, juice reserved
½ cup plus 2 tablespoons Kahlua liqueur
1 tablespoon lemon juice
2 tablespoons cornstarch
1 11-ounce can mandarin oranges, drained
¼ cup green onion, chopped
Freshly cooked rice or noodles

Dry chicken parts well. Combine browning sauce and oil; brush generously over chicken. Sprinkle with garlic powder, salt, and ginger. Arrange skin side down in shallow oval baking dish, with larger pieces toward outside of dish. Cook covered with waxed paper 10 minutes on High (600–700 watts). Add pineapple juice to baking dish, along with ½ cup Kahlua liqueur and lemon juice. Turn chicken skin side up, and cook covered with waxed paper on High

10–14 minutes or until chicken is done (allow 7 minutes per pound). Remove chicken with slotted spoon and set aside.

Skim fat from baking dish. Combine cornstarch with remaining liqueur, and stir until cornstarch is dissolved. Stir into sauce. Cook on High until thickened and clear, about 2–3 minutes. Arrange chicken in baking dish. Add pineapple and mandarin oranges and spoon sauce over chicken. Sprinkle with green onion. Reheat chicken to serving temperature, about 2 minutes. Serve immediately over freshly cooked rice or noodles.

TUTTI-FRUTTI CHICKEN

Serves 4

Combining chicken with dried fruits and fresh mushrooms enhances the taste and beautiful appearance of this dish. It is great for holiday entertaining, guest dinners, and for a sweet way to enjoy chicken. Choose an attractive cook-and-serve dish to simplify serving.

1 3½- to 4-pound chicken, disjointed; or 4 chicken breasts
1 cup Russian dressing (8-ounce bottle)
1 cup pineapple-apricot jam
½ cup white wine
1 envelope dry onion soup mix
½ pound fresh mushrooms, sliced
1 6-ounce package dried apricots
1 cup pitted prunes
½ cup sliced almonds

Arrange chicken skin side up in oval or round baking dish, with large pieces facing outside of dish. Combine all ingredients except almonds in a bowl. Stir well; pour over chicken. Cover with waxed paper or parchment. Cook on High (600–700 watts) 25 minutes (7 minutes per pound), turning dish once halfway through cooking time.

Sprinkle with almonds. Cover and allow to stand 5 minutes before serving. The fruit will caramelize and attach to the chicken.

Serve with Curry Rice (see index).

Note: Tutti-Frutti Chicken may be made ahead of time and reheated on Medium High (400–500 watts).

STUFFED ROAST CHICKEN
Serves 3–4

Just because this is an old fashioned dish doesn't mean new technology can't handle it. This can start a family tradition. Use the heel of the bread to hold the stuffing in—a trick I learned from my mother. My sister and I loved to share the wonderful flavors it absorbed. It is a perfect technique for microwave, since you cannot use metal skewers.

½ **cup finely chopped celery**
½ **cup finely chopped onion**
2 **tablespoons vegetable oil**
1 **cup finely chopped mushrooms**
2 **tablespoons finely chopped fresh parsley**
½–1 **cup chicken broth, heated; or 1 cup water**
   plus 1 teaspoon chicken granules
1 **6-ounce package corn bread stuffing mix**
1 **4-pound chicken cleaned (kidneys removed),**
   rinsed, and patted dry
1 **slice bread, preferably the heel of an egg bread**
   loaf
½ **teaspoon paprika**
¼ **teaspoon salt**
⅛ **teaspoon pepper**
⅛ **teaspoon garlic powder**

Combine celery, onion, and oil in a 2-quart glass measure or bowl. Cook on High (600–700 watts) for 4 minutes, stirring once. Stir in mushrooms and parsley. Continue to cook for 1 minute. Add ½ cup of broth. Lightly toss in the corn bread stuffing mix. Add just a bit of broth at a time until mixture is lightly moistened. Don't allow it to become too moist, or stuffing will be soggy.

Spoon the stuffing into the chicken cavity. Cover the opening with the heel of bread. Stuff the neck of the chicken, and secure with wood toothpicks. Put any remaining stuffing into a small dish.

Place chicken in a shallow au gratin or baking dish. Sprinkle with paprika, salt, pepper, and garlic powder (or if you prefer, use a microwave shake product for chicken).

Cook chicken breast side up, covered with parchment or wax paper, on High (600–700 watts) for 15 minutes. Baste chicken with drippings. Carefully turn chicken over and continue cooking covered for an additional 15 minutes, until the juices in chicken run clear—or if using a probe, when the internal temperature reaches 170°F. (after standing it should go up 10 degrees). If using a smaller or larger chicken use 7–8 minutes per pound as a cooking guide.

Turn chicken over; baste with drippings. Cover and allow to sit 5 minutes for juices to redistribute before carving. If you enjoy experimenting, try this way of carving the chicken. It will give you thick chunks of succulent chicken, instead of thin slices:

Cut the entire breast away from the bone in one piece. Place it on a cutting board. Cut thick slices across the grain. Arrange on a platter, with slices slightly overlapping. Place stuffing in center of platter. Reheat on Medium High (400–500 watts) before serving, about 2–3 minutes.

To keep chicken moist when reheating and to crisp the skin, remove the skin in one piece before you slice into the breast area. To reheat, use the skin of the chicken to cover the slices of chicken and stuffing. Heat on High until skin is crisp.

You can use this technique just to crisp the skin of chicken or turkey, even when not reheating the meat.

OVEN-FRIED CHICKEN
Serves 3–4

Trust me—this oven-fried chicken is delicious!

This recipe, without the Parmesan cheese, was a favorite for large family get-togethers in our home. I prepared the chicken in the morning in large lasagna pans rather than attempt to barbecue it. It is good served at room temperature, and best if cooked and served the same day without having been refrigerated. However, leftovers do taste good—just not as crisp.

I also use this recipe to prepare a fast chicken dinner for two. I use paperboard throwaways to prepare the chicken, then serve it on dinner plates with baked potato and fresh vegetable. The cleanup? Two dinner plates.

1 **cup corn flakes**
⅓ **cup Parmesan cheese, grated**
½ **teaspoon paprika**
1 **fryer, cut up (about 3–3½ pounds)**
¼ **cup butter, melted (may substitute salad oil or**
   1 egg white)

Place corn flakes in a paper bag. Using a rolling pin, wine bottle, or your hands, crumble the flakes to make it easy to coat the chicken. (I never use the prepared corn flake crumbs for this recipe, because they do not provide the same crunchy texture I get when I crumble the corn flakes myself.) Add the cheese and paprika and shake bag to combine well.

Place coating mixture in a shallow plate.

Dip each chicken piece into melted butter, oil, or egg white, then into crumbs, coating well. Arrange pieces in a shallow oval or round baking dish, with thickest section of chicken facing outside of dish. Cover with white paper towel to catch any splatter and keep microwave cavity clean.

Cook on High (600–700 watts) 7 minutes per pound. Rotate dish if chicken appears to be cooking unevenly. No need to turn chicken over; it will brown underneath from the butter or oil. To ensure that chicken is completely cooked to the bone, continue to cook the chicken on Medium Low (200–250 watts) for an additional 5 minutes.

CHICKEN CACCIATORE
Serves 4

When this recipe was adapted to microwave, the oil was cut from ¼ cup to 2 tablespoons and the wine cut from 1 cup to ½ cup. Also cut was the step requiring the onion and green pepper to be browned in a skillet on the cook-top, the sauce cooked separately, then both added to the chicken, which was then baked for almost 1 hour.

A big advantage to microwave, then, is no frying pan and stove top to clean; a minimum amount of fat required; shorter cooking time; and all cooking done in one baking dish, which can double as a server.

1　3½- to 4-pound fryer, cut into pieces
1　large onion, thinly sliced
1　medium green pepper, thinly sliced
2　tablespoons olive oil (may substitute regular salad oil)
¼　cup all-purpose flour
1　28-ounce can whole peeled tomatoes, with liquid
½　pound fresh mushrooms, sliced
1　bay leaf
2　cloves garlic, minced
2　tablespoons chopped parsley
1　teaspoon paprika
½　teaspoon salt
⅛　teaspoon pepper
½　teaspoon oregano
¼　teaspoon basil
½　cup dry red wine

Wash chicken; pat dry and set aside.

Place onion, green pepper, and oil in a 3-quart oval or round casserole. Cook on High (600–700 watts) for 5–7 minutes or until onion is transparent, stirring once. Stir in the flour. Add tomatoes and stir until flour is absorbed. Blend in remaining ingredients, except chicken. Cover and continue to cook on High 5 minutes. Arrange chicken parts in casserole with thinner portions facing inside and the white meat placed in center. Spoon sauce over chicken, covering well. Cover. Continue to cook on High 25–30 minutes, or until chicken is fork tender.

Note: The sauce makes this a good dish to serve over a bed of simple rice (see index). Or cook a pound of pasta on your cook-top while this is cooking in your microwave, and have a whole meal. Add a green salad with oil and vinegar dressing, and garlic bread (see index). Pass some Parmesan cheese at the table—and you will enjoy a touch of Italy.

This reheats well, so if you are only two, do the whole recipe anyway and enjoy it two nights in a row.

PARMESAN CHICKEN
Serves 1

Dining alone need not be a sandwich. Easy to prepare, turns a breast of chicken into a feast for one. You might even decide to invite a guest the next time around. Goes well with a simple baked potato and a fresh seasonal vegetable and sliced tomatoes. If you increase recipe, use about 5 minutes per pound as timing for boned chicken breast.

2　tablespoons dry bread crumbs
2　tablespoons grated Parmesan cheese
⅛　teaspoon dried oregano, crumbled
⅛　teaspoon paprika
⅛　teaspoon freshly ground pepper
1　whole chicken breast (about 8 ounces), boned (skinned if desired)
1　egg white or 2 tablespoons melted butter

Combine first 5 ingredients in small bowl and blend well. Dip chicken in egg white, then in coating mixture, turning to coat evenly. Arrange skin side up on small shallow dish or plate. Cover loosely with paper towel and cook on High (600–700 watts) until chicken is just tender, about 4 minutes.

CHICKEN MARENGO
Serves 4

Although I do not use many packaged seasoning mixes, some are so well blended that I don't feel the need to mix my own. This recipe is a good example.

Lawry's printed this recipe in one of their recipe folders well over 10 years ago. I used to make it in the conventional manner: I seasoned the chicken parts, fried the chicken in oil on a cook-top, transferred the browned chicken to a baking dish, poured the sauce and mushrooms over the top, and baked it for an hour.

Look what I save in the microwave: No oil needed for frying, no big frying pan to scour, no cook-top to clean off splatter, no baking dish to wash, and no hot oven in my kitchen for almost an hour!

To microwave, I simply place the chicken into the casserole I will later serve in. I brown and crisp the coating with the help of an egg white, then add the remaining ingredients and let it finish cooking in the sauce. Results —the same; time saved — approximately 35 minutes.

This technique of pre-crisping and pre-cooking the chicken is an important part of my workshops. Notice the timing on this recipe. The 3-pound chicken is pre-cooked without the sauce for 15 minutes (5 minutes per pound); then the sauce is added to finish the recipe.

It is usual to cook chicken 7 minutes per pound in the microwave. This leaves 2 minutes per pound for the chicken to cook in the sauce. Once the sauce is added the microwaves are attracted to the moisture and very little cooking takes place in the chicken. Therefore it is important to remember to increase the amount of *the pre-cooking time* if you increase the amount of chicken. For example, for 4 pounds of chicken you would pre-cook the cooked parts for 20 minutes before adding the sauce. The time for heating the sauce — 10 minutes —would stay the same.

This is a good company dish, as well as one your family will enjoy. If you are only cooking for two, I recommend you still cook the entire recipe —it is excellent cooked ahead and rewarmed the next day.

This recipe is also delicious made with just the coating, sans sauce.

1 **3-pound chicken, cut up**
1 **egg white**
2 **cups fresh bread crumbs**
1 **3-ounce package spaghetti sauce mix**
1 **15-ounce can peeled tomatoes, undrained (pear-shaped with basil, if available)**
2½ **cups mushrooms, freshly sliced**

1 **cup dry white wine**
Parsley for garnish (optional)

Rinse chicken and pat dry with paper towels. Dip in egg white. Blend bread crumbs and spaghetti sauce mixture. Heavily coat each piece of chicken with crumbs. Place pieces in deep round or oval 3-quart casserole or tureen, with white meat on bottom (it needs less energy) and legs and wings on top. Arrange legs so large portion is facing toward outside of dish. Sprinkle any remaining crumbs over top. Cook uncovered on High (600 to 700 watts) 15 minutes to crisp chicken.

With a scissors, cut tomatoes into pieces (carefully as they are quite juicy and have a tendency to squirt). Add tomatoes, mushrooms, and wine to chicken. Cover; cook on High 10 minutes. Check at bone of leg for doneness and cook 5 more minutes if needed.

Before serving, sprinkle with touch of parsley if you like.

SHERRIED CHICKEN FLORENTINE
Serves 4

Florentine means the addition of spinach. This dish will become a tradition for family gatherings, entertaining friends, or just dinner at home. It is easy to prepare and the flavors are so good together. I have also prepared it with jumbo shrimp instead of chicken; either way, it is a treat.

You may use the Poached Chicken Breast recipe (see index) or cook an entire chicken, which is less expensive and just as easy. I use a 3½-pound chicken to get 2½ cups of shredded chicken for this recipe.

1 **small onion, chopped**
4 **tablespoons butter or margarine**
2 **10-ounce packages frozen chopped spinach, thawed and well-drained**
2½ **cups shredded cooked chicken**
1 **10½ ounce can cream of chicken soup**
1 **cup shredded sharp cheddar cheese**
3 **tablespoons dry sherry**
2 **slices fresh bread, coarsely crumbled in a blender or food processor**
3 **tablespoons butter or margarine**
Paprika
2 **teaspoons finely chopped fresh parsley**

Place onion and 1 tablespoon butter in a 2-quart bowl. Cook on High (600–700 watts) until the onion is tender, about 4 minutes. Add the spinach and blend together lightly. Spread on the bottom of a 10-inch quiche dish. Arrange the chicken on top of the spinach.

Combine the soup, cheese, and sherry in a 4-cup glass measure. Cook on High 4 minutes, stirring once. Stir again until cheese is melted.

Combine the bread crumbs and remaining butter in a small glass measuring cup. Cook on High for 1–2 minutes, stirring once, until the crumbs begin to brown. Stir through crumbs several times to blend the butter.

Pour the cheese sauce over the chicken. Sprinkle the browned crumbs over the chicken. Sprinkle with paprika. Cook on High for 10–12 minutes until heated through. Sprinkle with fresh parsley just before serving.

CHICKEN CORDON BLEU

Serves 2–4

When I buy chicken for this recipe, I always buy two small fryers weighing about 3 pounds each and bone the breasts myself. The whole breasts are quite large and can serve four people, depending on their appetites.

2 whole chicken breasts, boned
4 slices prosciutto ham, thinly sliced
4 slices Monterey Jack cheese
1 egg beaten

Sauce

1–2 tablespoons flour
2 tablespoons freshly grated onion
¼ cup dry white wine
8 medium-sized mushrooms, sliced
1 cup shredded Monterey Jack cheese
3 tablespoons finely chopped fresh parsley

Place each chicken breast in a plastic bag and pound, skin side down until even and thin. Place a slice each of ham and cheese on each breast half and fold over (you may fasten sides together with wooden toothpicks, but I seldom find it necessary).

Dip the breasts in the beaten egg. Place them skin side down in ring fashion in a shallow round or oval dish, leaving the center empty. (It is all right if the ends touch each other.) Cover with parchment or wax paper. Cook on High (600–700 watts) for 5 minutes. Baste with drippings. Turn chicken over. Continue to cook for an additional 4 minutes, until chicken is just tender. Remove chicken from dish and set aside, covered, to keep warm while you make the sauce.

Stir flour into drippings, adding enough to give the sauce some body. Slowly stir in onion. Cook sauce on High for 1 minute. Slowly stir in wine and mushrooms. Continue to cook on High 2–3 minutes, until mushrooms are just cooked and sauce has thickened slightly. Stir in cheese; continue to cook 1–2 minutes, until cheese is melted.

Arrange chicken as before; spoon sauce over top. Sprinkle with parsley. If necessary reheat on Medium High (400–500 watts) for 1–2 minutes, until sauce begins to bubble slightly.

LOW-CALORIE PINEAPPLE CHICKEN

Serves 4

This is a low-calorie favorite I adapted for my low-calorie classes. If you don't tell, they won't guess. You can make it ahead and reheat.

1 cup crushed pineapple (unsweetened, canned in its own juices, drained)
¼ cup soy sauce
1 tablespoon wine vinegar
2 teaspoons prepared mustard
½ teaspoon ground ginger
1 3-pound frying chicken, cut into parts, skin removed
2 cups fresh mushrooms, sliced
1 small green pepper, cut into chunks
1 scallion, cut into small sections
Fresh parsley for garnish

In a large glass measure, combine drained pineapple, soy sauce, vinegar, mustard, and ginger. Cook on High (600-700 watts) until it reaches boiling point.

Place chicken in a shallow oval dish, with larger pieces facing outside. Pour pineapple mixture over chicken, turning it well to coat each piece. Cover with wax paper; cook on High for 10 minutes. Turn chicken over, baste, and add mushrooms and green pepper. Cook 12–15 minutes more until chicken is tender (check for doneness near bone). Sprinkle with chopped scallions and fresh parsley and serve.

CHICKEN BREASTS WITH GARLIC, WINE, AND TOASTED PINE NUTS
Serves 2-3

If you visited a friend and the entire house gave forth an aroma that made your mouth water, you would head for the kitchen as I did and plead for the recipe. Shirley Hart should write a cookbook, so that I could adapt as many of her recipes to microwave as possible.

To adapt to microwave, I cut the amount of oil to a minimum and browned the pine nuts first. This is to ensure the nice, crisp texture that is important to the recipe. The advantage to cooking it microwave is that it is all prepared in a single serving dish, uses less fat, and is finished in just a few minutes.

Nice company dish, but ideal for an easy dinner for two or three. If you wish to increase the recipe to serve 4–6, add another whole breast, and increase all other ingredients by ½. Increase cooking time about 5 minutes after adding the chicken.

You may find my servings a bit on the generous side. When the whole chicken breast is split, it does make four sections. But I do find that men prefer two pieces of chicken.

½ **cup flour**
½ **teaspoon salt**
½ **teaspoon paprika**
⅛ **teaspoon pepper**
2 **whole chicken breasts, split and pounded**
2 **tablespoons olive oil**
2 **cloves garlic, minced**
¼ **cup pine nuts**
½ **cup dry white wine**
3 **tablespoons lemon juice**
½ **cup chicken stock, or ½ cup water plus ½ teaspoon chicken concentrate granules**
½ **cup parsley, freshly chopped**

Combine flour, salt, paprika, and pepper. Dip chicken pieces and coat well on both sides. Set aside.

Place oil, garlic, and pine nuts into shallow baking dish, just large enough to contain recipe. Cook on High (600–700 watts) for about 2 minutes, just until nuts are slightly brown. Stir; add chicken and continue to cook on High 3 minutes. Turn chicken over; spoon juices over top. Cook on High 2 more minutes, or until just done.

Remove chicken and set aside, covered. Stir remaining flour mixture, wine, lemon juice, and chicken stock into the baking dish. Cook on High 2–3 minutes until slightly thickened, stirring once.

Stir in parsley. Place chicken in dish; spoon sauce over to baste. Heat on High for about 45 seconds to heat the chicken through. Serve immediately.

BAKED APRICOT CHICKEN
Serves 4–6

This was one of those easy-to-prepare recipes that appeared when we all began to experiment with prepared seasonings and mixes. It readily adapts to microwave and was an early favorite for teaching microwave cooking because it not only tastes good, but looks so attractive. I always prepare it in an oval or round large, shallow baking dish that fills the entire cavity. If you prefer to cut the recipe in half by using less chicken, cut the other ingredients in half as well.

4–5 **pounds chicken fryer parts**
1 **cup apricot preserves**
½ **cup bottled Russian dressing**
¼ **cup mayonnaise**
1 **envelope dry onion soup mix**

Rinse chicken, dry with paper towels, and arrange skin side down in a large, shallow baking dish, placing thickest pieces facing outside of dish and thinnest toward the center.

Combine remaining ingredients. Spread over chicken, coating each piece. Cover with wax paper or parchment. Cook on High (600–700 watts) for 15 minutes. Turn chicken over with tongs, and baste with sauce. Continue to cook, covered with wax paper or parchment, for an additional 15 minutes, or until the juices near the bone of the chicken are no longer pink.

If you reduce the amount of chicken, use 7 minutes per pound as your guide, turning and basting halfway through the timing.

CASHEW CHICKEN
Serves 4

The popularity of light eating, but not at the expense of good flavor and nutrition, is a sign that we are beginning to be aware that we are what we eat.

Typical of Oriental dining is this combination of chicken, vegetables, a bit of chicken stock for low fat flavor, and the lovely cashew for crunch and protein. Taken from a wok recipe, it adapts well to microwave.

2 tablespoons dry white wine (may substitute water)
1 tablespoon soy sauce
1 tablespoon oil
1 tablespoon cornstarch
⅛ teaspoon freshly ground pepper
⅛ teaspoon hot sauce
2 whole chicken breasts, skinned, boned, pounded slightly
1 medium onion, cut in half, then cut into slices
1 red or green pepper (or both), cut into chunks
2 tablespoons oil
1 cup whole cashews
½ cup chicken stock, or ½ cup water and 1 teaspoon chicken granules
1 6-ounce package frozen pea pods (removed from freezer and rinsed with cold water to separate, or placed in the microwave for 2 minutes on High)

In a small bowl, combine wine, soy sauce, 1 tablespoon oil, cornstarch, pepper, and hot sauce. Stir until cornstarch is completely dissolved. Cut each chicken into 6 pieces. Place chicken pieces in a shallow plate, pour wine marinade over top and turn chicken to coat. If time permits, allow it to marinate for 45 minutes.

In a 2-quart bowl, combine onion, peppers, oil, and cashews. Cook on High (600–700 watts) for 5 minutes, stirring once. Stir in chicken stock. Drain marinade from chicken. Add to vegetable mixture. Stir and set aside.

Cook chicken pieces in the same plate in which they were marinating. Cover with parchment or wax paper, and cook on High (600–700 watts) for 3 minutes. Turn pieces over, continue to cook for 2–3 minutes, just until chicken loses its pink color. Set aside while you prepare the sauce.

Cook sauce, covered, on High 5–6 minutes, or until thickened. Stir in pea pods and chicken pieces. Heat on High 1–2 minutes, just until heated through. Serve in attractive shallow platter.

CORNISH HEN WITH WILD RICE STUFFING
Serves 4

If using a frozen hen, thaw it slowly, preferably overnight in the refrigerator. If time is short, thaw in microwave for 2 minutes on High (600–700 watts). Allow to rest 5 minutes, then rinse with cold water and let it finish thawing at room temperature. Too much microwave energy for thawing will begin to cook the wings. Turn hen breast side down during final cooking time for more succulent white meat.

½ cup sliced almonds
1 tablespoon butter
1 11-ounce can mandarin orange segments, liquid reserved
1 6-ounce package long-grain and wild rice mix
4 Cornish hens, thawed
1–2 teaspoons bottled browning sauce or microwave shake or paprika or seasoned salt
Parsley sprigs or orange segments for garnish

Combine almonds and butter in small measuring cup and cook on High (600–700 watts) until almonds are crisp, 2½–3 minutes.

Drain mandarin oranges, reserving liquid. Add enough water to liquid to measure 1½ cups. Pour into 1½ quart casserole. Add rice mix and seasoning packet and blend well. Cover and cook on High 10 minutes. Let stand covered 5 minutes. Stir in the mandarin oranges and almonds.

Fill hen cavities and close with wood toothpicks, or place ¼ piece from the heel of a bread loaf over the opening. Reserve any remaining stuffing. Place hen breast side up in baking dish just large enough to accommodate. If not using liquid browning sauce, sprinkle with microwave shake or paprika.

Cover with parchment or waxed paper and cook 10 minutes per pound on Medium (300–350 watts). Halfway through cooking time, baste hens with pan drippings. (At this point, only if using browning sauce, add the 2 teaspoons to the pan drippings and baste with a pastry brush.)

Turn hens breast side down and continue cooking until juices run clear when you press down on the hens and the leg portion moves easily. If using microwave with automatic meat probe, set probe after you have turned hens over, because it will not give you any information during the first period and will be awkward to turn with probe in. Set temperature at 170°F. Internal temperature will rise about 10°F. after being removed from microwave.

To keep hens warm in the microwave after cooking, set power level at Low (10%, 65–200 watts) until ready to serve.

Note: Hens do not have a fat layer to promote good browning. There are three suggestions to follow. If you have microwave shake for chicken, this will give the hens good color and flavor. Paprika is an old standby and works well. If using a liquid browning sauce, I prefer to add it to the pan drippings, stir it with the pastry brush, then brush the hens.

Salt and pepper have not been listed because some of the products suggested are already seasoned. If using paprika, you should add salt and pepper to taste.

When a traditional Thanksgiving turkey is impractical, but you just can't do without it, try cutting it down to more manageable proportions. Half a breast is just the right size for one or two, and with a traditional bread stuffing or a fresh vegetable garnish it can duplicate all the best-loved features of Thanksgiving dinner, without all those leftovers.

TURKEY BREAST WITH OLD FASHIONED DRESSING
Serves 1–2

¼ cup onion, diced
¼ cup celery, diced
1 tablespoon oil or butter
1 cup mushrooms, diced
⅔ cup chicken stock, turkey stock, or bouillon
1½ cups corn bread stuffing mix
½ turkey breast
Paprika
Minced fresh parsley
Salt and pepper to taste

Combine onion, celery, and oil in au gratin–type dish just large enough to accommodate all ingredients. Cover with wax paper and cook on High (600–700 watts) 3 minutes. Stir. Add mushrooms and cook 1 minute. Add stock or bouillon and blend well. Add stuffing mix and toss lightly. Mixture should be moist but not soggy.

Set turkey breast on dressing. Sprinkle with paprika and parsley, and salt and pepper if desired. Cover with parchment or wax paper and cook on High 7–10 minutes per pound. For additional flavor you may wish to baste the turkey with a touch of oil or butter.

BREAST OF TURKEY ON BED OF GARDEN VEGETABLES
Serves 1–2

A boned chicken breast also works well with this recipe. While you may choose any of the julienne vegetables in combination, I like to use them all!

1 medium carrot, julienne
1 celery stalk, julienne
1 very small onion, julienne
1 very small potato, julienne
1 tablespoon minced fresh parsley

2 tablespoons butter
Salt and freshly ground pepper
½ turkey breast (remove skin if desired)
Paprika

Place first 5 ingredients close together in small au gratin dish just large enough to accommodate all ingredients. Dot top with butter. Season lightly with salt and pepper. Cover with plastic wrap and cook on High (600–700 watts) for 7 minutes. Stir vegetables, making certain they are still tight together. Set turkey breast on vegetables and sprinkle with paprika. Cover with parchment or wax paper and cook on High 7–10 minutes per pound.

For additional color, baste turkey with melted butter along with the paprika.

ROASTED BONELESS TURKEY
Serves 6–8

During the holidays these boneless, easy to prepare turkeys are perfect for small gatherings. They provide an ideal solution for couples or small families who like the traditional Thanksgiving turkey but don't want to buy a 25-pounder. This boneless version weighs between 5–5½ pounds, is easily sliced at the table, and leaves enough for another Thanksgiving tradition: a turkey sandwich the next day.

1 5- to 5½-pound uncooked boneless young turkey, rolled and ready to cook (do not use precooked turkey roll)
Oil
½ teaspoon garlic powder, or to taste
Salt and freshly ground pepper
Paprika

Set turkey on rack. Rub with oil. Sprinkle with garlic powder, salt, pepper, and paprika. Cover with wax paper or parchment, and cook on medium (300–350 watts) for 30 minutes. Turn roast over and baste with drippings. If you have a meat probe, insert horizontally; set temperature to 160°F. Continue cooking until meat probe registers 160°F. Remove turkey from microwave, cover with foil, and let rest until internal temperature reaches 175°F., about 10 minutes. Cut into slices and serve.

If you do not have a probe, you may use a microwave thermometer and watch for the rise in temperature. Or use timing of about 9–10 minutes per pound for poultry cooked on a Medium setting.

9
MEAT

DEFROSTING GUIDE: MEAT

Food	Amount	Power Setting	Time (in minutes per pound)	Standing Time (in minutes)	Comments
BEEF Ground Beef	1 lb. 2 lb. ¼ lb. patty	Medium Low (200–250 watts)	5–6 5–6 1 min. per patty	5 5 2	½ way through defrost time remove defrosted portions with fork. Return remainder.
Pot Roast Chuck	Under 4 lb.	Medium Low (200–250 watts)	3–5	10	Turn over once.
	Over 4 lb.	Medium (300–350 watts)	3–5	10	
Rib Roast Rolled	3–4 lb.	Medium Low (200–250 watts)	6–8	30–45	Turn over once.
	6–8 lb.	Medium (300–350 watts)	6–8	45–60	
Rib Roast Bone in	2½–4 lb.	Medium Low (200–250 watts)	5–6	45–60	Turn over once.
Rump Roast	3–4 lb.	Medium Low (200–250 watts)	3–5	30	Turn over once.
	6–7 lb.	Medium (300–350 watts)	3–5	45	
Round Steak	2–4 lb.	Medium Low (200–250 watts)	4–5	5–10	Turn over once.
Flank Steak	2–4 lb.	Medium Low (200–250 watts)	4–5	5–10	Turn over once.
Sirloin Steak	½" thick	Medium Low (200–250 watts)	4–5	5–10	Turn over once.
Tenderloin	2–4 lb.	Medium Low (200–250 watts)	5–6	10	Turn over once.
Steaks	2 or 3, 1½–3 lb.	Medium Low (200–250 watts)	4–5	8–10	Turn over once.
Stew Beef	2 lb.	Medium Low (200–250 watts)	3–5	8–10	Turn over and separate once.
LAMB Cubed for Stew	1½–3 lb.	Medium Low (200–250 watts)	7–8	5	Turn over and separate once.

DEFROSTING GUIDE: MEAT

Food	Amount	Power Setting	Time (in minutes per pound)	Standing Time (in minutes)	Comments
LAMB (cont.)					
Ground Lamb	1–4 lb.	Medium Low (200–250 watts)	3–5	20–30	½ way through defrost time remove defrosted portions with fork. Return remainder.
	Over 4 lb.	Medium (300–350 watts)	3–6	30–45	
Chops	¾–1″ thick	Medium Low (200–250 watts)	5–8	15	Turn over once.
Leg of Lamb	4–8 lb.	Medium Low (200–250 watts)	4–5	15–25	Turn over once.
PORK					
Chops	½″ thick	Medium Low (200–250 watts)	4–6	5–10	Separate and turn over ½ way through defrost.
	1″ thick	Medium Low (200–250 watts)	5–7	10	
Spareribs, country style	2–5 lb.	Medium Low (200–250 watts)	5–7	10	Separate and turn over ½ way through defrost.
Roast	under 4 lb.	Medium Low (200–250 watts)	4–5	30–45	Turn over once.
	over 4 lb.	Medium (300–350)	5–7	30–45	Turn over twice.
Bacon	1 lb.	Medium Low (200–250 watts)	2–3	3–5	Separate strips as they defrost.
Bulk Sausage	1 lb.	Medium Low (200–250 watts)	2–3	3–5	½ way through defrost time remove defrosted portions with fork. Return remainder.
Sausage Links	1 lb.	Medium Low (200–250 watts)	3–5	4–6	Separate pieces and turn over once.
Hot Dogs	1 lb.	Medium Low (200–250 watts)	5–6	5	Turn over once.
VEAL					
Roast	3–4 lb.	Medium Low (200–250 watts)	5–7	30	Turn over once.
	6–8 lb.	Medium (300–350)	7–9	60	Turn over twice.

DEFROSTING GUIDE: MEAT

Food	Amount	Power Setting	Time (in minutes per pound)	Standing Time (in minutes)	Comments
Chops	½–¾" thick	Medium Low (200–250 watts)	4–6	20–30	Separate and turn over once.
VARIETY MEAT Liver	1–2 lb.	Medium Low (200–250 watts)	5–6	10–15	Turn over once.
Tongue	1½–3½ lb.	Medium Low (200–250 watts)	7–8	15–20	Turn over once.

SUCCESS WITH BEEF ROASTS

What I appreciate most about cooking tender cuts of meat in the microwave is that I can trim off all the fat and cut down on unnecessary calories. With conventional ovens in which hot air cooks the food, the fat surrounding the roast serves the important function of keeping the meat from drying out. But cooking with microwave energy eliminates the need for a layer of fat for constant basting.

I always find it difficult to persuade a butcher to remove the fat from a roast. I finally realized the price includes the tied-on layer of fat. To reduce the negotiating time, I now simply ask the butcher to give me the roast weighed with the fat, but without additional fat tied to it. If it needs more trimming, a good sharp knife can remove the layer of fat, which will allow browning to take place right on the meat. *A thick layer of fat interferes with good browning,* since the microwaves are then cooking the fat rather than the meat. (Perhaps one day butchers will feature a microwave roast sans fat!)

While there are many ways to cook meat in the microwave, for tender cuts I have a favorite method: cover the roast with dehydrated onion soup and sliced fresh mushrooms to give it a rich brown color and enhance the flavor of the natural meat juices. If you prefer not to use the soup, simply cover the meat with chopped fresh mushrooms, packing them firmly over the entire roast. The natural brown juices of the mushrooms will brown the meat. Other good browning aids include Micro Shake, the first product of its kind to appear on the market, developed for microwave use by Dr. Gasi Taki. Liquid browning

sauces like Gravy Master and Kitchen Bouquet were not developed for microwave use, but have been used in restaurants and kitchens for many years to bring attractive color to gravies and sauces. These add color and flavor to meats. For many recipes, soy sauce or teriyaki sauce can be used to enhance flavor and, again, bring color to the meat. After all, we do eat first with our eyes.

A tender cut of beef should not be covered because it would promote steam. However, you can use a paper towel, because it is not an airtight cover and can be draped over the meat to catch splatter. The need for covering is the same as in conventional cooking. You would not cover a prime rib, but would cover pot roast to promote steam and tenderizing.

A low-sided dish just deep enough to hold the meat and juices snugly is the best for these recipes. I prefer a medium-size au gratin dish. If the container is too deep, the meat will not brown as well and will steam rather than roast; if too large, the food will spread out and will cook unevenly. Cook on High power (600–700 watts) first to promote as much surface browning as possible, then later lower cooking to allow microwaves to penetrate the center of the roast without overcooking the outside. (This is effected through the conduction of heat from the outside of the roast toward the center.)

If your unit does not have a Medium High setting (400–500 watts) you may use a Medium setting (300–350 watts). If your unit has only High (600–700 watts) and Medium Low or Defrost (200–250 watts) settings, use Medium Low as the lower power. Since meat juices are close to the surface on completion of cooking, standing time is important because it allows the juices to be distributed evenly as the roast "relaxes." The juices then remain in the meat rather than run away with the first slice. For this reason you should not penetrate meat with a fork during turning—use tongs or paper towels and your hands to turn meat.

I prefer cooking this type of roast without a rack. Since fat is trimmed the need for the rack is eliminated. The meat absorbs flavor from the onions and mushrooms, and heat from the dish increases browning. Rotate the roast so that each side has a turn cooking against the bottom of the dish. It may take a few minutes of your time, but is worth the effort. It deepens the flavor, promotes even cooking, and the roast will retain more moisture.

To judge doneness of meat if you do not have a meat probe thermometer, press down on the meat with your finger. If the juices are very red it needs further cooking; pink juices indicate that the inside is rare; brown juices suggest it is becoming well done.

TIPS ON GROUND BEEF

Working with a gas-fired barbecue for many years made me aware of the great differences in ground meat. The smoking and shrinking of hamburger patties that contained too much fat, and the great improvement in flavor and texture when high-quality meats were ground, brought me to the conclusion that the only way for me to use ground meat was to have it ground for me.

Chefs I have known always preferred chuck meat to round or sirloin. A lean chuck roast, or a chuck roast trimmed of fat, still has marbleizing to add flavor. I look for packages of lean stew meat (which is usually chuck) and have the butcher grind it for me. If I cannot find stew meat, I will select a boneless chuck roast, then ask the butcher to trim off any fat, grind it, and place it into 1-pound packages. I freeze the extra packages for future use.

When shopping for meat, ask for the butcher in charge—he knows his meat better than anyone, and will be happy to assist you in making a selection. Since we use a great deal of hamburger meat, it is in my best interest to establish a good relationship with my local butcher—as it is yours.

Stew meat is usually less expensive than ground round—but even if it was more, it is worth the difference in flavor.

I seldom have fatty juices to pour off, because of the control I use in selecting the meat. For that reason, I prefer to cook ground meat in a bowl in its own juices, which provide flavor. The plastic colander—a popular microwave accessory—has its value only if fatty ground beef is used. Otherwise the meat will absorb more flavor if allowed to cook in its own juices.

PRIME RIB
Serves 4

It was this recipe that began my association with Dr. Decareau, who changed the course of microwave teaching for those of us who pioneered.

Dr. D. was invited to participate in the first microwave workshop in Los Angeles, sponsored by our Department of Water & Power. It was in 1973 and I had been cooking this prime rib for a microwave commercial, and in my classes. Although we only had High power then, I discovered if I would cook the roast in 5 minute segments, and let it rest an equal amount of time, I could cook it medium rare. Many of the home economists and other professionals attending had been to my workshops and tasted the roast. But Dr. Decareau explained how microwaves penetrated the food about 1½" from the outside in, and did not do well with large dense foods. He said, "When you see Barbara Hale's prime rib on TV, don't you believe it!" With all around me waiting, I had to defend that TV roast, since I had prepared it! So I did and we then had the opportunity to explore what had happened with my testing.

This was a most exciting area of pioneering, because variable powers soon followed and manual control for cooking was no longer necessary. It was Dr. D.'s newsletter that gave us the education and understanding we needed to better understand the technology we had available to us. This is the exact recipe for the roast . . . the only thing that has changed is the equipment.

We now have restaurants that prepare this roast in a microwave, because they can reheat it without loss of flavor—after all, the microwave does not remove the moisture as it cooks. It remains in the roast. It is also important to trim the fat, so the microwaves are cooking the meat, not the fat layer.

In this recipe, I do not use a rack. I find the contact of the meat with the drippings give it color and flavor. The baking dish also becomes quite hot from the meat drippings and sears the meat. Use a paper towel to catch any splatter. Any other covering will boil the meat.

1 5-pound prime rib, fat layer removed
1 package dry onion soup mix (Lipton's)
1 pound fresh mushrooms, sliced

Use a shallow oval baking dish to just contain recipe. Sprinkle soup mix over roast and pat as much as you can on all the surfaces allowing the rest to remain in the dish. Arrange the mushrooms over and around the roast.

Place roast "fat" side down, cook on High (600–700 watts) for 10 minutes. Turn roast over to one side, spoon mushrooms over top. Cook on High 5 minutes. Turn roast to other side, spoon mushrooms over top, continue to cook on High 5 minutes.

At this point the roast has cooked for 20 minutes to promote browning of the outside surface. We now must slow it down, to prevent the outside from overcooking before the inside can begin to cook. Turn roast fat side up.

Continue to cook, at Medium High (400–500 watts) for 10–15 minutes, or until the internal temperature reaches 120°F. if using a probe. (If using a probe do not insert it until this final stage, it will just be in your way when turning and will not give you any information until this stage in any case.)

Timing on rare meat is 6–7 minutes per pound, even when reducing to a Medium High setting. This is minimum timing and one can add from there.

For medium rare the timing is 7–8 minutes per pound, starting on High and reducing to Medium High. Stop cooking at an internal temperature of 130°F. After cooking the temperature will rise about 10°F. degrees to 140°F., which is medium rare.

If you prefer meat well done, this is not a proper roast to choose. During the rest time of about 10 minutes, I like to set my microwave at a low power level, depending on the equipment. Medium Low (200–250 watts) or Low (100–250 watts) will keep the roast warm during the rest period. Allowing the roast to rest before carving is important, since it allows the juices to be redistributed throughout the roast.

BEEF TENDERLOIN (FILLET ROLL)
Serves 4

Prepared this way, the tenderloin looks like a miniature roast. This marvelous fillet can be cut into generous steaks for four or it can be thinly sliced and presented with a savory mushroom mixture over the top just before serving.

1 2- to 2½-pound beef tenderloin at room temperature
2–3 tablespoons dehydrated onion soup mix
1 pound fresh mushrooms, sliced

Place roast in shallow dish and pat soup mix evenly over meat. Arrange mushroom slices over and around roast. Place paper towel loosely over top to catch splatter. Cook on High (600–700 watts) for 5 minutes. Turn roast over and spoon mushrooms and any drippings over top. If available, insert microwave meat probe thermometer into thickest part of roast. Cook on High an additional 5 minutes for medium rare, or until probe registers 130°F. For extremely rare cook to an internal temperature of 120°F.

(Cooking time may vary with the thickness of the fillet of beef. A thinner roast may cook in less time, while the thicker butt end of fillet may need additional time.)

Let stand 5 minutes. Cover with foil tent to keep warm. Internal temperature will increase about 5–10 degrees.

OLD-FASHIONED POT ROAST
Serves 4–6

It *is* possible to produce a tender, succulent pot roast in a microwave. What is necessary is to understand the cooking technique that makes it happen.

In the beginning of microwave technology, it was not possible to tenderize less tender cuts of meat, because High power was all we had. It cooked the meat too fast for the connective tissue to break down and tenderizing to take place. In conventional cooking, we always cook this type of meat slowly and at lower temperature settings until it becomes fork tender. The same is true in microwave cooking—all you need is a fork for testing!

In preparing a pot roast, cook the vegetables, potatoes, and flavoring all together so that just a crisp fresh salad and dessert complete the meal. Leftovers reheat well, or can be frozen for future meals.

1 2½- to 3½-pound chuck roast
4 small potatoes, left whole
4 carrots, cut into large chunks
Seasonings to taste

Follow these simple guidelines for success:
1. Use a nylon cooking bag (or casserole with cover) that *just* holds all of the ingredients. Too large a capacity allows the juices to spread out away from

the meat and attract the microwave energy away from the food needing to be cooked. The cooking bag has an advantage because it steams the ingredients in a closely packed environment. It is also easy to baste with the juices by simply moving the bag into a different position.

2. Always trim fat from the meat, so that the cooking takes place on the meat, not on the fat; this will contribute to browning and more even cooking.

3. Put in vegetables and seasonings at the beginning of cooking, instead of adding in the last 15 minutes of cooking time. The vegetables are sharing the microwave energy with the liquid and meat, and do not get tender when added later. Leaving the potatoes whole, and the carrots in large chunks, will ensure their holding together. I would rather have my potato so fork tender it falls apart than so firm it tastes underdone. Placing the vegetables in at the beginning also gives the meat more flavor, and helps to slow down the cooking even further. Be creative in combining herbs, spices, and sauces to produce tasty results.

4. Start at High power (600–700 watts) for about 10 minutes to get the roast started, then reduce the power level to Medium Low (200–250 watts). Cooking time for 2½–3½ pounds of beef will be about 1½ hours on Medium Low. (If you only have High and Defrost, Defrost is usually the same as Medium Low.)

5. There is no need to use a thermometer for pot roast—you are only interested in tenderizing.

Seasoning Suggestion

Add ½ cup dry sherry, ¼ cup each soy sauce and water, 3 cloves minced garlic, 1 teaspoon each dry mustard and thyme, 2 slices fresh ginger and ⅛ teaspoon ground pepper to the cooking bag for a touch of the Orient.

DEVILED BEEF BONES
Serves 4

If you can't behave like a *Henry the Eighth* movie script, perhaps you should skip this one. I would fight my dog for the last morsel on these bones!

These are the ribs cut from the prime rib and are available in many markets around the country. If you do not see them on display, ask your butcher about ordering some when he is cutting up spencer roasts (the inside eye of the prime rib). They are quite meaty and delicious on a barbecue. They have a delicious flavor when cooked with a sprinkling of onion soup

mix. Don't put these on a rack; they need to absorb the flavor from the drippings. It is best to turn them over once or twice.

If you prefer barbecue sauce, substitute your favorite variety or prepare the one in this book (see index). Cook the ribs for half the cooking time before adding the barbecue sauce. Because the sauce can only penetrate slightly into the meat, and the sugar in the sauce will burn before your cooking time is over, earlier basting is not only unnecessary but not advised.

3 **pounds beef rib bones, trimmed of heavy fat layer**
1 **envelope onion soup mix**

Place bones in a single layer in an oval or round shallow dish. Sprinkle with soup mix, covering all sides. Cover with a paper towel to absorb splatter. Cook on High (600–700 watts) 5 minutes per pound for rare, turning ribs once or twice during the cooking. If you prefer your ribs well done, cook for 6 minutes per pound.

Ribs will be extremely hot; leave covered and wait 5 minutes before tasting.

GRILLED CORNED BEEF HASH
Serves 4

If you love the flavor of corned beef hash but do not have the time or expertise to produce your own, a good canned variety can be a satisfying substitute. This recipe requires a browning dish in order to get a nice, crisp textured crust.

2 **English muffins, split and toasted**
1 **15-ounce can corned beef hash**
4 **teaspoons Dijon mustard**
½ **cup cheddar cheese, shredded**
1 **tablespoon fresh parsley, minced**

Preheat browning dish to its highest absorption (see browning dish information on page 24).

Remove both ends of can; slide a knife around edges to release the hash and press one end firmly until it slips out of the can. Slice into 4 equal patties.

Arrange in a circle on preheated browning dish. Cook on High (600–700 watts) 2 minutes. Turn patties over; cook on High 2 minutes. Lift each patty with a spatula and place muffins underneath; sprinkle tops with cheese. Cook on High 1–2 minutes until cheese is melted. Sprinkle with parsley and serve hot.

PERFECT HAMBURGERS WITH GRILLED ONION

Makes 4 hamburgers

As you may imagine, I have tasted many hamburger patties prepared in a microwave. Some were better than others. But cooking hamburgers that have the grilled texture that is so popular with American taste buds is a technique that can only be achieved in a browning dish. If you do not remove the dish after heating, the heat will remain intense and provide the best grilling affect. I use a long-handled spatula to make it easier to get the food in and out of the cavity.

Although you may add ingredients to ground beef, I prefer just the beef, and use ¼ pound for each hamburger, shaping them into thick, rather than flat shape. The number of hamburgers you can cook at once will depend upon the size of your browning skillet.

1   **pound beef (chuck) ground**
Salt and pepper
1   **large onion, cut into 4 ¼-inch thick slices**
4   **hamburger buns, split**

Season beef with salt and pepper. Moisten your hands and shape beef into 4 equal patties. (If you use a light touch when handling the beef, the texture of the hamburger will also be light, not heavy.)

Preheat browning dish to its highest absorption (see manufacturer's timing for hamburgers). Place meat patties and onion slice into preheated dish. Cook on High (600–700 watts) until juices appear on the top of the meat, which means it has cooked halfway through—about 1–3 minutes per hamburger, depending on the size of your browning dish and how many patties go in at once. Turn over patty and onion slice. Continue to cook on High 1–2 minutes, just until patty is almost cooked through. Leaving it a bit pink and allowing it to remain on the browning dish 1 minute will give you a perfect medium-cooked hamburger.

Place hamburger patty and onion slice into each bun. If you wish to heat the bun, place it into microwave and heat on High 15 seconds.

Note: Hamburgers may be frozen inside the buns. To reheat, remove top of bun, place in microwave, preferably on a rack to prevent the bottom of the bun from steaming from the heat being trapped underneath. Use defrost (Medium Low 200–250 watts) for 1 minute per hamburger. Allow it to rest about 3 minutes. Then use defrost again for 1 minute. Add top of bun and heat on High for 30 seconds. (If top of bun is no longer frozen, use only 15 seconds on High.)

MEAT LOAF TERIYAKI

Serves 4–6

Meat loaf does well in the microwave. There are as many variations to try as there are ethnic cultures in the United States. Simply changing the spices and flavorings makes the meat loaf a delicious new experience. Although you can use a loaf pan, I have always preferred a ring mold for more even cooking toward the center.

This recipe has a Far East flavor, so popular in Hawaii.

2   **pounds lean ground chuck**
1   **cup fresh soft bread crumbs (preferably white egg bread)**
2   **eggs, beaten**
1   **small onion, minced**
1   **cup green pepper, minced**
2   **tablespoons lemon juice**
2   **tablespoons soy sauce**
2   **tablespoons brown sugar**
1   **teaspoon salt**
¾   **teaspoon ground ginger**

Basting Sauce

1   **tablespoon soy sauce**
1   **tablespoon brown sugar**
1   **tablespoon flour**

Combine, with a light touch, all the ingredients but the basting sauce. Spoon into a 6-cup ring mold, or a 1½-quart casserole with a glass placed in the center. Cook on High (600–700 watts) for 10–12 minutes, until loaf begins to pull away from the edges. Turn dish if it appears to be cooking unevenly. If you have a probe meat thermometer, you may use it, set at 160°F.

Remove from microwave and allow loaf to remain in dish for a few minutes, then pour off juices into a 2-cup glass measure. Stir in 1 tablespoon soy sauce, 1 tablespoon brown sugar, and 1 tablespoon flour; stir until dissolved. If necessary, add water to make ½ cup.

Place flat serving plate over top of mold, and invert meat loaf onto plate. Add remaining juices to basting sauce. Heat sauce for about 1 minute on High (just long enough to cook flour). Pour sauce over top of loaf. Serve hot.

For a complete meal, place mashed potatoes in center of ring mold, and freshly cooked vegetables in a ring around the outside of mold.

MEAT LOAF ITALIANO
Serves 6

A layered meat loaf with chopped spinach, cheese, and aromatic Italian seasonings is a nice change from humble ground beef. A ring mold does the best job for meat loaf in your microwave—it provides even cooking. For more concentration of flavor, tomato paste is used in this recipe instead of sauce.

For best flavor and a minimum of fat, select a package of lean stew meat in the prepackaged fresh meat counter, or a small chuck roast. Then ask the butcher to grind it for you. It is much better to use chuck than round steak because it has more flavor. When ground meat is purchased already ground, it usually is quite fat and does not provide the same texture and flavor, nor does it brown as well because the fat is cooking down rather than the meat.

1 **10-ounce package frozen chopped spinach**
1½ **pounds lean ground chuck meat**
1 **6-ounce can tomato paste**
½ **cup onion, chopped**
2 **slices white bread, rinsed and squeezed dry, torn into pieces**
1 **egg**
1 **teaspoon garlic powder**
1 **teaspoon Italian herbs**
½ **cup Parmesan cheese, grated**
1½ **cups shredded Monterey Jack cheese**
1 **tablespoon chopped parsley for garnish**

Place unopened box of spinach on a plate. Defrost on High (600–700 watts) for 3 minutes. Set aside to continue defrosting.

In a large bowl, mix together the ground beef, tomato paste, onion, bread, egg, garlic powder, and Italian herbs. Place ½ the mixture into a 6-cup ring mold. Pat meat lightly into place. It is not necessary to pack the meat down—it will have a lighter texture if you treat it lightly.

Remove the spinach from the package and drain completely. Mix spinach with Parmesan cheese.

Sprinkle half of the Monterey Jack cheese over the beef. Arrange the spinach on top of the meat and cheese. Sprinkle with half of the remaining cheese. Place the rest of the ground beef on top, pressing gently into the sides of the ring mold.

Cover ring mold with piece of wax paper over top. Cook on High for 12 minutes, or until meat loaf begins to pull away a bit from the sides.

Let stand a few minutes. Then place a dinner plate over the top of the mold and invert. Immediately place the remaining cheese over the top and sprinkle with a touch of chopped fresh parsley.

To serve, cut into wedges.

OLD WORLD MEAT LOAF
Serves 6

My mother always tucked hard-cooked eggs in the meat loaf, enough so that each slice would produce a lovely round egg section in the center. It is never meat loaf to me without it! This is the way I remember her preparing it, with catsup and onion and bread that was rinsed and squeezed dry. I added the Worcestershire sauce to give it more color in the microwave. This is good cold and makes excellent sandwiches. I always use lean stew meat or a lean chuck roast and have the butcher grind it. See page 93.

1½ **pounds lean ground chuck or beef stew meat**
½ **cup catsup**
2 **eggs**
1 **medium onion, chopped**
1 **clove garlic, minced**
2 **slices egg bread, rinsed with cold water and squeezed dry**
1 **teaspoon Worcestershire sauce**
½ **teaspoon salt**
¼ **teaspoon pepper**
2 **hard-cooked eggs**
¼ **cup catsup, room temperature, for topping**

Combine first 9 ingredients in mixing bowl and blend well. Pack lightly and evenly into 6-cup ring mold or 9"x5" loaf pan. Tuck hard-cooked eggs into loaf so they are completely covered. Cook on High (600–700 watts) until loaf has begun to pull away from the edges, about 10 minutes. Turn if it appears to be cooking unevenly. Pour off any accumulated juices. Invert onto serving plate. Spoon remaining catsup over top and serve.

PORK BASICS

Fresh pork comes in many varieties and shapes—a true challenge to the microwave cook. In addition to selecting cuts of pork which lend themselves well to microwave cooking, there are some guidelines you can follow to ensure that the pork is done to its proper internal temperature, without the overcooking that causes it to become tough.

Boned pork cuts work well, since microwave energy can cook the roast more evenly without interference from bone. Many recipes for conventional roasting recommend precooking the pork in water to ensure even temperatures throughout. This can also be done in your microwave.

Cooking bags designed for oven use provide a stable environment for pork, because they keep the moisture and heat inside the bag, rather than allowing the cool oven temperature to slow down heat penetration toward the center of the roast. A bonus from this method of cooking is, of course, the elimination of a pan to wash!

Large cuts, such as bone-in roasts, should be set first on High power (600–700 watts) to get them started, then be finished on low power settings, as low as Medium Low (200–250 watts).

If you do not have many power levels to choose from, use your lowest setting—it might be called *Defrost,* which should be the same as Medium Low. It will work well for slowing down the cooking process.

All pork, with the exception of sausage and links, benefits from lower power settings. In addition to lower power, an excellent technique for reaching proper internal temperatures of 165°F. to 170°F. is to wrap the pork in aluminum foil after reaching a temperature of 160°F. and allow it to reach 170°F. without further cooking inside the microwave.

If you do not have a thermometer, you may test for doneness by piercing the thickest part of the meat with a skewer or other sharp instrument: the juices will run clear, with no tinge of pink, when the meat is fully cooked.

When cooking a boned roast such as a loin, the ends will tend to become dry if allowed to cook without shielding. Since *rare* is not permitted in pork, use aluminum foil on both ends for part of the cooking time to allow the center to catch up. Remember, microwaves cook from the outside in, just like conventional cooking—except it happens much faster.

PERFECT BACON

If you are preparing one piece or just a few strips of bacon, you can cook the bacon on a white paper towel placed on a paper plate. On the other hand, a pound of bacon is more bacon than a paper towel and paper plate can handle—you are likely to end up with fat drippings on the floor and poorly cooked bacon.

When I bring a pound of bacon home, I like to deal with the fat drippings just once! I use my large round rack and place a 2-quart casserole underneath, which permits the fat to drain away from the bacon, leaving it crisp and evenly cooked. The rack should not permit the fat to touch the food; bacon sitting in fat drippings does not cook evenly.

Cooking time on bacon will vary with the quality of the bacon: the amount of fat and sugar and the thickness of the slices will determine the final cooking time. Cook bacon on High (600–700 watts). You can use the following as approximate times:

1 slice—about 1 minute
2 slices—about 1½ minutes
3 slices—about 2 minutes
For each additional slice, add about 15 seconds

To cook a whole pound of bacon, place bacon on large round rack in 2 layers with paper towels in between. Cover with paper towel. Place 2-quart casserole under rack to catch drippings. Cook on High (600–700 watts) for 6–8 minutes, or until crisp.

Then freeze the crisp bacon slices in packages that suit your needs—for example, 2–4 slices in each package. When rushed in the morning, simply remove the bacon from the package, place on a paper towel, and reheat on High about 30 seconds per slice of bacon. It will taste as though just made.

Here are several ways to use precooked bacon:

- Crumble over baked potatoes, or into a spinach or mixed green salad
- Chop and sprinkle over scrambled or poached eggs, or use in quiches
- Have on hand for quick bacon, lettuce, and tomato sandwiches
- Use crumbled bacon as a topping for vegetables or casseroles, or in soups

CHINESE PORK ROAST
Serves 4

If you enjoy the flavor of Chinese ribs, you will find this similar. Because it is boned, it is easy to carve. Serve it with plain rice and fresh vegetables. Leftover roast makes a delicious sandwich filling when sliced thin.

2 **tablespoons flour**
1 **large onion, thinly sliced**
1 **2-pound boneless pork loin**
2 **tablespoons sherry**
2 **tablespoons soy sauce**
1 **tablespoon brown sugar**
1 **teaspoon salt**
½ **teaspoon freshly ground pepper**
¼ **teaspoon ground ginger**

Cut a 1-inch strip from the open end of a regular-size cooking bag. Place flour in bag. Arrange onion slices in bag. Place roast on top of onion. Combine remaining ingredients in small bowl and blend well. Pour over meat. Tie end of bag loosely with reserved strip. Place bag in shallow baking dish for ease of handling.

Simmer on Medium (300–350 watts) for 15 minutes. Turn bag over. Insert probe horizontally through bag into center of roast. Continue to cook on Medium until probe registers 160°F., about 15 minutes. Remove roast from microwave. Turn bag over and cover entirely with foil, leaving probe exposed. Let stand at room temperature until probe registers 170°F., about 15 minutes.

Note: Boneless roasts benefit from being prepared in plastic cooking bags that seal in moisture and heat, providing more even cooking.

SWEET AND SOUR PORK
Serves 6–8

Pick up some fortune cookies and chow mein noodles and treat yourself to a home-cooked Chinese dinner. Because the vegetables used in this recipe are not fragile it can be made ahead and reheated just before serving. Also nice as a leftover—even to take to the office and reheat in the office microwave.

4 **medium carrots, thinly sliced at angle**
¼ **cup vegetable oil**
2 **pounds lean pork, cut into 1-inch cubes**
1 **large onion, thinly sliced, or cut Oriental style in chunks**
2 **green peppers, seeded and cut into chunks**
1 **8-ounce can pineapple chunks in unsweetened juice**
¼ **cup cornstarch**
½ **cup soy sauce**
½ **cup light brown sugar**
¼ **cup vinegar**

1 **tablespoon Worcestershire sauce**
¼ **teaspoon hot pepper sauce**
¼ **teaspoon pepper**

Combine carrots and oil in 3-quart casserole. Cover. Cook on High (600–700 watts) 6 minutes. Add pork, onion, and green peppers. Cover; cook 5 minutes. Drain pineapple chunks, reserving ½ cup syrup. Transfer syrup to bowl and stir in cornstarch until it dissolves. Blend in remaining ingredients. Add to pork; blend in pineapple. Cover and cook on High 10 minutes, or until sauce has thickened and pork is done. Stirring once or twice during this last stage is helpful for even cooking of the sauce.

Serve immediately over rice or chow mein noodles.

STUFFED PORK CHOPS
Serves 4

A popular way to enjoy pork is with apples and raisins. Adding a sprinkle of gravy mix or seasoned Micro Shake gives the chops a nice rich color and flavor, and using a cover and a lower setting makes the chops soft and tender.

2 **tablespoons butter**
1 **cup coarse dry bread crumbs**
½ **cup apple, chopped**
2 **tablespoons raisins, chopped**
½ **teaspoon salt**
2 **tablespoons sugar**
2 **tablespoons minced onion**
¼ **teaspoon pepper**
Pinch sage
2 **tablespoons hot water**
8 **thick pork loin chops (fat trimmed)**
½ **package brown gravy mix, or generous sprinkle of seasoned Micro Shake**

Melt butter on High (600–700 watts) in 4-cup glass measure. Add bread crumbs, apple, raisins, salt, sugar, onion, pepper, and sage, mixing lightly. Moisten slightly with hot water (but not too much water or it will make stuffing soggy).

Place 4 chops into an 8-inch round shallow baking dish. Divide stuffing and place portion on top of each chop. Cover with remaining chops, pressing together lightly. Sprinkle gravy mix through a small strainer, or use Micro Shake. Cover. Cook on Medium High (400–500 watts) 14–18 minutes, or just until done. Let stand 5 minutes, covered, before serving.

SAUSAGE LINKS
Serves 4

Unless you prefer to cook links in a skillet on your cook-top, you might like to try them in a browning dish. I was taught to cook them in water first to remove the fat—no reason why you can't do the same in your microwave. But don't try cooking the links in the microwave without a browning dish—they overcook on each end and won't be tender or attractive.

1 pound sausage links
Water to cover

Place links in a 1-quart shallow baking dish, adding enough water to just cover. Cover dish, and cook on High (600–700 watts) 4–5 minutes, until juices are no longer pink. Remove and drain on paper towels.

Preheat browning dish to its highest absorption (check your book for steak preheating setting). Place sausages on heated dish. Cook 1 minute on High. Turn sausages over and continue cooking for an additional 1–2 minutes until done to your liking. Turning sausages during cooking will give a more uniform browning.

BRATWURST

Use same technique as above, but cook longer in the browning dish.

POLYNESIAN SPARERIBS
Serves 4–6, or makes approximately 36 appetizers when cut in half and into sections

For those who enjoy eating well-flavored, fat-free ribs right off the bone, this is certain to become a favorite standby. Cooking the pork ribs in water first gets rid of the fat, and ensures the even cooking of the pork also.

4 pounds pork spareribs, cut in half and into sections
3 cups hot water (or more)
1 large onion, sliced
1 lemon, thinly sliced
1 cup bottled teriyaki marinade

OR if you prefer making your own, use the following:

1 cup pineapple juice
¼ cup cornstarch
½ cup soy sauce
½ cup firmly packed brown sugar
2 tablespoons honey
1 tablespoon Worcestershire sauce
½ teaspoon pepper
¼ teaspoon hot pepper sauce

Arrange ribs in a 4-quart casserole, layering if necessary. Add enough hot water to cover. Place onion and lemon slices over top. Cover and cook on High (600–700 watts) for 15 minutes. Reduce power to Medium (300–350 watts) and continue cooking 20 minutes. Turn ribs over and rearrange so those on bottom are on top. Continue cooking covered on Medium until ribs are fork tender, about 25 minutes. Let remain covered until cool enough to handle. Drain. Use a scissors to cut between bones to separate, leaving the smaller sections intact.

If making your own sauce, combine pineapple juice, cornstarch, and soy sauce. Stir until cornstarch is dissolved. Add remaining ingredients; stir to mix thoroughly. Dip each rib into sauce, coating completely. Place remaining marinade mixture in 1-quart measure and cook on High 1½ minutes. Pour over ribs. Cook ribs on High until crisp and sauce begins to thicken, about 10–12 minutes.

If using bottled teriyaki sauce, dip ribs in Teriyaki sauce, then pour remaining sauce over ribs. Continue cooking as above.

COUNTRY-STYLE PORK RIBS WITH SAUERKRAUT
Serves 6

An instant hit with our tasters. Old country flavors are brought up to date with the combination of sauerkraut and red cabbage. It is attractive on the table and goes well with mashed potatoes. You can prepare it ahead of time and reheat on Medium (300–350 watts) or Medium High (400–500 watts).

3 pounds pork loin country-style ribs, trimmed of fat
7 cups water
1 24-ounce jar sauerkraut, rinsed and drained

1 16-ounce jar sweet-sour red cabbage,
  undrained
1 medium onion, chopped
Salt and pepper

Arrange ribs in 4-quart baking dish. Add water. Cover and cook on High (600–700 watts) for 20 minutes. Drain ribs well and set aside.

Combine sauerkraut and red cabbage in shallow 2½-quart baking dish. Arrange ribs over top, with thickest portions facing outside of dish and any smaller ribs in center. Sprinkle with onion and season with salt and pepper. Cover and cook on Medium (300–350 watts) 15 minutes. Check for even cooking, shifting slower cooking ribs to outside of dish if necessary.

Turn ribs over. Test with fork for tenderness. If almost fork tender, remove from microwave and cover dish with foil. Let stand at room temperature until ribs test done, about 10 minutes.

BAKED HAM WITH PINEAPPLE
Serves 6–8

For a traditional baked ham you might enjoy this recipe. Again note the limited use of liquid in basting. Use enough to give the ham good flavor, but not enough to draw microwave energy away from the ham, which would keep it from acquiring the lovely baked color that makes this recipe work.

1 5-pound precooked shank or butt end ham
  (with bone in)
Whole cloves
1 cup orange marmalade
¼ teaspoon paprika
1 8-ounce can sliced pineapple, drained (juice
  reserved)

Place ham fat side down in baking dish. Cook on High (600–700 watts) for 5 minutes. Turn ham over. Score top in diamond shapes using tip of sharp knife. Place a clove in center of each diamond.

Combine marmalade and paprika in measuring cup and cook on High 1½ minutes. Brush some of glaze over ham. Arrange pineapple slices over ham and secure with wooden toothpicks.

Place about 2 tablespoons pineapple juice in bottom of baking dish. Blend remaining juice with glaze and spoon over ham. Cook on High 10 minutes. Drain off some of excess liquid. Baste with remaining

drippings. Turn dish, reduce power to Medium High (400–500 watts) and continue cooking 10 minutes, or until thermometer inserted in thickest part of meat (not touching bone) registers 120°F. Cover lightly and let stand 5–10 minutes before slicing.

The reason for dropping power level to Medium High is that the shank or butt end of ham is irregular in shape, and the bone makes heating less even. By slowing the energy down it heats more slowly and evenly.

SCALLOPED HAM AND POTATOES
Serves 4–6

One of the nice things about cooking a ham is the leftovers — there is so much you can do. In addition to the usual sandwiches (made even more tasty by melting cheese over thin slices of ham) there is the variety in casserole combination. If you do not have 4 to 6 people in your family, cut the recipe in half and cook 10–12 minutes on High.

For more speed, you can substitute a can of whole potatoes, drained and sliced.

2 large onions, thinly sliced
4 tablespoons (½ stick) butter or margarine
4 medium potatoes (about 2 pounds), peeled
  and thinly sliced
1½–2 cups cooked ham, cubed
3 tablespoons flour
½ teaspoon salt
¼ teaspoon freshly ground pepper
1½ cups shredded sharp cheddar cheese
Paprika
1 cup milk

Combine onion and 2 tablespoons butter in 2-quart casserole. Cover and cook on High (600–700 watts) for 10 minutes, stirring once. Remove onion from dish and set aside.

Layer half of potatoes and half of ham in bottom of dish. Combine flour, salt, and pepper and sprinkle half of mixture over the ham and potatoes. Top with half of onion and half of the cheese. Sprinkle with paprika. Repeat layering, except for paprika.

Heat milk on High in measuring cup until scalded, about 2 minutes. Pour over casserole. Sprinkle with paprika. Cover and cook on High until potatoes are fork tender, about 15–20 minutes.

BAKED HAM WITH RASPBERRY APRICOT GLAZE

Serves 6-8

A rich liqueur made with fruits and herbs makes a magnificent glaze for a holiday ham. Using a minimum amount of liquid to concentrate the flavor gives the ham a glaze you would expect to get only from long oven baking. Since hams can be purchased already cooked, heat it through to bring out all the flavor possible. Any good quality canned ham will do; however we found a good flavor in the honey-glazed variety.

1 **5-pound precooked, honey-glazed canned ham**
Whole cloves
½ **cup orange marmalade**
1 **6-ounce package extra fancy choice dried apricots**
¼ **cup black raspberry liqueur (Chambord is excellent)**
¼ **teaspoon paprika**

Place ham fat side down in a baking dish just large enough to contain ham and juices. Spoon liquid from can over top and allow it to drip down the sides of the ham. Cook on High (600-700 watts) for 5 minutes. Turn ham over. Baste with juices, then pour off liquid from bottom of dish.

Score top of ham in diamond shapes using tip of sharp knife. Place whole cloves at points where lines intersect. Spoon marmalade over top. Cook on High 10 minutes. Set aside and cover to keep warm.

Place apricots in 1-quart measure. Combine liqueur and paprika; stir to blend. Pour over apricots, stirring to coat. Cook on High 3 minutes.

Meanwhile, baste ham with ham drippings. Remove apricots from liqueur using slotted spoon. Arrange apricots over top of ham, and brush liqueur over ham and apricots. Cook on High 5 minutes until heated through. If using probe inserted in thickest portion of ham, it should register 120°F.

BAKED HAM WITH PINEAPPLE GLAZE

Serves 6-8

If you are a traditionalist and prefer the simple ham, pineapple, and brown sugar, you will enjoy the taste and appearance of this ham. I prefer the canned variety. The ham should be precooked when you purchase it. These are available either in a can or in the meat department of your favorite market.

1 **precooked ham, about 3-4 pounds**
1 **4-ounce can sliced pineapple**
¼ **cup brown sugar**
Whole cloves

Place ham fat side down in a shallow baking dish just large enough to hold it. Cook on Medium High (400-500 watts) for 5 minutes. Baste ham with drippings. Turn ham over and continue to cook on the same setting for 5 minutes.

Drain pineapple; reserve juice. Place 1 tablespoon pineapple juice in cup, and stir in the brown sugar to make a paste. Baste ham; place fat side up. Arrange pineapple slices over top, using wooden toothpicks if necessary. Stud with cloves.

Continue cooking on same setting 7-9 minutes, or just until internal temperature reaches 120°F. on your sensor probe.

LAMB: TIPS AND TECHNIQUES

Tender young lamb is one of spring's most delicious culinary gifts. It lends itself to many variations, making it ideal for any occasion from dinner parties to informal family suppers. Serve it roasted or richly napped, in a stew or cooked in a snappy tomato-chili sauce. Braise it and combine with eggplant, basil, and oregano for a meal with a Mediterranean flavor. Leftover leg of lamb can be cubed to add verve to favorite main dish casseroles or spicy curries. Or for an easy change-of-pace lunch, thinly slice lamb and spread with coarsely ground mustard. Top with a milky white cheese such as mozzarella or provolone, and arrange between slices of dark country bread. Cook on High (600-700 watts) until the cheese melts. Julienne strips of cooked lamb can even dress up main dish salads for stylish alfresco dining when warmer weather lightens appetites.

All of these tantalizing dishes are easily prepared in your microwave by following a few basic techniques:

- Always cook on Medium (300-350 watts) to ensure tenderness.
- Leg of lamb and lamb shanks will have more flavor served medium rare.

- Brushing with bottled browning sauce or sprinkling with a Micro Shake product will help to promote a rich brown color.
- If lamb is frozen, make sure it is completely defrosted before cooking.

SHASHLIK IN BURGUNDY
Serves 4

One of the most beautiful cookbooks I own is *A Treasury of Great Recipes* written by Vincent and Mary Price. Their flaming Shashlik inspired this adaptation. It was the lovely sauce that made me do it—it worked the first time.

2 pounds lamb (from the leg), cut into 2-inch cubes (pieces should be equal in shape)

Marinade

1½ cups red burgundy wine
1 small onion, minced
1 bay leaf
1 tablespoon Worcestershire sauce
2 cloves garlic, minced
1 teaspoon salt
¼ teaspoon ground pepper

Sauce

1 cup chili sauce
½ cup catsup
1 tablespoon honey
1 tablespoon prepared red horseradish
1 tablespoon chutney

Place lamb in a bowl small enough for the marinade to cover completely. Refrigerate overnight (or about 10 hours), stirring several times. Remove meat from marinade, place in an au gratin or round 10-inch shallow quiche dish, keeping meat together in a single layer.

Cook, covered loosely with wax paper, for 6–7 minutes on Medium power (300–350 watts). Stir several times for even cooking—smaller pieces will become overcooked if not kept in center of dish. Lamb should be rare at this point. Remove from microwave and set aside.

Combine sauce ingredients in a 4-cup glass measuring cup. Cook sauce on High (600–700 watts) for 3–4 minutes, or until it begins to bubble; it should come to a boil. Stir once or twice.

Pour off juices from lamb dish. Pour hot sauce over lamb, stirring to coat each piece. Cook uncovered on High 2–3 minutes, just until lamb is heated through, stirring once or twice. For best texture and taste, lamb should be pink in center. Overcooking will toughen the lamb. *Tip:* This dish looks lovely when served on a bed of rice.

LAMB WITH FRUIT AND A TOUCH OF HONEY
Serves 4–6

The addition of spices and the natural sweetness of fruit bring an exotic touch to this lamb casserole. It is a lovely blend of colors and goes well over a bed of rice. (Other fruits in season may be substituted.) It is excellent reheated—use a Medium setting (300–350 watts) to reheat, stirring several times to ensure even heating.

2 pounds lamb, cut into 2-inch cubes (meat from leg of lamb is good)
1 1-inch cinnamon stick
1 teaspoon coriander
Pinch each of turmeric, ginger, and salt
Fresh ground pepper
3 tablespoons olive oil
1 small onion, chopped
1 cup hot water
½ pound prunes
½ pound apples, cut in quarters
3 tablespoons flour
¼ cup honey
1 small orange, peeled and cut into small chunks
1 tablespoon toasted sesame seeds
Freshly cooked rice

Combine lamb, spices, oil, and onion in a 3-quart casserole. Cook on High (600–700 watts) 1 minute. Stir in water. Cook covered on High 10 minutes, stirring once. Remove cinnamon stick; continue to cook on Medium (300–350 watts) 15 minutes.

Add prunes and apples. Cook covered on Medium 20 minutes. Dissolve the flour in the juices. Add the honey and orange and cook uncovered on High until liquid boils, stirring once. Cook until sauce thickens slightly.

Sprinkle with sesame seeds. Serve over rice.

LAMB RIBLETS
Serves 4 –6

These are tasty little morsels in a delicious sauce that can be served over a bed of freshly cooked rice or pasta. The sauce is thickened with the addition of a small can of tomato paste.

2 pounds lamb riblets, trimmed of fat
1 large onion, sliced into thin rings
½ pound mushrooms, sliced
1 8-ounce can tomato sauce
1 6-ounce can tomato paste
2 tablespoons honey
1–2 tablespoons fresh lemon juice
¼ teaspoon freshly ground pepper
⅛ teaspoon chili powder

Place riblets in a 2-quart casserole and place onion rings over top. Cover and cook on Medium High (400 –450 watts) for 10 minutes. Drain fat. Add the mushrooms. Combine the remaining ingredients in a bowl, blending well. Pour over the meat. Cover and cook on Medium (300 –350 watts) until ribs are tender when pierced with a fork, about 50 minutes. Uncover and continue cooking on Medium for another 5 minutes to reduce moisture and promote additional browning. Serve hot.

Note: If you do not serve rice or pasta, a crusty French or Italian bread would be a great way to enjoy leftover sauce. Dunking is an old revered custom.

GRILLED LAMB CHOPS
Serves 2

For those of us who enjoy lamb and have a browning dish, this simple technique is pleasing. The preheated dish grills the meat perfectly, sealing in the juices and browning the outside. The lemon and garlic complement the flavor of the lamb.

½ lemon
4 loin lamb chops, about 2″ thick, fat trimmed
Garlic powder
Salt and freshly ground pepper to taste

Squeeze the lemon juice over the chops and sprinkle with garlic powder, salt, and pepper.
Preheat the browning dish to its maximum absorption, according to manufacturer's instructions.

The center of the dish should glow yellow.
Immediately arrange the chops in the corners of the dish, if possible, without removing the browning dish from the oven which makes it cool down too fast. Cook on High (600 –700 watts) for 3 minutes. With tongs, turn the chops over and continue to cook on High for 1 minute. Let the meat stand in the dish for several minutes to finish cooking.
Lamb is best and most tender when served medium pink. Overcooking lamb will make it tough.

OLD-FASHIONED LAMB STEW
Serves 6

For lamb lovers, a traditional old favorite. Lower wattage is used to ensure tenderness.

2 pounds lean lamb, cut into 2-inch cubes
2 teaspoons bottled browning sauce
1 large onion, thinly sliced
2 garlic cloves, minced
3 tablespoons vegetable oil
4 carrots, cut into sticks
4 potatoes, peeled and cubed
1 15-ounce can Italian plum tomatoes,
      undrained, cut up
1 cup diced celery
½ teaspoon freshly ground pepper
½ teaspoon crumbled dried rosemary
½ teaspoon crumbled dried marjoram
½ teaspoon paprika
3 tablespoons cornstarch
3 tablespoons dry white wine or water

Place lamb cubes in large bowl. Coat with browning sauce. Set aside. Place onion, garlic, and oil in a 3-quart casserole. Cook on High (600 –700 watts) for 7 minutes, stirring once. Cover and cook on Medium (300 –350 watts) for 10 minutes. Add carrots, potato, tomato and juice, celery, pepper, rosemary, marjoram, and paprika. Cover, and continue to cook on Medium for 1 hour, stirring once or twice during cooking.
Mix cornstarch and wine or water, and stir until cornstarch is dissolved. Drain off ½ cup stew liquid and add to dissolved cornstarch. Blend into stew. Cover, and continue to cook on Medium 10 –15 minutes until thickened. Let stand, covered, 20 minutes before serving.

TIME AND FLAVOR-SAVING BARBECUING

Get your cool summer barbecue off to a good start by precooking meats in the microwave, saving the coals for the final browning and crisping. Not only will you be spared the guesswork of determining when the meat is done, but you can retain more tenderness and eliminate many minutes from the total cooking time without sacrificing any wonderful barbecue flavor.

By microwaving first and then barbecuing, you retain the crisp texture of the food. To prevent burning, brush with barbecue sauce only during the last few minutes on the grill. Because the sauce can penetrate only about ¼ inch into the meat or poultry, there is little real advantage to adding it earlier — it will only burn and turn dark.

While the main course sizzles over the coals, the microwave can be cooking the corn.

While High power (600–700 watts) is fine for precooking chicken, turkey parts and spareribs need a lower power setting to produce more tender results. Covering is not necessary and does not affect cooking time; but particularly in the case of turkey parts, a cover further enhances tenderness. Wax paper and plastic wrap are excellent. A cover will trap more steam and this produces a tenderizing effect similar to parboiling. You may wish to use a covered casserole. Be sure to use tongs when turning the food; a fork will pierce the skin and meat and allow the wonderful juices to run out.

BARBECUED TURKEY PARTS
Serves 2

2 turkey thighs or legs
Oil
Barbecue sauce

Prepare barbecue. Brush turkey with oil. Cook covered on Medium High (400–500 watts) 10 minutes per pound. Turn turkey over about halfway through the timing. Transfer to grill and cook only until outside is crisp, turning and basting frequently with barbecue sauce the last few minutes of cooking.

BARBECUED CHICKEN PARTS

Chicken pieces
Barbecue sauce

Prepare barbecue. Place as many pieces as needed on a round or oval dish, placing thickest pieces toward outside of dish. Cook covered on High (600–700 watts) 5 minutes per pound, turning chicken over halfway through the timing. Transfer to grill and cook until crisp, turning and basting frequently with barbecue sauce.

BARBECUED SPARERIBS
Serves 4

5 pounds lean spareribs, cut into individual ribs
Barbecue sauce

Prepare barbecue. Place ribs in large baking dish. Cook covered on Medium (300–350 watts) 30 minutes, rearranging and turning ribs over after the first 15 minutes. Drain on paper towels. Transfer ribs to grill and cook about 10 minutes, turning frequently. Brush generously with sauce and cook an additional 5 minutes, turning as needed.

10
ONE-DISH MEALS

Enchilada Casserole

Green Enchiladas

Italian Sausage and Peppers

Stir-Fry Dinner

Cheese-Stuffed Zucchini

Tacos

Tex-Mex/Tamale/Noodle/Chili Casserole

Stir-Fry Chicken Livers

Paupiettes with a Mexican Flair

Stuffed Green Peppers

One-Step Lasagna

Fettucini

New England Boiled Dinner

Pasta Salad with Chicken and Vegetables

ONE-DISH SUPPERS

When we think of one-dish meals, we think of balance: a combination of meat and vegetables all cooked together for a satisfying lunch or dinner. As with conventional one-dish cooking, all of these meals can be cooked ahead and reheated. And because their flavors mellow with time, they offer an ideal way to get a head start on weekday meals as the season changes and the pace of life picks up again.

As a bonus to the busy cook with an eye on the family food budget, some recipes use economical cuts of beef in both traditional and surprising new guises.

ENCHILADA CASSEROLE
Serves 6–8

If you have never tried canned green chilies, this casserole will give you a good introduction to their mild, delightful flavor. It has been a family favorite for a long time.

Over the years I have added to and subtracted from the original recipe; you may wish to tailor it to suit your own tastes. For example, you might enjoy it without the chilies and olives, or you may wish to add a 7-ounce can of Mexicorn or whole kernel corn.

1½ **pounds lean ground beef (see page 93)**
1 **large onion, chopped**
2 **large cloves garlic, minced (or ½ teaspoon garlic powder)**
1 **package dry enchilada seasoning mix (or 1 tablespoon chili powder, 1 teaspoon cumin, ¼ teaspoon paprika, and 1 tablespoon flour, blended together)**
1 **15-ounce can tomato puree**
1 **4-ounce can diced green chilies**
6 **corn tortillas**
2½ **cups grated cheddar cheese**
1 **2¼-ounce can sliced black olives**
Cilantro or parsley for garnish

Crumble beef into a 2-quart bowl. Add onion and garlic. Cook on High (600–700 watts) 3 minutes, stirring to keep beef crumbly. Continue to cook an additional 2 minutes, just until meat loses its pink color. Add enchilada seasoning and tomato puree. Cook on High 3–4 minutes until bubbly. Stir in chilies.

To assemble the enchiladas, use a 2-quart round casserole or soufflé dish. It should be slightly larger than the tortillas. If it is too large the tortillas will not be properly stacked and the dish will not be as attractive to serve.

Set aside ½ cup of the cheese to use for topping. Alternate layers of tortillas, meat sauce, and cheese in casserole, starting with tortillas and ending with cheese. Cook covered on High 7–8 minutes until hot. Sprinkle with reserved ½ cup of cheese.

Garnish with sprigs of fresh cilantro or parsley and sliced olives. Serve immediately. Cut into wedges, like a pie. Use a pie server to remove each wedge from the bottom. All the layers can be seen; it is most attractive.

May be served as a main dish with rice and salad.

GREEN ENCHILADAS
Serves 6–8

This recipe was given to me by a student who cooked from a rich Mexican heritage. Like many professional women she used a microwave shortcut, but not at the expense of flavor and attractive eye appeal.

1 **10-ounce can cream of chicken soup**
1 **16-ounce carton dairy sour cream**
1 **7-ounce can chopped chilies, drained**
12 **corn tortillas**
¾ **pound shredded Monterey Jack cheese**
Chopped parsley or cilantro for garnish

Combine soup, sour cream, and chilies. Place 1 tablespoon of the mixture at one end of each tortilla. Sprinkle with cheese. Roll and place seam side down in shallow oval dish. Pour remaining mixture over top and sprinkle with remaining cheese. Cover with wax paper.

Heat on Medium High (400–500 watts) 7–10 minutes or until heated through. Sprinkle with chopped fresh parsley or cilantro.

Serve with rice and salad for a lovely light luncheon or dinner.

ITALIAN SAUSAGE AND PEPPERS
Serves 6–8

The vegetables are cooked first and set aside to keep them firm and attractive while cooking the sausage.

The sausages are then precooked in water to eliminate the fat—an old method used to ensure that the pork is cooked through. The vegetables and sausage are wonderful together, and go well with pasta, rice, or even spooned into fresh-sliced crusty Italian bread for a "poor boy" sandwich.

1 **large green bell pepper, cored, seeded, and cut into wedges**
1 **medium onion, cut into wedges and separated**
1 **tablespoon olive oil (may substitute salad oil)**
1 **pound sweet Italian sausage**
1 **14½-ounce can Italian whole tomatoes, drained and sliced**
½ **pound mushrooms, sliced**
3 **tablespoons red wine**
½ **teaspoon dried oregano, crumbled, or 1 tablespoon fresh oregano**
Minced fresh parsley for garnish

Mix green pepper, onion, and oil in 2-quart round baking dish. Cook on High (600–700 watts) for 5 minutes. Remove vegetables from dish and set aside. Add sausages to dish with just enough water to cover. Cover dish and cook on High 10 minutes. Pour off liquid; drain sausages on paper towel. Cut sausages in half crosswise. Return to dish and cook on High, uncovered, 3–5 minutes, shifting sausages at the outside of dish to the center as they begin to brown. Pour off fat.

Return green pepper and onion to dish with tomatoes, mushrooms, wine, and oregano. Cover and cook on Medium (300–350 watts) until mushrooms are tender, about 10 minutes.

Garnish with parsley. Serve hot.

STIR-FRY DINNER
Serves 4

A simple way to enjoy wok cooking recipes without the wok. The pork can be replaced by chicken, seafood, or whatever pleases your palate. It can be a complete meal when served over a bed of rice or noodles.

½ **cup soy sauce**
½ **cup chicken broth**
¼ **cup dry sherry**
2 **tablespoons sugar**
1 **pound boneless pork loin, cut into ½-inch slices**
6 **large mushrooms, sliced**

1 **pound fresh spinach, stems removed**
½ **pound fresh bean sprouts**
¼ **pound fresh pea pods (may substitute frozen)**
½ **cup sliced celery**
1 **medium onion, thinly sliced**
1 **bunch green onions, halved lengthwise and cut into 3-inch pieces**

Combine soy sauce, chicken broth, sherry, and sugar in 2-cup glass measure. Cook on High (600–700 watts) for 2 minutes. Combine remaining ingredients in 3-quart casserole and toss lightly. Pour sauce over top; cover. Cook on High 5 minutes, stirring twice. Continue to cook 2–3 additional minutes, or until vegetables are tender. Serve immediately.

Pass additional soy sauce at the table.

CHEESE-STUFFED ZUCCHINI
Serves 4–6

There is something so attractive about a stuffed vegetable. The flavors and colors of this cheese-stuffed zucchini beautifully complement each other. It can be served as a family main dish as well as a side dish for company.

4 **medium zucchini, halved lengthwise**
½ **cup onion, chopped**
1 **large garlic clove, minced**
1 **cup shredded Monterey Jack cheese**
1 **cup shredded cheddar cheese**
¾ **cup corn bread stuffing mix**
1 **egg, light beaten**
1 **teaspoon fresh parsley, finely chopped**
⅛ **teaspoon freshly ground pepper**
¼ **cup grated Parmesan cheese**
Chopped fresh parsley for garnish

Scoop pulp from zucchini, leaving shell about ¼-inch thick. Chop pulp. Transfer to mixing bowl and add onion and garlic. Cover and cook on High (600–700 watts) for 5 minutes. Pour off accumulated liquid. Add shredded cheeses, stuffing mix, egg, 1 teaspoon parsley, and pepper and blend well. Fill zucchini shells with mixture. Arrange in 8″ x 12″ baking dish and sprinkle with Parmesan. Cover and cook on High for 8 minutes, turning dish once if zucchini appears to be cooking unevenly. Sprinkle with parsley just before serving.

TACOS
Makes about 20 tacos

Enjoy tacos as a complete dinner—they even include the salad in a most enjoyable fashion.

The only problem for me, when my children were younger, was preparing the taco shells by crisping them in oil in a frying pan. I don't believe I ever sat down with the family during the meal—I was so busy trying to keep up with their appetites.

To speed things up, and to avoid the mess on the cook-top, I began to crisp the shells on the racks in my regular oven until they were almost crisp, then would fold them and fill them. Now you can buy prepared crisp shells ready for filling. Of course, frying them is still the best, but if you do not have time, try it this way. There is a great taco rack designed specifically for microwave use with this recipe. I know, because I designed it—so I could make 10 at a time and enjoy eating at the table with my family.

1 **pound lean ground beef (see tips on ground beef)**
1 **1¼-ounce envelope taco seasoning mix**
10 **taco shells**
2 **cups shredded cheddar cheese or Monterey Jack cheese, or combination of both**
1 **16-ounce can refried beans, heated in casserole ahead of time and served on the side (optional)**

Fillings

1 **small, firm head lettuce, shredded**
1 **cup radishes, sliced**
1 **cup green onion, chopped**
1 **cup avocado, chopped**
1 **cup cucumber, chopped**
2 **firm tomatoes, peeled, seeded, and chopped**
Taco sauce and/or green chili salsa

Place beef in a medium-sized bowl. Cook on High (600–700 watts) 2 minutes, stirring until crumbly. Drain if necessary. Blend in taco seasonings and cook until meat is no longer pink, about 2–3 minutes.

Arrange taco shells upright in taco rack or shallow dish that will hold them upright. Spoon meat evenly among shells and sprinkle with cheese. Cook on High until cheese is melted and meat is heated through, about 2 minutes for 10 tacos.

Serve immediately with refried beans and assorted toppings.

Note: If you prefer meatless tacos, fill shells with refried beans and sprinkle with cheese. Heating time is the same.

TEX-MEX/TAMALE/NOODLE/CHILI CASSEROLE
Serves 8

In developing additional recipes for this book, I reached back into my past and from my old tattered cardboard file emerged this recipe, without a name, written on the back of an envelope. It is a winner, because it pleases everyone. And as you can see from the title I gave it, it has quite a bit going on!

Although I have indicated it serves 8, with other foods, at a buffet it will go much further. If you double the recipe for a party, use two separate dishes for heating and serving—it will reheat more evenly with less volume.

A 2-quart casserole about 12 inches round is ideal. If you do not have one, you can use a 9″ x 13″ baking dish. (The round is preferable because there is no chance of the corners overheating).

The original recipe specified layering the ingredients. In converting to microwave, I discovered it worked much better when all ingredients were combined, rather than layered. Original timing in a conventional oven was 40–50 minutes—I cut the time to a fourth. I use High power (600–700 watts) for this large a quantity; otherwise it takes too long to heat. However, the delicate cheese is not in danger of overcooking, since the volume in the receipe will automatically slow down the cooking process.

1 **12-ounce package wide noodles, cooked according to package directions**
2 **15-ounce cans tamales in chili gravy**
1 **15-ounce can chili, without beans**
1 **10½-ounce can beef broth**
½ **pound shredded cheddar cheese**
Freshly chopped parsley for garnish (optional)

Drain cooked noodles and combine with all other ingredients in a 2-quart round shallow baking dish about 12 inches round.

Cover with wax paper or parchment. Cook on High (600–700 watts) for 10 minutes, turning if it appears to be cooking unevenly.

Reduce power to Medium (300–350 watts) and cook an additional 3–5 minutes until it is heated all the way into the center.

Sprinkle with additional cheddar and freshly chopped parsley for color, if desired.

STIR-FRY CHICKEN LIVERS

Serves 4

Let's eat out—out of the freezer, that is!

The frozen food industry has presented us with a gardenful of vegetable varieties. When I began to find Chinese, Japanese, and almost any other combination of vegetables I would hope for in a frozen package, I began to collect them in my freezer. By combining with livers, which I can also freeze in a package the correct size for my family, this recipe becomes a quick last-minute meal. I find this a good way to combine freezer and microwave.

If the livers are frozen, remove from the package (they will pop right out if you rinse them with water). Place livers in a bowl, cover, and defrost on Medium (300–350 watts) for 2 minutes per pound. Let stand 5 minutes and repeat until defrosted. They do not need to completely defrost to start the recipe—since you will be cutting them into pieces and rinsing, they will be just about defrosted when you are ready to cook them.

To prevent the livers from popping because of the tight membrane, I cut the livers apart and into chunks before cooking. If defrosted, you may like to use a scissors; but if they are still slightly frozen, a sharp knife may be easier.

The rice is added as a suggestion; it is optional.

1 **cup long grain rice (see page 131 for cooking directions)**
1 **pound chicken livers**
1 **large onion, cut in half and sliced**
2 **tablespoons oil**
1 **10-ounce package frozen Chinese or Japanese stir-fry vegetables with seasonings (if only available in a pound bag, use that instead)**
1 **tablespoon soy sauce**

Cook rice for 12 minutes (see recipe page 131) and set aside, covered. It should be just ready for serving when the recipe is complete. If it cools down, simply add 3 tablespoons of water and reheat on High (600–700 watts) for 3 minutes.

Cut livers into chunks, rinse, and set aside. In a 1½-quart casserole, place onion and oil. Stir. Cook on High 3–4 minutes, until cooked through. With a slotted spoon, remove onions and set aside while you cook the livers (otherwise, the "juice" from the liver will dilute the rich flavor of the onions).

Stir livers into remaining oil. Cover with casserole lid. Cook on Medium (300–350 watts) for 6–7 minutes or until livers just lose their pink color.

(Overcooking makes liver tough.) Stir and set aside, covered.

Place vegetables in a 1-quart bowl. Cook on High 5 minutes. Stir in the soy sauce and seasoning packet. Drain juices from the livers, and combine with the vegetables and onions. Serve over a bed of hot rice.

Note: If you feel the livers and the rice could be hotter for serving, combine the livers with the vegetables and heat for about 2 minutes on High.

PAUPIETTES WITH A MEXICAN FLAIR (STUFFED WHOLE GREEN CHILIES)

Serves 4

This is a Mexican version of the Paupiette. This recipe may not be in the true Mexican tradition, but the ingredients are traditional and the flavors blend in an easy, fun serving.

1 **7-ounce can whole green chilies**
1 **1-pound can refried beans**
¾ **pound medium sharp cheddar cheese**
Fresh parsley or cilantro, minced, for garnish

Cut the chilies down one side and carefully remove seeds. Stuff the chilies as full as possible with the beans, allowing the sides to separate if necessary.

Cut strips of cheese about ½-inch thick and place in center of beans. Place chilies carefully, slit side up to prevent the stuffing from seeping out, into a round 9-inch quiche dish or oval au gratin dish, just large enough to hold chilies in a circle. They should touch and make a complete ring around the outside of dish. If some refried beans remain, place in the center of the dish.

Cover dish with wax paper and cook on High (600–700 watts) for 5 minutes. Shred remaining cheese and sprinkle over chilies and refried beans. Continue heating, uncovered, on High power until cheese is completely melted (about 2 minutes). (If covered, the cheese will stick to the paper.)

Sprinkle with minced fresh parsley or cilantro. Serve immediately with thick dairy sour cream, sliced tomatoes, avocados, and tortillas.

This is best when freshly prepared. If leftovers are reheated, do so on Medium power (300–350 watts).

STUFFED GREEN PEPPERS
Serves 4

Stuffed vegetables are rather interesting because they can function as a complete meal, with perhaps a tossed green salad. They can be prepared ahead of time and reheated.

These stuffed peppers are attractive to look at and the flavors blend well together. When I first began to prepare this recipe, I would precook the green peppers, but it really is not necessary if you enjoy vegetables a bit on the crisp side. Using a covered casserole ensures that the peppers will cook through.

4 **large green peppers**
1 **pound lean ground beef**
1 **small onion, chopped fine (about ¼ cup)**
1 **large clove garlic, minced**
2 **tablespoons celery, minced**
1 **egg**
1 **cup catsup**
3 **tablespoons fresh parsley, minced**
1 **tablespoon Worcestershire sauce**
½ **teaspoon salt**
¼ **teaspoon pepper**
½ **cup cooked rice**

Wash peppers; remove tops, seeds, and membrane. Set upside down to drain.

Place beef, onion, garlic, and celery in a 2-quart bowl. Cook on High (600–700 watts) for 3 minutes. Stir to keep beef crumbly. Continue to cook on High 2 minutes. Stir in all remaining ingredients, reserving 4 tablespoons catsup.

Fill green peppers with mixture, mounding on top. Arrange peppers in a circle in a round or oval baking dish just large enough to contain peppers upright. If you have a casserole with its own cover, that would be a good choice.

Cover; cook on Medium High (400–500 watts) for 10–12 minutes. If you do not have a Medium High setting, cook on High for about 8–10 minutes. After 5 minutes of cooking time, turn dish halfway if it appears to be cooking unevenly.

Spread 1 tablespoon of catsup on top of each pepper. Serve with a crusty garlic bread (see index).

ONE-STEP LASAGNA
Serves 6–8

An interesting concept began to develop several years ago with recipes using noodles: When enough liquid is added to the recipe it is possible to use uncooked noodles, which will cook in the sauce—thus eliminating the need to precook them on your cook-top.

The important element in constructing these recipes is to determine the amount of liquid needed to produce a tender noodle, without reducing the quality of the sauce. Each time I prepare this recipe, I add a touch to try to perfect the technique. It is such a help to the cook to use this idea, you might like to experiment with some recipes yourself.

An important part of the success of this recipe is to allow the noodles standing time to soften after the cooking time is completed (leaving the plastic wrap on during that period).

The addition of the egg in the ricotta cheese has nothing to do with microwave cooking—it was taught to me years ago by a wonderful Italian cook, who always added eggs to the ricotta; this makes the cheese easier to spread, and helps bind it all together. If ricotta cheese is not available in your area, you may substitute cottage cheese.

Although I am extremely fond of mozzarella cheese, I prefer to use a good quality Monterey Jack or Sonoma Jack cheese in the microwave. It melts well and gives a more creamy texture.

1 **pound lean ground chuck roast**
1 **15-ounce jar Ragu spaghetti sauce**
1 **8-ounce can tomato sauce**
½ **cup water**
1 **teaspoon salt**
2 **cups ricotta cheese (or cottage cheese)**
1 **egg, beaten**
1 **8-ounce package lasagna noodles, uncooked**
4 **cups shredded Monterey Jack cheese, or mozzarella**
½ **cup Parmesan cheese, grated**
Chopped fresh parsley for garnish

Place beef in a 2-quart bowl. Cook on High (600–700 watts) for 3 minutes. Stir to keep meat crumbly and continue to cook 2 minutes. Stir and drain if necessary (although lean ground meat usually does not leave a fat residue).

Combine spaghetti sauce, tomato sauce, water, and salt. Stir to blend well; add to the cooked meat. Set aside.

Combine ricotta cheese and egg; blend well. Set aside. Assemble lasagna in a baking dish approximately 12″ x 7″. Layer as follows:
1 layer sauce—use ⅓ of sauce
1 layer noodles—use ½ of noodles
1 layer ricotta—use ½ of cheese

1 layer Monterey Jack cheese—use ⅓ of cheese
1 layer sauce—use ⅓ of sauce

Repeat layers, ending with sauce. Top with Parmesan cheese.

It is important for the noodles to steam. Therefore, triple wrap baking dish with a microwave-recommended plastic wrap. I usually place one sheet of plastic wrap down the very center of the baking dish, then overlap toward the center from each side, using 3 sheets of wrap. Vent one corner of the plastic wrap.

Cook on Medium (300–350 watts) for 30 minutes. Let stand covered for 20 minutes, or longer if there is time. Before serving, sprinkle with additional Monterey Jack, Parmesan, and chopped parsley.

To reheat, use Medium power for about 3 minutes per serving if at room temperature; longer timing may be necessary if taken from the refrigerator.

Note: If you would prefer to make your own sauce, use the spaghetti sauce in this book (see index) instead of the Ragu. You will need 2 cups of sauce instead of the jar. Use the remainder of ingredients as suggested.

FETTUCINI
Serves 8

This recipe comes from a fine Italian chef. Serve with garlic bread and a salad.

2 **9-ounce packages extra-long fettucini egg noodles, cooked and drained**
½ **pound sweet butter**
⅔ **cup light cream (half & half)**
2 **egg yolks, beaten**
1 **teaspoon salt**
½ **teaspoon freshly ground pepper**
1 **cup Parmesan cheese, grated**
¼ **cup freshly chopped parsley**

Cook noodles according to package instructions. While noodles are cooking, this rich sauce can be made in minutes.

Melt butter in large glass measure on High (600–700 watts) for 1 minute. Whisk together cream and egg yolks; add to melted butter. Add seasonings and Parmesan cheese. Heat on High for 1 minute.

Combine with cooked noodles, stirring thoroughly. Transfer to serving dish, and sprinkle with parsley and additional grated Parmesan cheese.

NEW ENGLAND BOILED DINNER
Serves 4

Using microwave for cooking less tender cuts of meat is definitely a timesaver. Before we had lower power settings it was impossible to break down connective tissue in tough cuts of meat by the use of High power only. Now we can save time by using a combination of high and low. To get the liquid started, we can use High power (600–700 watts) for a short time, then reduce the setting to Medium (300–350 watts) or a bit lower, perhaps to Medium Low (200–250 watts).

With corned beef, it is important that the meat be covered by liquid the entire time—whatever sticks out of the water will be overcooked and tough. Therefore cut the meat in half to make it easier to submerge. Although traditionally the potatoes and carrots are added after the meat cooks for about 1 hour, my experience has been that the vegetables do not get tender unless they are placed in at the beginning. With so much liquid absorbing microwave energy, it takes longer for the food inside the liquid to cook. We are not only using lower power, but the water also slows down the cooking action.

1 **2½- to 3-pound corned beef brisket, cut in half (rinsed if desired to reduce salt)**
4 **small potatoes, peeled and left whole**
3 **carrots, cut into chunks**
1 **medium head cabbage, cut into wedges**

Combine corned beef, potatoes, and carrots in 4-quart casserole with enough water to cover completely. Cover and cook on High (600–700 watts) for 20 minutes. Turn meat over; add more water if necessary. Cover and cook on Medium (300–350 watts) for 1 hour 15 minutes. Test doneness of beef; if not fork tender, cover and cook for an additional 15–30 minutes on Medium, or until fork tender (time will vary with the meat). For additional tenderness, allow meat to sit covered for 15 more minutes.

Arrange cabbage over top of liquid in a circle. Cover and cook on High about 3–5 minutes. Cabbage is at its best when just barely cooked and still fairly crisp and green.

Thinly slice meat across grain and serve with vegetables.

PASTA SALAD WITH CHICKEN AND VEGETABLES

Serves 8–10

Cold pasta salads have become so popular, I decided to experiment with my own. This is an attractive luncheon or dinner dish that can be made a day ahead. Serve with croissants, or a crusty garlic bread and a rich, rich dessert...perhaps chocolate?

⅓ **cup pine nuts**
1 **teaspoon butter**
6 **chicken breast halves, boned (about 1½ pounds total), or 1 four-pound chicken cooked [see index] and meat removed from bones and shredded**
½ **cup chicken broth, or ½ cup water and 1 teaspoon chicken granules**
1 **pound linguine, cooked "al dente" and drained well**
1 **15-ounce can garbanzo beans, well drained**
2 **6-ounce jars marinated artichoke hearts, with liquid reserved**
1 **10-ounce package frozen peas, rinsed with cold water to separate**
½ **pound fresh mushrooms, sliced**
½ **pound Monterey Jack cheese, cut into ½" cubes**
1 **2-ounce jar stuffed green olives, sliced**
1 **2-ounce jar pitted black olives, drained and sliced**
1 **red or green bell pepper, seeded and cut into thin strips**
1 **cup olive oil**
⅔ **cup red wine vinegar**
¼ **cup finely chopped fresh parsley**
2 **teaspoons Dijon mustard**
½ **teaspoon curry powder**
1 **clove garlic, finely chopped, or ¼ teaspoon garlic powder**
Salt and freshly ground pepper

Combine the pine nuts and butter in a 1-cup measure. Toast them on High (600–700 watts) for 2–2½ minutes, stirring once, cooking just until the nuts begin to brown. Set aside to cool.

Arrange the chicken, skin side up, in a circle in a round or oval shallow baking dish, just large enough to hold chicken. Pour the chicken broth over the chicken. Cover with parchment or wax paper. Cook on High for 5 minutes, then turn the pieces over, continue to cook for another 4–5 minutes, just until chicken is tender when pierced with a fork and the juices are no longer pink when chicken is pressed with your finger. Let the chicken cool in the stock. (I always like to baste it several times during standing with the pan juices.) When cooled, drain, discard the skin, and shred the meat. (If anyone enjoys crisp cracklins you can place the skin from the chicken on a rack and cover with a paper towel, cook on High several minutes, until it is crisp and brown.)

In a large mixing bowl, combine the nuts, chicken, linguine, beans, artichoke hearts, peas, mushrooms, cheese, olives, and bell pepper and toss to blend. Combine the oil, vinegar, parsley, mustard, curry, garlic or garlic powder, salt and pepper in a glass measure and blend well. Pour the dressing over the salad and toss to blend the seasonings. Refrigerate until ready to serve.

Tip. As soon as the pasta is finished cooking, drain it in a colander. Then place it in a bowl, or back into the cooking pot and pour the oil from both jars of marinated artichoke hearts into the still warm pasta. The oil is too tasty to discard, and will keep the pasta threads from sticking together while they cool.

11

VEGETABLES, PASTA, AND GRAINS

COOKING GUIDE: VEGETABLES
All cooking is done on a power setting of High (600–700 watts)

Food	Amount	Preparation	Time (in minutes)	Water	Standing Time (in minutes)	Comments
Artichokes Approx. 3–3½″ in diameter	Fresh 1 2	Wash thoroughly. Cut off top of each leaf.	9–10 11–12	¼ cup ½ cup	2–3 2–3	Done when leaf pulled comes out easily.
	Frozen 10 oz.	Slit pouch.	5–6	none	3	
Asparagus	Fresh 1 lb.	Wash, cut off tough base.	7–8	¼ cup	2	Rearrange once during cooking time.
	Frozen 10 oz.	Slit pouch	4–5	none	2–3	
Beans, Wax	Fresh 1 lb.	Wash, trim ends. Leave whole or cut.	12–14	¼ cup	2–3	Stir once during cooking.
Beans, Green, French Cut	Frozen 10 oz.		6–7	none	0	
Beets	4 medium	Scrub, leave 1″ stem on top.	16–18	¼ cup	0	After cooking, cut or leave whole.
Broccoli	Fresh whole 1–1½ lb.	Remove leaves. Slit stems.	10–11	¼ cup	3	Stir or rearrange during cooking time.
	Fresh chopped 1–1½ lb.		9–10	¼ cup	3	
	Frozen chopped or whole		8–10	none	2	
Brussels Sprouts	Fresh 1 lb.	Cut off stems and wash.	8–9	¼ cup	3	Stir once during cooking time.
	Frozen 10 oz.		6–7	none	0	
Cabbage	½ head shredded	Remove wilted leaves.	5–6	¼ cup	2–3	Rearrange wedges ½ way through cooking time.
	1 head quartered		10–12	¼ cup	3–4	

COOKING GUIDE: VEGETABLES
All cooking is done on a power setting of High (600–700 watts)

Food	Amount	Preparation	Time (in minutes)	Water	Standing Time (in minutes)	Comments
Carrots	1 lb.	Cut into ½" slices.	9–10	¼ cup	2	Stir once during cooking time.
	Frozen 10 lb.		7–8	none	0	
Cauliflower	Fresh 1 medium whole	Remove core and outside leaves.	8–9	¼ cup	3	Stir ½ way through cooking time.
	florets		7–8	¼ cup	3	
	Frozen 10 oz.		6–7			
				none	0	
Celery	2½ cups	Clean and trim stalks.	8–9	¼ cup	0	
Corn kernels	Frozen 10 oz.		5–6	¼ cup	2	Stir ½ way through cooking time.
Corn-on-the-Cob	1 ear	Leave in husks.	3–4	none	2	
	2 ears	Cook no more	6–7	none	2	Rearrange ½ way through cooking time.
	3 ears	than 4 at a time.	9–10	none	2	
	4 ears		11-12	none	2	
	Frozen:	Covered dish.				
	2 ears		6–7	none	2	
	4 ears		9–10	none	2	
Mushrooms	Fresh ½ lb. sliced	Add butter or water.	2–4	2 tbsp. (or butter)	2	Stir ½ way through cooking time.
Okra	Fresh ½ lb.	Leave whole or cut into chunks.	3–5	¼ cup	2	Stir ½ way through cooking time.
	Frozen 10 oz.		6–8	none	2	
Onions	1 lb. small pearl	Add 1 tbsp. butter.	6–7	¼ cup	3	Stir ½ way through cooking time.
	1 lb. medium large	Peel and quarter. Add 1 tbsp. butter.	7–9	¼ cup	3	
Parsnips	4 medium quartered	Peeled and cut.	8–9	¼ cup	2	Stir once.

COOKING GUIDE: VEGETABLES
All cooking is done on a power setting of High (600–700 watts)

Food	Amount	Preparation	Time (in minutes)	Water	Standing Time (in minutes)	Comments
Green Peas	Fresh 1 lb.	Shell, rinse well.	7–8	¼ cup	2	Stir once.
	Frozen 10 oz.		6–7	none	2	Stir once.
Pea Pods (Snow Peas)	Frozen 10 oz.		5–6	none	2	
Potatoes, Sweet 5–6 oz. each	1	Scrub, pierce with fork.	4–5	none	3	
	2		6–7	none	3	
	4		8–10	none	3	
	6		10–11	none	3	
Potatoes, White, Baking 6–8 oz. each	1	Scrub, pierce with fork. Place on paper towel or rack.	4–6	none	3	
	2		6–8	none	3	
	3		8–12	none	3	
	4		12–16	none	3	
	5		16–18	none	3	
Potatoes, Russet Boiling	3	Wash, and peel. Cut into quarters.	12–16	½ cup	0	Stir once.
Rutabaga	Fresh 1 lb.	Wash; remove wilted or tough stems.	6–7	¼ cup	2–4	Stir once.
	Frozen 10 oz.		7–8	none	2	
Spinach	Fresh 1 lb.	Wash well. Remove tough stems.	6–7	none	2	Stir once.
	Frozen 10 oz.		7–8	none	2	
Squash, Acorn or Butternut	1–1½ lb. whole	Scrub. Pierce with fork.	10–12	none	0	Cut and remove seeds to serve.
Spaghetti Squash	2–3 lb.	Pierce with fork. Place on rack.	6 per pound	none	5	
Turnips	4 cups cubed	Peel, wash.	9–11	¼ cup	3	Stir ½ way through cooking time.
Zucchini	3 cups ¼″ slices	Wash; leave peel on.	6–8	¼ cup	2	Stir once.

BLANCHING FRESH VEGETABLES

Blanching (quickly heating fresh vegetables or fruit to stop the enzyme action that causes them to spoil) can be easily accomplished in a freezer bag, which is also a cooking bag.

There are bag sealers on the market like Seal-a-Meal which provide a variety of sizes to suit the needs of individual families. It is important to realize that these are not the same as sandwich bags, which are not designed for cooking and should not be used in your microwave. Limit your use of plastic bags in the microwave to those marked for microwave use or for boiling in hot water.

Blanching is ideal for the increasing number of people in our country who grow their own vegetables. It is such a bonus, I often wonder why more people don't take the time to do it. In the old days people did not need to join exercise classes or jog, because they got their exercise digging in the garden— accomplishing two things at once. Think about it!

The concept of blanching in the microwave was proposed in the mid 1970s by Oster Corporation for their sealer in a pamphlet for microwave. Here are three blanching suggestions; experiment with them and find the method that you prefer.

Blanching Method 1

Place 4 cups washed, cut vegetables in a 4-cup glass measure or glass casserole so you can observe the vegetables. Add ¼ cup water. Cover with a glass that fits the opening, or use a dinner plate to cover. Blanch on High (600–700 watts) for 5–6 minutes, or just until vegetables turn a bright color. Immediately plunge into ice water to cool.

To freeze, pack into desired size boilable bags. Season to taste with butter, salt, and pepper, a few tablespoons of the blanching water, or your favorite cream or cheese sauce. Freeze.

To use, cut a corner off the bag. Place straight up on a small plate. Heat on High until vegetables are fork tender (7–8 minutes). Timing will depend upon amount and texture of vegetables.

Blanching Method 2

Place 2 cups washed, cut vegetables into a boilable bag of correct size, leaving room at the top for sealing and expansion (follow directions from your manufacturer).

Add ¼ cup water to each bag. Blanch on High (600–700 watts) for 2½–3 minutes, just until vegetables turn a bright color. Immediately plunge into ice water to cool. Freeze in the bag.

To use, cut a corner off the bag. Place straight up on a small plate. Heat on High until vegetables are fork tender, about 5–7 minutes.

Blanching Method 3 (if you do not have a Seal-a-Meal)

Follow directions for blanching in Method 1. Place vegetables in a zip-lock bag for freezing, removing as much air as possible. To use, transfer vegetables from zip-lock bag to a small casserole and heat with the liquid from the freezer package and seasonings of your choice.

ARTICHOKES

Since this book is about cooking for taste and appearance, the recipes used for artichokes do not include what I consider an unfortunate technique that began to appear some years ago: You were to take an artichoke, rinse it, wrap it in either wax paper or plastic wrap, and cook it in the microwave. When I first observed this being done in a demonstration on-stage, I went up to taste it afterwards, a bit unhappy with myself for not having thought of it first! But I could not taste it, because it had been tossed into the wastebasket.

When I tried it at home, it tasted just like an artichoke that had been wrapped in plastic and cooked.

The Italians know what to do with their lovely homegrown varieties—and to me the best-tasting is the first recipe given below. You may agree that there is no need for melting butter, that the sauce it is cooked in is sufficient for flavor. But if you like, do melt some butter to serve for dipping the leaves.

Selecting Artichokes

Choose artichokes that have compact leaves and good green color. A bronze tinge on outer leaves indicates "winter kissed"—a sign of slow maturity and premium flavor. If not used immediately, moisten artichokes lightly and refrigerate in plastic bags.

To prepare: wash well; remove small leaves at bottom. Cut off thorny tips of leaves with scissors. Cut about one inch off top. Leave the stem intact and just cut off the discolored parts; it will give you more of the artichoke to enjoy. The stem becomes very tender, almost like the heart.

Use a 1-quart glass measure, or bowl just large enough to contain the vegetable. By adding a touch of oil, the leaves remain soft; and by using a cover and water, the steaming effect produces a moist, tender artichoke. Cooking time is determined by the size of the artichokes.

TO COOK ONE ARTICHOKE
Serves 1

1 artichoke, prepared for cooking
1 large clove garlic, cut in half
½ lemon, sliced
Water
1 tablespoon olive oil (may substitute salad oil)

Set one large artichoke upside down in a bowl-type container or casserole just large enough to contain recipe. Add garlic, arrange lemon slices around artichoke, and add water to cover ⅓ of the artichoke. Pour oil over top of artichoke. Cover. Cook on High (600–700 watts) for 10 minutes or until the stem becomes fork tender. Immediately turn artichoke in water to moisten all leaves. Allow to remain covered in liquid about 5 more minutes to soften leaves.

If time permits, you may wish to try cooking artichoke 15 minutes using Medium High (400–500 watts) power. I have noticed it produces an even more excellent, tender result and I usually cook it that way for myself.

TO COOK FOUR ARTICHOKES
Serves 4

4 artichokes, prepared for cooking
4 lemon slices
4 tablespoons oil

Place artichokes in a circle in a round casserole, upside down. Add water to cover ⅓ of the artichoke. Add 4 lemon slices; pour 1 tablespoon oil over each artichoke. Cover and cook on High (600–700 watts) for 16 minutes, or until stems are fork tender. Immediately, turn artichokes around to moisten all the leaves. Re-cover, and let stand 5 minutes before serving.

Spices and Seasonings for Your Artichoke

Be creative and add a variety of flavors with herbs and spices. Cook with:
A Greek accent—Add a clove of garlic and a pinch of oregano for each artichoke
Italian zest—Add a garlic clove, two tablespoons oil, 1 teaspoon red wine vinegar, and a pinch of basil for each artichoke
A French touch—Cook with garlic and lemon juice; serve with Hollandaise Sauce (see index).

LOW-CALORIE MARINATED ARTICHOKES
Serves 2, or 4 as an appetizer

¼ cup water
¼ cup wine vinegar
¼ teaspoon salt
1 clove garlic, crushed
¼ teaspoon thyme leaves
¼ teaspoon crushed basil leaves
¼ teaspoon crushed oregano leaves
2 tablespoons olive oil
2 artichokes, cooked (see above)

Place water, vinegar, salt, garlic, thyme, basil, and oregano in large glass measure. Heat on High (600–700 watts) until marinade reaches a boil. Stir in oil; blend well. Pour over cooked artichokes. Refrigerate and serve cold.

LOW-CALORIE YOGURT HERB DIP
Serves 4

¼ cup finely chopped celery, cucumber, or carrot, or combination
¼ teaspoon salt (or to your taste)
½ teaspoon dill weed
1 8-ounce cup plain yogurt
Additional raw chopped vegetables for garnish
4 cooked artichokes, chilled (see above)

Gently stir chopped vegetables and seasonings into yogurt. Chill and top with additional chopped vegetables as a garnish. Serve as a dip for cooked artichoke leaves.

ARTICHOKE STUFFED WITH CRAB
Serves 2

1 artichoke, cooked (see above)
3 ounces canned shredded crab meat
¼ cup celery, cut fine
French dressing as needed

After cooking artichoke, remove from water and turn upside down to drain well. Remove choke with a spoon. Open petals out to form a cup. Set aside. Combine crab meat, celery, and just enough French dressing to moisten. Fill artichoke with mixture. May be refrigerated until ready to serve.

DRUNKEN GLAZED CARROTS
Serves 4

An old recipe gets a new treatment. If you prefer "sober" carrots, increase the orange juice to two tablespoons and leave out the liqueur. Either way, they are a treat.

1 pound carrots
3 tablespoons water
3 tablespoons butter
1 tablespoon orange liqueur
1 tablespoon fresh orange juice
½ teaspoon cornstarch
¼ teaspoon grated orange rind
Pinch salt
Pinch white pepper

Peel and slice carrots diagonally, about ¼ inch thick, with entire "eye" showing. Place in small oval or round casserole, just large enough to contain recipe. Add water; cover. Cook on High (600–700 watts) for 7 minutes. Drain liquid. Stir in butter. Combine liqueur, orange juice, and cornstarch. Stir until cornstarch is dissolved. Stir into carrots, along with orange rind, salt, and pepper. Cover; cook on High 2 minutes, or until mixture is slightly thickened.

Note: The reason for a small casserole is to contain the carrots and not allow them to spread out, because the pieces on the outside would overcook before the rest of the carrots received enough microwave energy to cook.

BROCCOLI CASSEROLE
Serves 6

In the interest of consumer education on the microwave, Mary Marshall of the Department of Agriculture invited me to do a workshop for the San Bernardino community. We were all amazed and delighted at the response, since it was early 1970s—the room held 300 people, and we had to turn people away and schedule a second workshop, even though there was a registration fee.

The interest in the workshop was intense, especially since I had cooked a prime rib, which was unheard of in those days of cooking on High power.

When it was over, a very excited tall, blonde, handsome young woman came over, and with eyes gleaming and the southern accent fighting to slow down her speech, she grabbed my attention and said, "I want to do what you do. I don't care what it costs or how long it takes—*you* are going to teach me!" Well, that was protégé Martha Green, a smashing lady who always gets what she wants. Within a few days, she appeared at my doorstep and we began. She was a sponge and need I tell you, she now is the owner of three shops! They are all successful because she builds a following wherever she goes and her students adore her.

Martha happens to be an excellent cook and will attempt anything once. Nothing is too much trouble and she will experiment until she feels it is right. Several of her recipes appear in this book—including this one.

2 10-ounce packages frozen chopped broccoli
2 cups Ritz crackers, spread with margarine
1 small onion, grated
1 cup mayonnaise
1 10½-ounce can cream of mushroom soup
2 eggs, beaten
1½ cups shredded cheddar cheese

Place both packages of broccoli on a plate to catch any drippings. Defrost on High (600–700 watts) for 5–6 minutes. Set aside to complete defrosting.

Crumble half the buttered crackers in bottom of a 10-inch quiche dish. Combine onion, mayonnaise, mushroom soup, and eggs and blend into a sauce. Drain broccoli well and blend into sauce. Pour over crackers. Sprinkle with remaining crackers. Cook on High until mixture is set, about 12–14 minutes. Sprinkle with cheese and heat for 1–2 minutes on High, just until cheese is melted.

BRUSSELS SPROUTS WITH GARLIC AND PARMESAN
Serves 6–8

A blend of flavors that enhances these miniature cabbage heads. If you have passed these up in the produce section, be brave—you are in for a treat.

1 pound fresh brussels sprouts
¼ cup water
2 tablespoons (¼ stick) butter
1 garlic clove, minced
Salt and freshly ground pepper
¼ cup freshly grated Parmesan cheese

Discard any dry outside leaves from sprouts. Trim stems. Using small sharp knife, cut a shallow *X* in bottom of each stem. Combine sprouts and water in shallow 1-quart dish. Cover and cook on High (600–700 watts) for 7 minutes. Let rest covered 3–4 minutes.

Combine butter and garlic in small glass measuring cup and cook on High 1–2 minutes. Drain water from sprouts. Add butter mixture, salt, and pepper and toss lightly to coat. Add cheese and toss again. Serve hot.

BRUSSELS SPROUTS WITH A TOUCH OF DILL
Serves 6–8

If using fresh sprouts, timing may vary slightly. These are undercooked slightly to give them a crisp and crunchy texture. You may cook them longer if you wish, but it would be a pity.

2 10-ounce packages frozen brussels sprouts
¼ cup Italian salad dressing
1 teaspoon dill weed
1 scallion, minced

Place sprouts in a small casserole, just large enough to contain them. Add ¼ cup salad dressing. Cover. Cook on High (600–700 watts) for 6–7 minutes, until heated through.

Add dill weed and scallion; stir. Cover and refrigerate for several hours. Serve cold. May be served as an appetizer.

FRESH CAULIFLOWER IN A SHALLOT MARINADE
Serves 6

1 medium to large cauliflower
¼ cup water
¾ cup salad oil
½ cup white wine vinegar
2 tablespoons fresh lemon juice
3 tablespoons shallots, chopped
1 clove garlic, chopped
1 teaspoon salt
¼ teaspoon pepper
1 teaspoon fresh minced parsley
Pimiento for garnish

Trim florets from stem. Cut any large florets in half, leaving small ones whole. Place in a 1-quart casserole; add ¼ cup water. Cook, covered, on High (600–700 watts) for 5–7 minutes or until fork tender. (Timing will depend upon size of cauliflower.) Allow to cook in water.

While cauliflower is cooking, combine all remaining ingredients except parsley. Drain cauliflower and add florets to marinade, stirring to coat. Sprinkle with parsley. Cover; place in refrigerator until ready to serve. Stir through once or twice.

To serve, remove from marinade with slotted spoon. Serve cold on lettuce or green leaves on an attractive serving platter. Reserve marinade to use as a salad dressing.

Garnish with pimiento for a nice holiday touch.

CAULIFLOWER GRATINÉED NOREEN
Serves 4

Named for a favorite niece, who challenged me to adapt this recipe 11 years ago. It was my first success with staggering cooking times of tomatoes and cheese so that all ingredients were done at the same time. Since microwave energy cooks from the outside in, if all ingredients were layered at once as in the original recipe, the cheese and tomatoes would be overcooked before the cauliflower began to heat.

¼ cup (½ stick) butter, or 3 tablespoons water
1 large head cauliflower, broken into florets
Garlic salt
Freshly ground pepper

2 **firm medium tomatoes, cut into wedges**
¼ **cup seasoned Italian bread crumbs, or Italian herbs**
1½ **cups Swiss cheese, shredded**
¼ **cup freshly grated Parmesan cheese**
Touch of chopped fresh parsley for garnish

Melt butter in attractive 1½-quart serving bowl (if using water skip this step). Add florets and turn to coat evenly with butter.

Season to taste with garlic salt and pepper. Cook covered on High (600–700 watts) for 5–6 minutes, just until fork tender. Arrange tomatoes over top and sprinkle with bread crumbs. Cover and cook an additional 2 minutes. Top with cheese; cook uncovered 1–2 minutes, or until cheeses are melted.

Sprinkle with parsley. Serve immediately.

Note: For even fewer calories, cook cauliflower with 3 tablespoons water instead of butter, and sprinkle tomatoes with Italian herbs instead of bread crumbs.

GREEN BEANS WITH TOASTED ALMONDS
Serves 3–4

A timesaving technique: Use your microwave to sauté nuts for any recipe.

1 **10-ounce package frozen French-cut green beans**
½ **cup sliced almonds**
2 **tablespoons (¼ stick) butter**
Salt and freshly ground pepper to taste

Cook beans in unopened package on High power (600–700 watts) for 6 minutes. Set aside.

Combine almonds and butter in measuring cup and cook on High 1–2 minutes until nuts are lightly browned, stirring after 1 minute. Transfer beans to serving dish. Add nuts, salt, pepper and toss lightly. Heat on High 1 minute. Serve hot.

BOILED BEETS
Serves 4

Sliced beets can enhance a salad, or can produce a wonderful cold borscht to be served with sliced cucumbers and sour cream on a hot summer day. You may purchase them in a jar or a can, but you have not tasted beets until you cook them yourself—nothing can replace freshly cooked beets.

1½–2 **pounds fresh beets of uniform size, washed well**
½ **cup water**

Trim beets, leaving about 1½ inches of the tops attached to prevent bleeding during cooking. Place beets and water in a 3- to 4-quart casserole. Cover and cook on High (600–700 watts) for 15–17 minutes, or until just fork tender.

Drain. Peel and slice or dice. May be served with butter, salt, and pepper, or used for your favorite recipe.

CORN ON THE COB

Long before the microwave came into my life, there was the barbecue. In keeping with my cooking concept of good eating without cleanup, I used to roast corn, Indian style—I would soak the corn in the husks to keep it from burning, then cook it on the hot coals until done. The husks and silk peeled back just like a banana skin.

The first time I served this, with the husks pulled back and the succulent corn just brimming with bursting juices, my husband queried, "Where am I supposed to put the corn-holders?"

To avoid such a confrontation in your dining room, may I share my solution: Before placing corn on the dish for cooking, take a sharp knife and cut ¾ of the way into corn through the husk, just above the stem end. After cooking it can simply be broken off or cut the rest of the way with a knife.

Fresh ears of corn, with husks intact
Water for soaking

To prepare corn, remove outside soiled leaves. Place cold water in sink or pan and soak corn for about 5 minutes. Place corn on dish to make it easier to remove from microwave when it is hot. Cook for 3 minutes per ear of corn on High (600–700 watts). Allow to stand a few minutes before peeling. (They will be quite hot.) The size and age of the corn determines the exact timing—naturally, a smaller, more delicate kernel will take less time.

You may serve it with melted butter if you wish; however, I find cooking the corn intact keeps all of the moisture inside nature's own package.

EGGPLANT ITALIAN STYLE
Serves 4

Sautéing eggplant in a frying pan on a cook-top requires a lot of oil because the eggplant absorbs so much, and frying requires oil to keep the pan from burning.

By using microwave, you eliminate this need and cut the oil to a minimum. Since the eggplant takes much longer to become tender, it is started first; the other vegetables are added later.

This is a good side dish for meat or fish. It can also be spooned into pita bread for a great sandwich: Heat vegetables first, fill pita bread, then heat entire sandwich for just 45 seconds to warm the pita.

3 **cloves garlic, minced**
3 **tablespoons olive oil (may substitute cooking oil)**
1 **medium eggplant (about 1 pound), cut into chunks**
1 **green pepper, cut into chunks**
1 **red pepper, cut into chunks (if in season)**
1 **small onion, sliced into rings and separated**

Place garlic and oil in shallow oval or round baking dish. Cook on High (600–700 watts) for 1 minute. Stir in eggplant, cover; cook on High 6 minutes, stirring once or twice. Stir in other vegetables; continue to cook, 4–5 minutes, covered, until eggplant is soft and tender, stirring once or twice.

Note: You may need to add oil during cooking, but only add what is needed, a small amount at a time. Too much oil will make vegetables soggy.

LENTILS
Serves 6

If you have never tried this energy-giving, tasty vegetable, now is a good time to experiment. Having a package on your shelf makes it easy to add it to an evening meal. It is a good substitute for potato, rice, or any starch, and adapts well to your favorite seasonings. Instead of soaking overnight, try this technique.

1 **cup dry lentils, washed and sorted**
4 **cups water**
1 **teaspoon salt**
⅛ **teaspoon pepper**
Butter to taste

Place all ingredients except butter in a 2- or 3-quart casserole. Cover. Cook on High (600–700 watts) fo 15 minutes. Remove and set aside for 1 hour (you may leave it inside microwave if not needed for other cooking).

After 1 hour of soaking, stir and continue cooking on High, covered, for 22–25 minutes, or until lentils are soft and tender. Taste for seasoning, adding more salt and pepper if needed. Stir in butter and serve hot.

To reheat, add 2–3 tablespoons of water for each cup of lentils and reheat on High.

FRESH MUSHROOM SAUTÉ WITH PEPPERS, ONIONS, AND ZUCCHINI
Serves 2–3

While traveling in Italy we fell in love with the fresh, colorful vegetables served in the countryside by the local chefs—we could always see the well-tended vegetable garden surrounding the restaurant. Filled with a variety of warm-climate vegetables, it reminded me of my father's love for gardening and the patches of vegetables he always planted each season. And it made me appreciate my early exposure to fresh vegetables at our table.

Of course, in "those days" we did not have the liberating frozen vegetables—but we did have canned. Fortunately for us, they seldom entered our kitchen; we had our garden.

6 **fresh mushrooms, sliced**
1 **green pepper, sliced thin**
1 **red pepper, sliced thin (if in season)**
1 **small onion, thinly sliced in rings**
1 **zucchini, sliced thin**
2–3 **tablespoons olive oil (may substitute cooking oil)**
Freshly chopped parsley for garnish
Season to your taste with any combination of the following: salt, pepper, oregano, parsley, basil, garlic powder, or your choice

Combine all ingredients in a small casserole. Cover. Cook on High (600–700 watts) for 4–5 minutes, or just until all ingredients are fork tender, stirring once.

This is nice spooned into pita bread, or a side dish with meat.

Note: If fresh tomatoes are in season, add 1 or 2 small, firm red tomatoes, cut into wedges after other vegetables cook about 3 minutes. Continue cooking for about 1–2 minutes, uncovered, to keep tomato wedges crisp tender, rather than cook them so soft they fall apart.

HOT PEA SALAD
Serves 4

From my protégé, the charming Martha Green.
   This simple and delicious treatment of the unassuming pea will bring raves.

1 **10-ounce package frozen peas**
6 **slices bacon**
½ **cup green onions, thinly sliced**
Mayonnaise
Fresh ground pepper

   Place unopened box of peas on plate in microwave. Cook on High (600–700 watts) 4 minutes. Set aside to complete defrosting.
   Place bacon slices on paper towel on a paper plate. Cook on High 5–6 minutes until crisp.
   Drain peas and place in bowl. Crumble bacon and add to bowl. Add green onions and just enough mayonnaise to moisten. Sprinkle ground pepper on top. Serve at once.
   Can also be served chilled.

POTATOES—BAKED AND BEYOND

   Almost all new microwave owners develop an instant fascination, as I did, with baked potatoes. There is something almost miraculous about popping a potato in to cook and serving it minutes later—and the results are equally miraculous. Because it is not cooked with hot, dry air, a microwaved potato retains its moisture and does not require the ritual dressing of butter or sour cream—or both. It's delicious plain. This makes it a great boon for the weight-conscious, who should be reminded that a medium potato, sprinkled with a little salt and pepper, contains approximately 90 calories.
   Several years of indulging my fascination prompted a member of my family to remark one

evening, "There must be something else you can do with this potato!" Should you grow weary of eating baked potatoes before you tire of cooking them, why not try one of the following different approaches.

Baked Potatoes

   Although baking a potato in a conventional oven may be the easiest "recipe" in the world short of boiling an egg, speedy microwave cooking eliminates some of the steps of traditional preparation. Simply elevate the potato on a rack and cook on High (600–700 watts) until the outside feels slightly soft. (A medium-sized potato will usually take about 6 minutes.) Let stand for a few minutes to finish cooking before cutting into it. If it is elevated you may not have to turn it over—elevating it will prevent heat from being trapped underneath, thus keeping the potato from steaming.

One Potato, Two Potatoes, Three Potatoes, Four

   A simple way to calculate for more than one is to increase cooking time 5 minutes for each additional potato. Place potatoes in a circle if cooking more than one. If they are not all the same size, the smaller ones will be finished first just as they are in conventional cooking.
   If you like a crisp potato: Instead of letting it stand to finish cooking, transfer the potato to a 400°F. toaster oven and bake until skin is crisp, about 5 minutes. But remember, you will then need to add butter or sour cream to replace the moisture that has been lost through conventional cooking.

PARSLEY NEW POTATOES
Serves 4–6

1 **pound small new potatoes**
¼ **cup water**
2 **tablespoons butter**
2 **tablespoons fresh parsley, minced**
Salt and freshly ground pepper to taste
Touch of garlic powder (optional)

   Wash potatoes, but do not peel. Place in a 2-quart casserole. Add water, and cook covered on High (600–700 watts) for 12–14 minutes. Stir once during cooking. Cook until fork tender.
   Drain. Stir in butter, parsley, salt, pepper, and garlic powder (if desired), coating potatoes well.

ROASTED BROWNED POTATOES
Serves 4

If you still believe you cannot get a lovely, browned potato in your microwave, do try this—you may be pleasantly surprised. Liquid browning sauces like Gravy Master, Kitchen Bouquet, and others were around long before microwave came on the scene. I have not added salt because there is salt in the browning liquid. Taste for flavor and adjust the seasoning—salt does improve potatoes. I always enjoy a touch of garlic; however, it may be left out if you prefer not to use it.

3   **tablespoons butter or oil**
1   **teaspoon liquid browning sauce**
½   **teaspoon paprika**
1   **teaspoon garlic powder**
3   **tablespoons fresh chopped parsley (optional)**
4   **medium-sized potatoes, peeled**

Combine butter, browning sauce, paprika, and garlic powder in a 1-quart casserole. Heat on High (600–700 watts) 1 minute. Stir in potatoes and parsley, making sure they are well coated with mixture. Cover; cook on High 10–12 minutes or until potatoes are fork tender, stirring once or twice to coat with mixture. Serve hot.

Adjust cooking times accordingly if smaller or larger potatoes are used.

POTATO SOUFFLÉ
Serves 6

½   **cup (1 stick) butter**
1   **pound yellow onions, thinly sliced**
2   **pounds potatoes (about 5 medium)**
¾   **cup milk**
½   **cup sour cream**
1   **teaspoon baking powder**
2   **eggs, well beaten**
1   **teaspoon salt**
¼   **teaspoon white pepper**
1¼   **cups cheddar cheese, grated**
1   **teaspoon fresh parsley, minced**
Minced fresh parsley for garnish

Heat ¼ cup butter in 1½-quart soufflé dish on High (600–700 watts) until butter is melted, about 30 seconds. Add onion, stirring to coat evenly. Cover (try

using a microwave-safe dinner plate) and cook on High (600–700 watts) until onion is light brown in spots, about 15–20 minutes, stirring several times. Remove dish from microwave and set aside. Keep onions covered.

Arrange unpeeled potatoes in a circle and elevate on rack. Cook on High until just soft, about 5–6 minutes per potato. (If one or two are done before the others, remove and continue cooking remainder.) Let stand 5 minutes.

Peel, quarter, and place potatoes in food processor or large mixing bowl. Add remaining butter, milk, sour cream, and baking powder and whip until smooth. Add eggs, salt, and pepper and continue whipping until fluffy. Stir in reserved onion, 1 cup cheese, 1 teaspoon parsley, and any butter remaining in soufflé dish (do not wash dish). Spoon into soufflé dish and sprinkle with remaining cheese and some additional minced parsley. Cook on Medium High (400–500 watts) for 15 minutes. If you do not have variable power, use either Medium (300–350 watts) or Medium Low (200–250 watts) (sometimes called Defrost) and increase cooking time 5–7 minutes or until heated through. Serve immediately.

Reheat any leftovers on Medium High. High power will overcook outside edges.

TRADITIONAL LYONNAISE POTATOES
Serves 4

The ultimate microwave side dish. This is the first of two versions of Lyonnaise potatoes—the second is even easier.

3   **tablespoons butter**
1   **pound yellow onions, very thinly sliced**
2   **garlic cloves, minced**
1½   **pounds potatoes, peeled and sliced ¼ inch thick**
1   **teaspoon salt**
¼   **teaspoon freshly ground pepper**
Paprika (optional)
Minced fresh parsley for garnish

Heat butter in 2-quart casserole dish on High (600–700 watts) until butter is melted, about 30 seconds. Add onion and garlic and stir to coat evenly. Cover and cook on High (600–700 watts) 15–20 minutes, or until onion is lightly browned in spots, stirring once or twice. Add potatoes, salt, pepper, and paprika; blend evenly. Cover and cook on High 10 minutes. Stir thoroughly and continue cooking until potatoes are fork tender, about 5–10 minutes. Sprinkle with minced parsley.

QUICK AND EASY LYONNAISE POTATOES

Serves 2

Keeping oil to a minimum is the secret to the crisp texture of these potatoes.

2 medium potatoes, peeled, rinsed, and patted dry
Garlic salt
Garlic powder
Paprika
⅓ cup dehydrated onion flakes
2 tablespoons oil
Parsley flakes (see index for dehydrating parsley)

Slice potatoes thinly and evenly. Pat dry with paper towels. Arrange half of slices in dish just large enough to accommodate all potatoes being used. Sprinkle lightly with garlic salt, garlic powder, and paprika; top with half of dehydrated onion. Repeat layering. Pour oil over top. Cover and cook on High (600–700 watts) until potatoes are fork tender, about 10 minutes. Sprinkle with parsley flakes.

PARMESAN POTATOES

Serves 4

A quick appetizer, easily adaptable to any number of servings. Keep a batch of the coating on hand in the refrigerator so you can whip up hors d'oeuvres at a moment's notice. The topping, incidentally, is especially good on chicken.

¼ cup (½ stick) butter
1 pound russet potatoes, peeled and cut into 1-inch cubes
¼ cup grated Parmesan cheese
8 Ritz crackers
1 teaspoon garlic powder
¼ teaspoon salt, or to taste
½ teaspoon freshly ground pepper
½ teaspoon paprika

3 tablespoons fresh parsley, minced
1 tablespoon grated Parmesan cheese

Heat butter on High (600–700 watts) in pie plate or au gratin dish just large enough to accommodate potatoes in single layer, until butter is melted, about 30 seconds. Add potatoes, stirring to coat evenly. Remove with slotted spoon and set aside. Pour off any remaining butter and reserve.

Combine ¼ cup Parmesan, crackers, garlic powder, salt, pepper, and paprika in food processor or blender and process to fine crumbs. Transfer to plastic bag. Add potatoes in batches, shaking to coat evenly. Return potatoes to dish in single layer. Cover with plastic wrap and cook on High (600–700 watts) for 5 minutes. Add reserved butter and stir potatoes well. Cook uncovered on High until potatoes are fork tender, about 2–3 minutes. Combine parsley and remaining cheese and sprinkle over top. Spear potatoes with toothpicks and serve hot.

Note: Add a sprinkle of dill weed, oregano, tarragon, or other favorite herb at beginning of cooking time for variation, if desired.

POMMES DE TERRE AU GRATIN

Serves 6

¼ cup (½ stick) butter
2 pounds yellow onions, very thinly sliced
2 pounds russet potatoes, peeled and thinly sliced
1 teaspoon freshly grated nutmeg
Salt and white pepper
1½ cups Swiss cheese, grated
1½ cups milk

Heat butter in round 2-quart casserole or soufflé dish on High (600–700 watts) until butter is melted, about 30 seconds. Add onion, stirring to coat evenly. Cover and cook on High (600–700 watts) until onion is lightly browned in spots, about 25 minutes, stirring several times. Remove onion and set aside.

Combine potatoes, nutmeg, salt, and pepper and toss to coat evenly. Arrange half of potato slices in dish and top with half of onion. Sprinkle with ¾ cup cheese. Repeat layering of potato and onion. Heat milk on High power 1½ minutes. Pour evenly over top layer. Sprinkle with remaining cheese. Cover and cook on High until potatoes are just fork tender, about 20 minutes.

SWEET AND SIMPLE SWEET POTATOES
Serves 6

Both sweet potatoes and yams are cooked on lower settings to ensure even cooking. Because of their irregular shape, the narrow end sometimes has a tendency to overcook. Timing is approximately 4 minutes for each potato.

6 medium (about 3 pounds) sweet potatoes

Pierce potatoes. Arrange in circle on rack in microwave. If size of potatoes varies, place large ones outside the ring and smaller ones inside. Cook on Medium High (400–500 watts) until potatoes are soft on outside but still slightly firm in center, about 20 minutes. Cover and let stand 3–4 minutes to equalize moisture and finish cooking.

Potatoes can be cooked in advance and reheated on Medium High. Allow 1–2 minutes per potato.

ORANGE-GLAZED YAMS
Serves 6–8

Easy combination to prepare, and may be made ahead. The addition of the brown sugar helps to caramelize the sauce and makes the dish taste as though oven-baked for hours.

1 40-ounce can yams, drained; or 3 large fresh
**   yams, cooked, peeled, and cut into chunks**
1 large orange, peeled and cut into chunks
¼ cup firmly packed brown sugar
¼ cup sugar
1 tablespoon cornstarch
⅛ teaspoon salt
1 cup fresh orange juice
1 teaspoon grated orange peel
2 tablespoons (¼ stick) butter

Arrange yams and orange chunks in a 1½-quart round or oval baking dish. Combine sugars, cornstarch, and salt in a 4-cup measure. Stir in orange juice and peel; stir until cornstarch is dissolved. Cook on High (600–700 watts) for 2 minutes. Whisk through several times; continue cooking on High for 2 more minutes. Add butter, stirring until melted. Pour sauce over yams. Cook on High until heated through, about 3–5 minutes.

MONTEREY JACK RATATOUILLE
Serves 4–6

This recipe beautifully melds the flavor of eggplant, zucchini, and tomatoes, and is easy to prepare because the eggplant cooks quickly and easily.

1 eggplant (about 1½ pounds)
¼ cup olive oil
2 large garlic cloves, minced
1 large onion, thinly sliced into rings
½ pound zucchini, thinly sliced into rounds
1 green pepper, thinly sliced into rings
1 celery stalk, thinly sliced
3 firm large tomatoes, cut into wedges; or 1
**   14½-ounce can plum tomatoes, coarsely**
**   chopped**
1 6-ounce can tomato paste
3 tablespoons flour
1 teaspoon salt
1 teaspoon fines herbes
½ teaspoon freshly ground pepper
¼ teaspoon oregano
Pinch of dried thyme, crumbled
2 cups Monterey Jack cheese, shredded
Chopped fresh parsley for garnish

Set eggplant on rack and pierce well with fork. Cook on High (600–700 watts) for 7 minutes. Set aside to cool.

Combine oil, garlic, and onion in 3- to 4-quart casserole. Cover and cook on High 5 minutes. Stir in zucchini, green pepper, and celery. Peel eggplant and cut into 1½-inch cubes. Add to vegetables, mixing well. Cover and cook 5 minutes. Combine tomatoes and all remaining ingredients except cheese and parsley; blend well. Spoon half of tomato mixture over vegetables, and sprinkle with half of cheese. Cover with remaining tomato mixture and cheese. Cook on High until mixture is hot and bubbly, about 2 minutes. Sprinkle with parsley just before serving.

SAUERKRAUT AND APPLE TZIMMES
Serves 6–8

A tasty side-dish for the holidays.

2 tablespoons oil
½ large onion, sliced into rings

3 large cooking apples, chopped (about 4 cups)
1 1-pound can sauerkraut
1 tablespoon sugar
½ teaspoon salt

In a 1-quart oval or round casserole, place oil and onion rings. Cook on High power (600–700 watts) for 5–7 minutes, covered, until onion begins to brown slightly.

Add apples, sauerkraut, sugar, and salt. Stir until all ingredients are well blended. Cook covered on High power 12–15 minutes, or until apples are tender. Stir once or twice during cooking.

Allow to remain covered 5 minutes before serving.

MEDLEY OF WESTERN VEGETABLES
Serves 6–8

This vegetable combination had its first introduction on a national TV commercial over 10 years ago — it was Barbara Hale's favorite.

One of the nice things about doing these commercials was that I had to sign a statement that all foods were prepared in a microwave, exactly as they were presented to the public. So the food was the best possible, and the crews adored us. They also all went out and bought microwaves!

1 large zucchini squash
1 large crookneck squash
1 large summer squash (pattypan)
1 small cauliflower
2 bunches broccoli
3 large fresh mushrooms
1 red pepper
1 green pepper
1 cube butter
Garlic salt and seasoned pepper to taste
1 tomato, cut into wedges
½ cup cheddar cheese, shredded
½ cup Monterey Jack cheese, shredded

Slice squashes into rounds about ¼ inch thick. Break cauliflower into florets. Cut broccoli into florets, leaving some of the stems. Split stems several times to speed cooking. Slice mushrooms. Cut peppers into strips.

Select a large round platter that will fill the entire microwave range cavity. Place broccoli in circle around outside of platter. Place cauliflower inside broccoli circle. Arrange other vegetables in center, alternating for color.

Heat butter in small measuring cup on High (600–700 watts) until melted (about 30 seconds), and pour lightly over vegetables; sprinkle with garlic salt and seasoned pepper.

Cover with plastic wrap and cook 8 minutes on High until vegetables are just fork tender. Remember, they will continue to cook for a few minutes after removing from microwave.

Arrange tomato wedges in center; sprinkle with shredded cheeses. Cook uncovered on High (600–700 watts) for 1–2 minutes until cheeses are just melted.

SPINACH SALAD
Serves 4

A simple salad is made even easier by the fact that the bacon can be "grilled" quickly in the microwave. Just dice the raw bacon, place in a measuring cup, and cook until crisp. Even the dressing is prepared in the measuring cup. Simply add the ingredients to the remaining bacon drippings and cook the dressing hot.

6 slices lean bacon, diced
¼ cup wine vinegar
2 tablespoons water
¼ teaspoon freshly ground pepper
¼ teaspoon dry mustard
1 pound fresh spinach, stems removed
4 green onions, thinly sliced
½ pound fresh mushrooms, sliced
1 hard-cooked egg, grated

Place bacon in 4-cup measure and cover with paper towel. Cook on High (600–700 watts) until bacon is crisp. Timing will depend on thickness and fat content of bacon. Stir once or twice to keep bacon separated.

Remove bacon with slotted spoon and drain on paper towel; put to one side. Add next four ingredients to bacon drippings and blend well. Cook on High until mixture boils, about 1–2 minutes.

Combine spinach, onion, and mushrooms in large salad bowl. Pour hot dressing over top and toss lightly; taste to see if salt is needed. Sprinkle with grated egg and reserved bacon and serve immediately.

TOMATO/MOZZARELLA SNACK
Serves 2

Whenever I see tomatoes in the height of their season—fully vine-ripened, thick-skinned, and juicy—I am tempted to repeat this wonderful combination of flavors we learned to enjoy while traveling in northern Italy. It was on the menu so often, it must be extremely popular.

For me, this snack is at its best when the tomato is just warm and still has its fresh taste. So I cut the cheese quite thick—and the moment it begins to melt, I remove it and let it stand for just a moment before serving. You can make a number of these at once—just arrange them in a circle for more even melting of the cheese.

2 **thick slices tomato**
2 **thick slices mozzarella cheese**
2 **teaspoons olive oil**
1 **teaspoon basil, or oregano, or Italian herbs—or simply fresh chopped parsley**

Place tomatoes on small dish; cover with slice of cheese. Pour 1 teaspoon oil over each and sprinkle with ½ teaspoon herbs.

Heat on High (600–700 watts) for 1–2 minutes, just until cheese begins to bubble and melt.

CORN-STUFFED TOMATOES
Serves 6

A nice, filling accent to a dinner or luncheon when tomatoes are plentiful.

6 **large, firm tomatoes**
Salt
2 **tablespoons (¼ stick) butter**
1 **tablespoon chopped onion**
1 **tablespoon chopped green pepper**
1 **17-ounce can corn, drained**
½ **cup corn bread stuffing mix, crushed**
2 **eggs, well beaten**
½ **teaspoon salt**
¼ **teaspoon freshly ground pepper**
¼ **cup grated Parmesan cheese**

Cut stem end out of tomatoes; remove core. Slice

off top. Scoop out pulp, leaving a ½-inch shell. Sprinkle inside with salt and invert onto paper towels.

Combine butter, onion, and green pepper in 1-quart baking dish. Cook on High (600–700 watts) for 2 minutes. Add corn, stuffing mix, eggs, salt, and pepper and blend well. Fill tomatoes with mixture. Sprinkle with cheese. Arrange in circle on 9-inch shallow pie plate. Cook on High until heated through but still firm (not soggy), about 8 minutes, turning if tomatoes appear to be cooking unevenly.

ZUCCHINI MEDLEY
Serves 4

Attractive, easy way to enjoy seasonal vegetables.

Thanks to the limited need for fat, we can consider this a low-calorie dish—but believe me, it does not taste it.

No, I did not forget the salt; it does not need any.

2 **medium zucchini, sliced into rounds**
1 **medium onion, sliced and separated into rings**
1 **teaspoon dried oregano, crumbled (or 3 teaspoons fresh)**
2 **medium tomatoes, sliced**
½ **green pepper, halved, seeded, and cut into 1-inch slices**
2 **tablespoons olive oil (may substitute salad oil)**
½ **cup grated Parmesan cheese, or shredded Monterey Jack or cheddar cheese**

Arrange zucchini in a 1½-quart round or oval casserole. Top with onion rings; sprinkle with oregano. Arrange tomatoes and green pepper over onion. Pour oil over top.

Cover and cook on High (600–700 watts) for 4–5 minutes. Sprinkle with cheese. Cook uncovered an additional 1–2 minutes to melt cheese. Serve immediately.

FRESH ZUCCHINI IN A CUSTARD SAUCE
Serves 4–6

Through my teaching relationship with the University of California at Northridge, CSNU, I have had young

Home Economics majors intern with me in the test kitchen of the Microwave Cooking Center.

During one of these periods, seeing an abundance of leftover zucchinis, one student suggested this easy recipe and we tried it. What a nice way to treat zucchini, or any fresh vegetable!

3 cups fresh zucchini, sliced about ¼-inch thick
2 tablespoons butter
2 eggs, beaten
2 cups cheddar cheese, shredded
½ cup french-fried onion rings (canned variety)

Place zucchini and butter in a 1-quart round casserole. Cover; cook on High (600–700 watts) for 3 minutes. Stir.

Combine beaten eggs with cheese; blend well. Pour over zucchini. Cover. Cook 8 minutes on Medium (300–350 watts). Arrange onion rings over top. Heat uncovered about 1 minute on High.

ZUCCHINI CUSTARD
Makes 6–8 servings

A great dish for bumper crop growers.

This is almost like a zucchini pie. It can be a base recipe for almost any other vegetable as well—just use the same amount of shredded vegetable.

It is important to remember that zucchini has a great deal of water that needs to be drained; otherwise, the custard will not turn out as it should.

This recipe works best in a 6-cup ring mold. In a baking dish the center will not cook without stirring the custard, which would spoil its nice, firm texture.

5 cups shredded zucchini, packed
1 teaspoon salt
1½ cups shredded cheese (cheddar, Monterey Jack, or combination of the two)
⅛ teaspoon pepper
⅛ teaspoon garlic powder
¼ cup chopped fresh parsley
¼ cup prepared biscuit mix (like Bisquick)
4 eggs, well beaten
Vegetables for garnish

Sprinkle shredded zucchini with salt and set aside for 45 minutes. Then place into a colander and press out all liquid.

Combine zucchini, cheese, pepper, garlic, parsley, and biscuit mix. Stir in eggs; blend well. Spoon into ring mold. Cook on High (600–700 watts) for 7–9 minutes, until cooked through. Use a wooden skewer for testing, as you would a cake. Also look for edges of zucchini to slightly shrink away from the sides of the dish. Wait about 10 minutes, then use a sharp knife to loosen edges. Unmold onto a 9-inch platter. Garnish with baby tomatoes, cooked carrots, or other vegetables of your choice.

May be served hot or cold.

PERFECT RICE
Serves 4

Cooking rice in the microwave will give you perfect results every time. This recipe, made with chicken and onion seasonings, adds just the right flavor to accompany chicken or meat dishes.

2 cups chicken stock, or 2 cups water with 2 teaspoons instant chicken granules
1 cup converted long-grain rice
¼ cup dehydrated onion

Combine all ingredients in 3-quart casserole. Cook covered on High (600–700 watts) for 12 minutes. Let stand covered 10 minutes until all water is absorbed.

To reheat, add about 2 tablespoons water for each cup of cooked rice. Stir until rice is moistened. This adds enough moisture to the dry rice to reheat the rice without drying it out. Cover and heat on High power for 2 minutes.

Note: If using a smaller casserole, the rice may boil over on High power. To prevent a boil-over, use the same technique used on a cook-top—bring the water to a boil, then reduce heat to a simmer. To duplicate this method in the microwave, place rice in a 2-quart casserole, cook covered on High 5 minutes, reduce power level to Medium (300–350 watts), and cook 18 minutes. Let stand covered 10 minutes until all water is absorbed. The timing is longer, but the results will be the same. (If the rice begins to boil over you can move the lid on the casserole slightly off center, just as you would if cooking on your cook-top.)

CHINESE FRIED RICE
Serves 8–10

This is traditionally cooked in a wok, but works well in the microwave — and it's easier to rinse a bowl than clean my wok. The flavoring is quite light and delicate; it complements chicken, fish, or meat dishes.

3 tablespoons oil
3 cups cooked rice (see above)
1½ tablespoons soy sauce
3 eggs
1 tablespoon water
¼ teaspoon sugar
¼ cup green onions, sliced

Place oil in 3-quart casserole. Cook on High (600–700 watts) for 1 minute. Stir in rice. Cook on High 1 minute, stir, then continue to cook 4 minutes; stirring once. Stir in soy sauce.

In a small bowl, beat eggs with water and sugar. Pour into center of rice. Cook covered on Medium High (400–500 watts) for 7 minutes, stirring once.

Stir in onion and serve immediately.

Note: To reheat 1 cup leftover rice, add 2 tablespoons water, cover, and heat on High 2 minutes. To reheat 2 cups rice, add 4 tablespoons water, cover, and heat on High 3–4 minutes.

BROWN RICE
Makes 3 cups – serves about 6

Although you only save about 10 minutes by cooking rice in your microwave, it does have the advantage of automatic timing — no scorched pan bottoms or boiling over on the cook-top.

The brown rice I use may be slightly different in texture or outer kernel than the rice you use, so use my method as a guide and develop your own perfect timing.

Start the rice on High (600–700 watts) to bring the water to a rolling boil. Don't remove the lid, unless you bring it back to a rolling boil. I do not find it necessary to stir the rice during cooking, since the water keeps the rice in a fairly even cooking pattern. After the water comes to a rolling boil, drop the cooking wattage to half and continue to cook until the water is almost completely absorbed. Then remove from the microwave and allow it to remain covered for

10 minutes so that the remaining moisture can be absorbed by the rice.

This is the method used for conventional brown rice cooking — but adapted to microwave. Although your rice package will suggest a simmer setting, if the wattage is too low the water does not stay at a high enough temperature to soften the rice. Medium (300–350 watts) is just the right power level to keep the water at a temperature similar to the cook-top simmer.

I like to use a 3-quart casserole with a glass lid so that I can watch the water level in the rice while it is cooking.

When reheating rice, stir in 3 tablespoons water for each cup of rice to keep the rice moist and tender. (You can also stir in butter or gravy.)

1 cup brown rice
2½ cups water
1 teaspoon salt

Place all ingredients in a 3-quart casserole. Cook covered on High (600–700 watts) for 10 minutes, or until rice comes to a rolling boil and boils several minutes.

Reduce setting to (300–350 watts). Continue cooking 25 minutes. At this point, just bubbles will appear during cooking. Remove from microwave and allow to remain covered for 10 minutes so remaining water can be absorbed.

CURRY RICE
Serves 4

Good with chicken, lamb, or beef dishes. Just a slight addition of seasonings gives the rice a faintly exotic taste.

1 cup converted long-grain rice
2 cups chicken broth, or 2 cups water and 2 teaspoons chicken granules
1 tablespoon butter
1 teaspoon curry powder
1 2-ounce jar chopped pimientos

Combine rice, broth, and butter in a 3-quart casserole. Cover and cook on High (600–700 watts) for 12 minutes. Remove from microwave and allow to remain covered 5 minutes. Stir in curry and pimientos. Cover until ready to serve.

To reheat, add about 2 tablespoons of water for each cup of rice. Stir and heat on High about 2 minutes per cup of rice.

TEX-MEX RICE
Serves 6–8

1   cup long-grain rice
¼   cup butter
1   small onion, coarsely chopped
½   green pepper, coarsely chopped
1   large celery rib, sliced
1   4-ounce can diced green chilies
1   8-ounce can tomato sauce
1   14½-ounce can whole tomatoes, with liquid

In a 4-quart casserole, sauté rice and butter on High (600–700 watts) for 2 minutes. Stir after 1 minute. Add onion, pepper, and celery. Continue to cook on High 7 minutes or until rice is slightly brown, stirring once.

Stir in chilies, tomato sauce, and tomatoes. Cover and cook 14 minutes on High, stirring after 10 minutes. Allow to sit covered 5 minutes until all the liquid is absorbed.

NOODLE A RONI
Serves 6 as a side dish

The combination of pasta and rice is available in "store bought" packages —why not do it yourself for less money? It makes a delicious side dish for meat, fish, or poultry. Or stir in some leftover chicken chunks, and serve it as a whole meal.

This is Roberta's version, and is just as simple as cooking plain rice in the microwave.

1   large onion, chopped
3   tablespoons butter or margarine
1   cup uncooked converted long-grain rice
½   cup uncooked thin spaghetti noodles, broken into 1-inch pieces
1   tablespoon instant beef bouillon granules
2½ cups water

Place onion and butter in a 3-quart casserole. Cook covered on High (600–700 watts) for 5 minutes, stirring once.

Stir in the rice, noodles, beef granules, and water. Stir until granules are completely dissolved. Cook

covered on High 15 minutes. Allow to stand 10 minutes covered, so liquid can be completely absorbed before serving.

To reheat add 1 tablespoon of water for each ½ cup of rice mixture. Cover and heat on High 2 minutes per cup of rice.

OATMEAL
Serves 1

⅓   cup regular oatmeal (not instant)
⅔   cup water
Pinch salt
Butter and/or milk to taste

Stir oatmeal, water, and salt into a 2-cup cereal bowl. Cook on High (600–700 watts) for 1½–2 minutes, just until mixture comes to a rolling boil (watch carefully so that it does not boil over). Stir; cook until it comes to a boil again, about 45 seconds. Stir and remove from microwave. Cover with saucer; allow to stand about 1 minute. Add a pat of butter and milk if you like, and it is ready to eat.

OATMEAL FOR A FAMILY
Serves 4–6

Because regular oatmeal is so quick to prepare in the microwave, there is no reason to buy instant. Once you taste the difference, you will enjoy the creamy texture of the longer-cooking oatmeal —it is worth waiting for!

A large casserole is necessary to avoid boiling over; that is also the reason for stirring. Best technique is to watch until the cereal boils up to the top, then stir and repeat once more. Setting your timer to stop for stirring will avoid a boil-over if you are distracted and do not get back in time —just like cook-top cooking.

1½ cups regular oatmeal
3   cups tap water
½   teaspoon salt, or to taste

Combine all ingredients in 2-quart casserole. Cook uncovered on High (600–700 watts) for 4 minutes. Stir. Continue cooking 4 minutes; stir. Cover and set aside for 3 minutes before serving.

SOUTHERN GRITS
Serves 8–10

Commonly found in the south, it is a delicious substitute for rice or potatoes. The addition of a sharp cheddar blends well with the bland flavor of the grits.

2 cups quick-cooking grits
1 teaspoon salt
4 cups hot water
2 cups milk
3 cups sharp cheddar cheese, shredded
4 egg yolks
¼ pound butter
Paprika

Combine grits, salt, and water in a 3-quart casserole. Cook on High (600–700 watts) for 5 minutes, stirring once. Stir in milk; cook on Medium (300–350 watts) for 7 minutes. Stir in 2 cups shredded cheese. Whisk egg yolks with some of the hot mixture. Add egg mixture to casserole, then butter, and stir until blended. Cook on Medium 25 minutes, stirring after 15 minutes. Sprinkle with remaining cup of cheese and paprika. Cook on High about 3 minutes, just until cheese melts.

GRITS WITH AN ITALIAN TOUCH
Serves 4

Not being from the South, I was not introduced to this delightful corn product until later in life. I have enjoyed it in many forms because it has great flexibility—and was impressed by the ingenuity of a chef from the Cafe Huberts in New York, when *The Cook's Magazine* printed a recipe of his called "Wild Mushrooms on Fried Grits." It was not a microwave recipe, since it ended by frying the grits into pancakes. However, my curiosity about his combination of flavors led me to this adaptation.

All cuisines go through changes when they leave their country of origin, simply because they cannot get the same ingredients. So sometimes it is hard to tell in a recipe where the old country stops and the new country begins. It is rather American to gather together all that wonderful knowledge from what we think of as ethnic foods, and use it to create new and exciting dishes. Perhaps this recipe might inspire you to try some on your own.

1 medium onion, chopped
3 tablespoons butter
½ pound fresh mushrooms, sliced (optional)
1¼ cups chicken stock, or 1¼ cups water and
    2 teaspoons chicken granules
1¼ cups milk
½ cup quick-cooking grits
Salt as needed
¼ cup Parmesan cheese, grated
2 drops Tabasco

In a 1-quart glass measure, place onions with butter on top. Cook on High (600–700 watts) for 4–5 minutes, until onions begin to turn slightly brown. Stir once. Remove onions with slotted spoon and set aside.

Using same glass measure, stir in mushrooms, coating them with remaining butter. Cook on High 2 minutes, until just barely cooked. Set aside.

In a 4-quart (or larger) casserole (large enough to prevent grits from boiling over) place chicken stock and milk. Cook on High, covered, until mixture begins to boil, about 5 minutes. Stir in grits; continue to stir until they are well blended. Cover, cook on High 3 minutes; stir, continue to cook 3 minutes, then stir again. At this point grits should have absorbed most of the liquid. If too much liquid remains, cook an additional minute. Like rice, grits continue to absorb liquid after cooking, so it is best to stop before all liquid is gone. Taste and add salt if necessary (depending upon saltiness of chicken stock). Stir in onions, mushrooms, Parmesan cheese, and Tabasco. Add a pat or two of butter only if necessary. Serve immediately.

Note: For best flavor, always precook onions until soft before adding to recipe.

12

SAUCES

Barbecue Sauce

Sauce Bercy

Basic Brown Sauce

Beef Gravy

Brown Gravy

Homemade Spaghetti Sauce

Perfect Hollandaise Sauce

Bearnaise Sauce

Tarragon Sauce

Simple White Sauce

Golden Pancake Syrup

Raspberry Sauce

Custard Sauce

Marshmallow Sauce

Apricot Dessert Sauce

Lemon Sauce

SAUCES: TIPS AND TECHNIQUES

Good cooks know that even a basic sauce can make the most everyday fare seem special. And if that cook has a microwave, preparing a smooth and flavorful sauce is no problem at all.

Making sauces in the microwave has many advantages. You can measure, mix, and cook in the same cup or bowl; the cooking time is much faster; there is no need for constant stirring; and, because there is no direct heat, cleanup is at a minimum—no scorched, sticky, or burned saucepans ever again.

This collection of recipes includes a simple White Sauce with a number of variations suitable for seafood, poultry, and eggs. The Tarragon Sauce is practically foolproof—a wonderful way to spruce up vegetables, or use on poached eggs for a light supper. The recipes for Barbecue Sauce and Spaghetti Sauce are quick and easy: prepare these in quantity and freeze so you will always have them on hand.

Here are a few basic techniques for successful sauces in the microwave:

- Prepare sauces in a microwave-safe container about twice the volume of the required ingredients. This will prevent boil-overs.
- Stir sauces through several times during cooking using a wire whisk. Opening the door for more frequent stirring may slow down cooking.
- Always use good quality unsalted butter for best results.
- When preparing sauces ahead, set them aside in a vacuum bottle or jar that has been rinsed in warm water and dried. This will keep them at the proper serving temperature.
- All sauces (except the Tarragon) can be reheated. Use Medium (300–350 watts) power. For ½ cup, start with 1 minute and add more time as needed. If sauce seems too thick, add a small amount of hot water before reheating and whisk through several times both before and after cooking.
- If ingredients such as butter or liquid are well-chilled at the time of preparation, cooking time will be longer.
- When adapting your own favorite sauce recipe to microwave cooking, increase the amount of flour or cornstarch, leaving the liquid the same. There will not be the evaporation there is in conventional sauce-making.

BARBECUE SAUCE
Makes about 1½ cups

⅓ **onion, chopped**
2 **cloves garlic, minced**
1 **tablespoon butter**
1 **8-ounce can tomato sauce**
2 **tablespoons dark brown sugar**
2 **tablespoons fresh lemon juice**
1 **teaspoon Worcestershire sauce**
½ **teaspoon salt**
¼ **teaspoon paprika**
¼ **teaspoon dry mustard**
¼ **teaspoon pepper**

In a 2-quart glass measure, combine onion, garlic, and butter. Cook on High (600–700 watts) power 3 minutes. Stir in remaining ingredients. Continue cooking 4–5 minutes until sauce is cooked through.

SAUCE BERCY
Makes 2 cups

Serve with roast beef or steak.

2 **shallots, finely chopped**
¼ **cup dry white wine**
2 **cups Basic Brown Sauce (see next recipe)**

Reduce chopped shallots and dry white wine by placing in a 2-cup measure and cooking on Medium High (400–500 watts) for 2–3 minutes, until about 2 tablespoons are left. Add to 2 cups of Basic Brown Sauce.

BASIC BROWN SAUCE
Makes about 3 cups

This may be used as a base for other brown sauces or to add to drippings of meat or poultry dishes.

3 **cups well-flavored brown beef stock**
2 **tablespoons arrowroot or cornstarch**
4 **tablespoons Madeira wine**

Place stock in a 2-quart measuring cup or bowl. Cook on High (600–700 watts) for 7–8 minutes, until it comes to a boil.

Mix arrowroot with Madeira until dissolved. Add to boiling stock. Stir well. Continue cooking until slightly thickened, about 2 minutes.

Sauce will be slightly thickened. For a thicker sauce, dissolve more arrowroot.

BEEF GRAVY
Makes about 4 cups

Use for turkey slices, meat, or mashed potatoes.

½ cup beef drippings
½ cup all-purpose flour
4 cups beef broth, heated
Salt and pepper to taste
Bottled browning sauce (optional)

Combine beef drippings and flour in a 3-quart bowl. Cook, uncovered, on High power (600–700 watts) 1 minute, stirring once. Stir in heated beef stock or broth. Continue cooking 4–5 minutes or until mixture becomes thick, stirring several times. Taste for seasonings, and add only if necessary. For deeper color, you may wish to use a touch of browning sauce.

To reheat, use Medium power (300–350 watts). Time will depend upon the amount to be heated—about 1 minute per ½ cup. If gravy becomes thick when refrigerated, add a bit of water before reheating.

BROWN GRAVY
Makes about 1 cup

It is quite simple to prepare gravy from your pan drippings. You may wish to do this while your meat has its standing time.

Pan drippings, minus fat
2 tablespoons skimmed fat
1½ tablespoons flour

Salt and pepper to taste
Garlic powder (optional)
Additional liquid to total 1 cup (other drippings, milk, water, or combination)

Pour pan drippings into a 1-quart glass measure; leaving the brown, crusty residue in the roasting dish. Wait until the fat rises to the surface; skim off the fat and set aside. Use the remaining drippings as the base for the gravy.

Place 2 tablespoons fat into roasting dish; stir in flour until dissolved. Heat on High (600–700 watts) for 2–2½ minutes, until slightly brown. Stir in remaining ingredients. Continue to cook 1–2 minutes, stirring several times to keep gravy smooth.

HOMEMADE SPAGHETTI SAUCE
Makes about 4 cups

This is a rich, full-bodied sauce that tastes as though you have been cooking it all day. Use it on pasta, for one-step lasagna (see index), or for the freezer.

1 medium onion, sliced thin
¼ cup celery, sliced
½ green pepper, sliced into thin strips
2 cloves garlic, minced
2 tablespoons olive oil (may substitute vegetable oil)
½ pound lean ground beef
1 14-ounce can whole peeled tomatoes, chopped, liquid reserved
1 can tomato paste
1 tablespoon fresh parsley, chopped
½ teaspoon oregano, crumbled
6 green mushrooms, sliced

Combine onion, celery, green pepper, garlic, and oil in 2-quart glass bowl. Cover; cook on High (600–700 watts) for 5 minutes. Stir in beef. Continue to cook on High 3 minutes. Stir to keep beef crumbly. Blend in tomatoes and liquid, tomato paste, parsley, and oregano. Cover; cook on High 5 minutes. Stir in mushrooms. Continue to cook on High 5–7 minutes, until sauce is slightly thickened.

PERFECT HOLLANDAISE SAUCE

Makes ⅔ cup

3 egg yolks
2 tablespoons fresh lemon juice
½ cup unsalted butter at room temperature
Salt and white pepper to taste

Whip egg yolks in a 4-cup glass measure, adding lemon juice while whipping. Cut butter into 3 equal sections. Add ⅓ of butter to egg yolk mixture. Cook uncovered on High (600–700 watts) for 30 seconds. Using a wire whisk, beat vigorously (the butter will not be completely melted until after you beat). Add the second piece of butter. Cook again for 30 seconds. Repeat procedure of beating well until butter is absorbed into the yolks. Add third piece of butter and repeat procedure. Season with salt and pepper.

If for any reason the sauce should curdle, add 1 tablespoon of boiling water and beat until it is creamy and thick.

The above procedure eliminates the problem of trying to add the butter too quickly for the eggs to absorb. Also, by adding cool butter to the mixture each time, it keeps the eggs from becoming too hot, which can cause sauce to curdle.

BEARNAISE SAUCE
(Hollandaise with Tarragon and White Wine)

Makes ⅔ cup

Nice to serve with steak or fish.

¼ cup tarragon wine vinegar
¼ cup dry white wine
1 tablespoon shallots, finely chopped
2 tablespoons fresh tarragon, finely cut; or 1 tablespoon fresh parsley, finely chopped, and 2 teaspoons dried tarragon
⅔ cup Perfect Hollandaise Sauce made using water instead of lemon juice (see recipe above)
Salt and white pepper to taste

Place vinegar and wine in a 2-cup glass measure. Add shallots and 1 tablespoon tarragon. Cook uncovered on High (600–700 watts) until reduced down, about 3 minutes. Strain the liquid through a fine sieve, pressing down on the herbs with a spoon.

Whisk the strained liquid into prepared Perfect Hollandaise Sauce along with 1 tablespoon of fresh tarragon or parsley. Season to taste with salt and white pepper (only if necessary).

TARRAGON SAUCE

Makes 1 cup

Serve over broiled meat or poultry, or over poached eggs or steamed vegetables.

½ cup butter
⅓ cup dry white wine
1 tablespoon tarragon vinegar
1 teaspoon dried crumbled tarragon, or 2 teaspoons finely chopped fresh tarragon
1 tablespoon chopped chives
½ teaspoon salt
¼ teaspoon pepper
Dash hot pepper sauce

Heat butter in 2-cup glass measure on High (600–700 watts) until melted, about 1 minute.

Add all other ingredients (except egg yolks) to butter in the glass measure, blending well. Cook on High (600–700 watts) 1 minute. Beat egg yolks in small bowl. Stir in a small amount of hot butter mixture, then combine with sauce.

Cook on Medium (300–350 watts) for 2 minutes, stirring once. Using a whisk, beat until smooth. Serve hot.

To reheat, use Medium power.

SIMPLE WHITE SAUCE

Makes 1 cup

3 tablespoons butter
3 tablespoons flour
¼ teaspoon salt
⅛ teaspoon white pepper
1 cup milk

Place butter in 1-quart glass measure and cook on High (600–700 watts) about 30 seconds, until completely melted. Stir in flour, salt, and pepper. Continue cooking for 45 seconds. Add milk slowly, beating mixture with a whisk. Continue cooking for about 2 minutes, stirring once or twice. Longer cooking will produce a thicker sauce.

White sauce stores well for about 2 days, covered, in the refrigerator.

To reheat, thin down with wine or milk (may use low-fat). Using Medium (300–350 watts), begin with 30 seconds and add small amounts of time until heated through.

SIMPLE WHITE SAUCE VARIATIONS

A basic white sauce can be turned into something new by the addition of wine, herbs, spices, or drippings from the food prepared.

Basic Cheese Sauce

Follow directions for simple White Sauce. Stir in ½-cup shredded sharp cheddar cheese, and beat until smooth. If cheese has not melted completely, cook on High (600–700 watts) for 30 seconds. (If cheese is at room temperature it is more likely to melt into sauce without further cooking.)

Herb Sauce

Instead of 1 cup milk, use ½ cup milk and ½ cup liquid from vegetable cooking. Add fresh herbs to complement recipe to be used.

Mornay Sauce

Add ½ cup shredded Swiss or Parmesan cheese, or combination of both, and a dash of cayenne pepper.

Curry Sauce

Add curry powder to your taste, beginning with ½ teaspoon.

Dill Sauce

Add 2 teaspoons dill weed, and lemon juice to taste.

GOLDEN PANCAKE SYRUP
Makes about 2 cups

In the old days, when Sunday breakfast was a leisurely affair and making pancakes went on all morning in our home, many of us made our own pancake syrup. It is easier in the microwave—and no preservatives!

1   cup water
1   pound brown sugar
½   teaspoon maple flavoring, or to your taste

Place water in a 2-quart glass measure. Heat on High (600–700 watts) for 3 minutes. Stir in sugar. Continue to cook for about 2–3 minutes, just until sugar is dissolved. Stir in flavoring.

Pour into serving pitcher and serve warm. May be stored covered. We always pour what we think we need for breakfast and heat the ceramic or glass pitcher in the microwave for about 1 minute.

Note: When preparing pancakes, mix more batter than you need. Continue cooking the batter until all is used up. Freeze pancakes in package for 1 serving each, with wax paper between pancakes. When ready to enjoy, reheat in microwave: about 15 seconds for each pancake if room temperature; about 30 seconds if frozen. Timing will also depend upon the size of the pancake.

RASPBERRY SAUCE
Makes about 1¼ cups

A not too sweet sauce that is delicious served over fruit, ice cream, angel food cake, pound cake, or a trifle. If you have the type of home that receives unexpected company, you might like to keep several packages of frozen raspberries in your freezer. This can be made in minutes.

1   10-ounce package frozen raspberries
1   teaspoon cornstarch
2   tablespoons water or raspberry liqueur (Chambord)

Place raspberries in a 1-quart glass measure and thaw on High (600–700 watts) for 3 minutes. Break up slightly with wooden spoon. Sieve and discard seeds if desired.

Dissolve cornstarch in water, blending well. Stir into berries. Cook on High until mixture thickens and becomes clear, about 1½-2 minutes. Remove from oven and stir with whisk to blend.

CUSTARD SAUCE
Makes 4 cups

Serve with ice cream, or as custard filling for a trifle, cream puffs, or layered cake. Instead of using a prepared mix, try making your own—it is so easy.

½ **cup sugar**
½ **cup cornstarch**
½ **teaspoon salt**
4 **cups milk**
4 **beaten egg yolks**
4 **teaspoons vanilla**

Combine sugar, cornstarch, and salt in a 2-quart measuring cup or bowl. Add milk gradually, stirring until cornstarch is dissolved. Cook on High (600–700 watts) for 8–10 minutes until mixture is brought to a boil, stirring twice.

When mixture has thickened, beat well with wire whisk and add egg yolks slowly, continuing to beat until well-blended. Cook 2 minutes longer. Stir in vanilla.

APRICOT DESSERT SAUCE
Makes about 1⅓ cups

To serve over ice cream, rice pudding, tapioca, or pound cake. You may use other fruit nectars and liqueurs for sauce variation.

¼ **cup sugar**
1 **tablespoon cornstarch**
1 **cup apricot nectar**
1 **teaspoon grated lemon peel**
3 **tablespoons apricot-flavored brandy**

Combine sugar and cornstarch in a 2-cup glass measure. Stir in apricot nectar and lemon peel. Stir until cornstarch is dissolved. Cook on High (600–700 watts) until mixture is thick and clear, whisking once. Allow to stand 5 minutes. Blend in brandy. Cook on High 1 minute; stir through several times. May be served warm or chilled.

MARSHMALLOW SAUCE
Makes 3 cups

Serve over ice cream or use as cake frosting. May be mixed with chocolate syrup as topping over ice cream layers to make ice cream cake.

1 **cup sugar**
⅔ **cup light corn syrup**
½ **cup hot water**
2 **egg whites**
Dash salt
¼ **teaspoon vanilla**
¼ **cup mayonnaise**

Combine sugar, syrup, and hot water in an 8-cup glass measure. Stir until sugar is dissolved. Cook on High (600–700 watts) uncovered for 12 minutes, without stirring, to firm ball or thread stage (248°F. on your candy thermometer).

While this is cooking, beat egg whites and salt until stiff. Gradually beat in the cooked hot syrup, using high speed on mixer, until thick and fluffy. Add vanilla. Fold in mayonnaise.

LEMON SAUCE
Makes about 1 cup

Serve over pound cake, use as a frosting, or use as a filling for pastries.

⅔ **cup water**
⅓ **cup sugar**
2 **tablespoons cornstarch**
3 **tablespoons fresh lemon juice**
1 **egg yolk**
1 **tablespoon butter**
1 **teaspoon grated lemon peel**
Pinch salt
Yellow food coloring (optional)

Combine all ingredients in a 1-quart glass measuring cup; blend well. Cook on High (600–700 watts) for 2½ minutes, stirring once. Mixture should be thick at this point. Use a wire whisk and beat until smooth.

If egg is light in color, the mixture will be pale. You must wait until completely cooked to see color, then add 1 or 2 drops of food coloring to deepen the yellow.

13

BREADS AND MUFFINS

REHEATING BREAD

Reheating bread is an apparently simple operation that confounds many microwave users. "Why is it nice and soft when I take it out of the microwave, but hard as a rock by the time it reaches the table?" is a frequently asked question.

The answer is that it is all a matter of timing. Excessive reheating actually cooks the bread, which is presumably cooked already. The result is overdone, hard bread.

In other words, since the bread is already cooked, you should do no more than bring it back to the point where it was when it left the oven. If you give it too much microwave energy, the gluten changes form and the bread is cooked beyond repair.

If you are careful, it is possible to reheat bread. The best way to learn is to feel the surface. However, don't rely on the way the *top* of the loaf feels, as this can be misleading; there will always be more heat *just under the surface* of the bread than on the top, since that is where microwaves penetrate.

Another important point to remember: A small single item absorbs all of the microwave energy which enters the cavity, while a large piece heats more slowly because the microwaves are dispersed. So a small roll or piece of bread takes only 15–20 seconds if fresh, and 20–30 seconds if frozen—while a larger piece or loaf of bread will take much longer.

When I try to determine timing on a loaf, I mentally cut the loaf into slices, and use about 10 seconds per slice. It may be a little undertimed, but I can always add to it.

Moisture content will also vary; a fresh roll may heat faster. Best results are obtained when the bread is elevated off the floor of the microwave with a rack or a paper-lined dish. This should be done to avoid trapping moisture on the bottom, which will cause retained heat and overcooking.

If bread is rather stale, sprinkle with a bit of water, wrap in a paper towel, and reheat on a rack.

Don't be discouraged—it is a lovely microwave concept once you get it under control. It is not any different to learn than placing garlic bread under the broiler and trying to estimate how long it will take. These are the variables in cooking that put the cook in charge of the equipment, rather than the other way around.

There is no smart equipment—without smart cooks.

BREAD FROM THE FREEZER

By using hot water and a low power setting, you can defrost frozen bread dough.

1 1-pound loaf frozen bread dough
1 cup water

Remove frozen dough from package. Place in 8″ x 5″ loaf pan or on a dish. Fill a 1-cup glass measure with water. Place in corner of microwave and cook on High (600–700 watts) for 2–3 minutes, until water is boiling. Leave cup in place.

Place the frozen dough plate in cavity. Set cooking control on lowest possible setting. Time for defrosting the dough will depend upon what settings are available in your microwave. Here are some examples:

10%–Low	65–100 watts	Time: 5 min.
30%–Medium Low	200–250 watts	Time: 4 min.
50%–Medium	300–350 watts	Time: 3 min.

After defrosting dough for the time indicated above for your power setting, turn dough over and repeat timing. Allow dough to remain in the microwave cavity, where the moisture and heat has built up slightly, until it is defrosted. It will be ready to work after 5–10 minutes.

HOT ITALIAN BREAD WITH GARLIC AND CHEESE
Serves 6–8

Because of the addition of cheese, this is a good choice to complete a meal where you are serving a large vegetable salad and soup. Very filling.

1 1-pound loaf Italian bread
½ cup butter or margarine
2 tablespoons grated Romano or Parmesan cheese
2 cloves garlic, minced; or 1 teaspoon garlic powder

¼ **cup grated Parmesan cheese**
¼ – ½ **cup shredded mozzarella cheese**

Place butter and 2 tablespoons Romano or Parmesan cheese in small glass measure. Melt on High (600 – 700 watts) for 45 seconds – 1 minute. Stir in garlic.

Cut bread in half lengthwise and brush butter mixture on both sides of bread. Sprinkle with shredded mozzarella and Parmesan cheeses. With a sharp serrated knife, cut shallow slices into bread. Do not cut through to other side of bread—just enough to be able to pull off pieces. Place on rack or in wicker basket on paper napkins. Heat on High about 1 minute. Timing will depend upon the freshness of the bread and how much you place in at a time. A slice about 2 inches thick would heat in about 25 seconds. Remember, you are reheating the bread—not cooking it. Too much cooking time results in a change in the gluten content of the bread, making it tough. Feel the bread just below the surface to best judge timing.

GARLIC BREAD
Serves 6

This is a great way to dress up soup, salad, pasta, or whatever. If there are several versions in this book, it is because I can never stop experimenting. This is an old standby.

If you prefer not to use fresh garlic, substitute a good quality garlic powder or chips (available in jars).

1 **loaf French, Italian, or sourdough bread**
½ **cup (1 stick) butter or margarine, melted**
2 **cloves garlic, minced**
½ **cup grated Parmesan cheese or to taste**
Paprika

Cut loaf into slices 1 inch thick without cutting all the way through to the bottom. Set loaf on a rack or in paper-napkin-lined basket.

Combine butter and garlic and blend well. Using a pastry brush, coat slices of bread with garlic butter. Sprinkle with cheese and paprika. Heat on High

(600 – 700 watts) until just heated through, 1 – 2 minutes. Feel bread with fingers for testing. As soon as it is slightly warm, just below the surface, it is ready to serve.

HOMEMADE CRACKERS
Makes about 100

This recipe was developed for Maxine Horowitz's book, *Inside the Food Processor*. Son Paul and I went through the excellent recipes and adapted the "microwave" ones. This turned out so well I'd like to share it. I have only made it in a food processor, but am certain it could be done in a blender as well.

Extra dough may be stored in the refrigerator in an airtight container for several days. Makes a nice snack food for guests or children—and would be interesting to serve with appetizers.

2½ **cups oats**
1½ **cups all-purpose flour**
½ **cup pecans or walnuts**
⅓ **cup coconut**
1 **teaspoon salt**
2 **tablespoons brown sugar**
⅔ **cup water**
½ **cup salad oil**
⅓ **cup sesame, poppy, or caraway seeds**
Kosher salt

Using a food processor with steel blade in place, place oats in work bowl and process 5 seconds. Add flour, nuts, coconut, salt, and brown sugar. Process until combined. With machine running, add water and oil and process until dry ingredients are incorporated.

Divide dough into thirds. Roll each piece on a cookie sheet to a rectangle at least 10″ x 14″ (dough will be very thin). Sprinkle dough with seeds and then with salt. *Press in gently.* Cut into squares with a knife. To bake, place 12 – 15 uncooked cracker dough squares on a shallow baking dish. Bake on High (600 – 700 watts) for 3 – 4 minutes, turning once after 1½ minutes. (Timing will vary depending on the thickness of crackers.) Crackers should be dry and hard when finished.

Continue cooking in batches until all dough is used.

PUMPKIN NUT BREAD

Serves 6–8

My son Richard developed such a love for nature, he decided to become a forest ranger. (He visualized school in a redwood tree, and camp songs every night.) While getting him settled in college up north, we visited a lumberyard to get supplies for bookcases which he planned to put together with bricks. While my husband and son bought out the lumberyard, I discovered a charming area for gardeners—filled with seeds, and even recipe folders to cook what you were about to grow so successfully. I thought it was masterful marketing!

In order to get this recipe, I even purchased the package of seeds. When I came home the recipe did just what I had hoped it would: adapt to the microwave.

What attracted me was the buttermilk and oil. The oil keeps the batter moist rather than dry, and buttermilk makes the batter a good texture for microwave baking. The only changes I made in the recipe were to cut down on the sugar by ⅓ cup (which I have been doing for years); to increase the pumpkin pie spice by 1 teaspoon; and since I prefer more nuts, to increase the amount by ½ cup. I did not find it necessary to reduce the amount of liquid.

As always, I prefer to bake this type of bread in a ring mold. (The center is always the hardest to cook.) If you do not own one you may use a glass in the center of a bowl—but it will not look as pretty!

The colorful folder gave some historical background for the pumpkin. Did you know that the American Indians gave the pumpkin to the pilgrims? And the pilgrims knew a good thing when they tasted it—it became so popular it was firmly established as the traditional last course of an American Thanksgiving dinner, in the form of pumpkin pie.

1 **cup sugar**
1 **cup mashed cooked pumpkin (fresh or canned)**
⅓ **cup oil (vegetable oil is fine)**
½ **cup buttermilk**
2 **eggs**
1⅔ **cups all-purpose flour**
1 **teaspoon baking soda**
3 **rounded teaspoons pumpkin pie spice**
½ **teaspoon salt**
1 **cup chopped nuts (walnuts are good)**

Blend first 5 ingredients in mixing bowl. Then add all remaining ingredients but ¼ cup of chopped nuts

and a little pumpkin pie spice. Beat at medium speed 1–2 minutes, until just blended. Use a 6-cup ring mold. Sprinkle ¼ cup nuts into the mold, along with a sprinkling of pumpkin pie spice.

Fill mold with mixture. If you have a rack, elevate the mold on the rack. Cook on Medium High (400–500 watts) for 13–15 minutes, turning only if it appears to be cooking unevenly. Bread will be done when area around the outside begins to move slightly away from dish. Allow to cool on a flat surface about 15 minutes before unmolding.

PUMPKIN NUT MUFFINS

Makes 1 dozen muffins

We used to make these for our visiting neighbor children for Trick or Treat. They loved it! If we ran out, we would invite them in to watch theirs being cooked.

1 **cup cooked pumpkin, mashed**
1 **cup sugar**
1 **cup oil**
½ **cup buttermilk**
1 **egg**
1⅔ **cups all-purpose flour**
1 **cup walnuts, chopped**
½ **cup golden raisins**
2 **teaspoons pumpkin pie spice**
1 **teaspoon baking soda**
½ **teaspoon salt**

Combine first 5 ingredients in large bowl and beat 1 minute. Add remaining ingredients and mix thoroughly. Pour batter into a microwave muffin ring, or 12 ¾-cup glass custard cups, filling ⅔ full. Arrange 6 cups in circle on a round platter, or place muffin ring in microwave (it holds 6 muffins also) and cook on High (600–700 watts) for 3–4 minutes, turning ring if it appears to be cooking unevenly. Repeat with remaining batter. Loosen muffins from cups with thin knife and turn onto racks. Serve warm.

PERPETUAL MUFFINS

Makes about 3 dozen

Not originated for microwave, but easily adapted and working well. It has been enjoyed for many years by my students, and I would recommend it to anyone who enjoys a freshly prepared hot muffin for breakfast.

It's easy to have them freshly prepared, because the recipe can be made up and left covered in your refrigerator for several weeks. Simply stir the batter and remove what you need, re-cover, and replace in the refrigerator. The batter may be refrigerated anywhere from 2–6 weeks. Our problem in testing was that the batter never lasted longer than 2 weeks (and we are only two)!

1 **cup Nabisco 100% Bran cereal**
2 **cups Kellogg's All-Bran cereal**
1 **cup boiling water**
2 **eggs, beaten**
2 **cups buttermilk**
½ **cup salad oil**
1 **cup raisins, nuts, or chopped dried fruit**
2 **teaspoons baking soda**
1 **cup sugar**
3 **tablespoons brown sugar**
½ **teaspoon salt**
2½ **cups all-purpose flour**

In large bowl, combine cereals with boiling water and stir lightly. Let cool; stir in eggs, buttermilk, oil, and fruit.

In another bowl, combine remaining ingredients. Stir it into bran mixture. At this point, batter may be covered and refrigerated.

To bake, stir batter well. Spoon batter into paper-cup-lined cupcake maker, filling about ½ full. Bake on High (600–700 watts) for 2½–3 minutes for 6 muffins. One muffin takes between 30–40 seconds. Allow 20–30 seconds for each additional muffin.

If you do not have a microwave muffin pan, you may use paper-cup liners in custard cups. If doing several at once, arrange custard cups in ring fashion for more even cooking.

GINGERBREAD RING

Serves 10–12

Use a ring mold for the gingerbread—it provides a more even cooking pattern.

2¼ **cups flour**
2 **teaspoons freshly grated ginger, or 1 teaspoon ground ginger**

1½ **teaspoons baking soda**
1 **teaspoon cinnamon**
½ **teaspoon salt**
⅛ **teaspoon ground cloves**
½ **cup butter, softened**
½ **cup packed brown sugar**
½ **cup granulated sugar**
2 **eggs**
1 **cup buttermilk**
1 **cup molasses**
2 **tablespoons grated orange peel**
Additional cinnamon

Mix flour, ginger, baking soda, cinnamon, salt, and cloves in a bowl and set aside. Cream together butter and sugars; combine eggs, buttermilk, molasses, and orange peel. Stir in flour mixture and blend.

Sprinkle a 10-cup Bundt pan with cinnamon (you may also wish to use a bit of brown sugar for additional browning). Pour mixture into pan.

Cook uncovered on Medium High power (400–500 watts) for 13–15 minutes, turning if gingerbread appears to be cooking unevenly. Allow to cool in pan 20 minutes before unmolding.

EASY COFFEE CAKE

Serves 6–8

1⅔ **cups graham cracker crumbs (about 22 squares)**
1 **cup finely chopped walnuts**
1 **cup sugar**
¾ **cup (1½ sticks) butter, room temperature**
4 **eggs**
3½ **ounces flaked coconut**
½ **cup chopped dates**
¼ **cup milk**
1 **teaspoon vanilla**
2 **tablespoons graham cracker crumbs**

Combine 1⅔ cups graham cracker crumbs, walnuts, sugar, and butter in large bowl and beat until creamy. Add eggs one at a time, beating well after each addition. Add coconut, chopped dates, milk, and vanilla. Mix until thoroughly blended.

Turn batter into 8½″ round cake pan. Cook on Medium High (400–500 watts) for 12–14 minutes, turning pan if cake appears to be cooking unevenly (cake will appear slightly moist on top). Sprinkle top with 2 tablespoons graham cracker crumbs. Let cake stand 15 minutes before serving.

ZUCCHINI BREAD
Serves 8

For several years I had the pleasure of teaching at the College of the Canyons, in the beautiful canyon country of California. One of my students who took my class seriously developed this recipe. I give it to you just as he gave it to me.

1 cup raisins
1 cup Madeira wine
2 eggs
⅔ cup salad oil
1 cup firmly packed brown sugar
1 cup whole wheat flour
1½ teaspoons soda
1 teaspoon ground cinnamon
½ teaspoon salt
2 cups grated zucchini
1 cup chopped walnuts
Additional cinnamon and nuts for bottom of
  Bundt dish

On day before, place raisins in small bowl, and cover with wine to soak overnight.

In bowl, beat eggs until just blended. Add oil and sugar; beat until thoroughly mixed. Stir together flour, soda, cinnamon, and salt. Stir into egg mixture. Add zucchini, well drained raisins and nuts.

Sprinkle bottom and sides of a 6-cup ring mold with cinnamon and finely chopped nuts. Pour mixture evenly into Bundt dish. (Drink wine!)

Cook on High power (600–700 watts) for 11–12 minutes, just until bread begins to pull slightly away from the sides. (The top will still be moist.) Use a toothpick or wood skewer to test. Turn only if it appears to be cooking unevenly.

Allow to cool on flat surface. Turn out on attractive round serving dish. You may sprinkle with powdered sugar, but it can stand on its own just as it is.

ENGLISH MUFFIN BREAD
Makes 2 loaves

This English muffin in loaf form is a wonderful breakfast surprise.

Cornmeal
2 cups milk
½ cup water
5 cups all-purpose flour
2 envelopes dry yeast
1 tablespoon sugar
2 teaspoons salt
¼ teaspoon baking soda

Use two 8½ x 4½-inch glass or ceramic loaf pans. Sprinkle with cornmeal, shaking out excess. Combine milk and water in 1-quart measure. Heat on High until warmed through, about 3 to 4 minutes. (If using probe, set at 125°F.) Mix 3 cups flour, yeast, sugar, salt and baking soda in large bowl. Add warm milk mixture and beat well. Blend in remaining flour and stir until dough is stiff. Divide dough between pans. Cover and let rise in warm draft-free area 45 minutes.

Cook loaves one at a time on High (600–700 watts) for 6 to 6½ minutes, turning once. Let stand 5 minutes before removing from pan. Slice loaves thinly and toast before serving.

14
DESSERTS

PIE SHELLS

For quiches and pies you can use the Basic Pastry Shell recipe that follows—or to make it simple, use one of the several varieties available in the frozen food section. Pick a preformed flaky pie shell ready to bake. Transfer the unbaked shell to a microwave-safe quiche or pie dish.

Here are a few tips to insure success:

Select a deep-dish variety uncooked pie shell; they come in a package of two. Remove one and place the other back in your freezer. Allow pie shell to remain at room temperature for about 5 minutes. Using an extra pie plate of the same size, place it inside the firm uncooked shell; invert and remove the original pie plate. Then simply place a 9-inch quiche dish (or pie plate suitable for microwaving) over inverted pie shell, and turn upright so that pie shell now occupies the inside of the quiche dish. Some people have been successful transfering the shell while still frozen. Carefully release edges with a sharp knife. Lift crust and place in a proper dish. Allow to defrost 5 minutes.

Without stretching the dough, firmly pat the inside edge of the pie shell with your fingers to the shape of the quiche dish. The center takes care of itself. Then working in a circle, press dough into quiche dish, bringing it up the sides to the edge of the dish. Prick the entire shell with a fork to keep it from puffing up when cooking.

To make the shell attractive in color and also to retain its crispness, I like to use an egg wash—either one beaten egg yolk plus 1 teaspoon water, or 1 whole egg beaten. Mix and brush over the entire shell, including sides and top. Cook on High (600–700 watts) for 5–6 minutes, just until brown spots appear. At that point the pie crust is crisp.

Be careful when pouring in the filling, because if it overflows the sides of the crust, liquid will get underneath the crust and make the crust soggy.

before filling. If it is not, the shell remains uncooked because all of the microwave energy is attracted to the filling rather then the shell. But not to worry—pastry shells work beautifully in your microwave: they become quite flaky, and they cook in minutes.

I have always brushed the outside of the shell with an egg wash as the French do with their pastries, to ensure that the color will be attractive and the shell will be sealed to keep it crisp. For shortening, I use a solid shortening like Crisco, or a combination of butter and solid shortening. I have never been successful with a pure butter shell, though I have tried many times. I love the flavor, but cannot get the crust to keep from slipping down off the sides of the pie plate.

1½ cup all-purpose flour
½ teaspoon salt
¼ cup solid shortening
¼ cup butter
3-4 tablespoons ice water
1 egg, or one egg yolk mixed with 1 teaspoon water

Mix flour, salt, and shortening with pastry blender, two forks, or a food processor until it just resembles coarse meal. Add water and mix just until it becomes a soft workable ball of dough. Press into a flat circle. Refrigerate for about 20 minutes. Roll dough out to fit a 9-inch quiche or pie plate. Place dough in plate without stretching, and build up edges to top of dish. With a pastry brush, coat pastry with egg wash. Prick all bottom and sides of shell with fork prongs to keep it from puffing up while baking.

To bake, cook on High (600–700 watts) for 6–7 minutes, until shell is crisp and brown spots begin to appear.

Use pot holders to remove shell from microwave; the sides will be hot.

Note: Shell may be made ahead, and it need not be refrigerated until filled.

BASIC PASTRY SHELL
Makes 1 pie shell

This is a conventional recipe that goes well with quiches and pies when you do not want them to be sweet.

A pastry or pie shell must be completely cooked

LEMON/ORANGE PASTRY SHELL
Makes 1 pie shell

Bert Greene is a New York-based food columnist with a passion for good American home cooking. I enjoy his column in our *Los Angeles Times* and often use his recipes. I recently was attracted to his recipe for

"My Grandmother's Cheesecake"—and adapted the pie shell to microwave. The fragrance that fills the house lingers for hours. It tastes almost like a favorite cookie.

I made a few minor changes: He lists seeds scraped from a 1-inch piece of vanilla bean, which I am sure his Grandmother had in her cupboard. Since my readers may not, I substituted vanilla extract.

His recipe uses unsalted butter. In the microwave, a pie shell made using an all-butter shortening slips down the sides of the pie plate as the butter heats; so I have substituted a part solid shortening.

I have better luck patting the pastry into the plate than rolling it—it does not roll well for me. It may not look as perfectly made this way as other pie shells do, but I assure you, it will taste the best!

1 cup flour
¼ cup sugar
1 teaspoon grated lemon peel
1 teaspoon grated orange peel
1 teaspoon vanilla
¼ cup unsalted butter
¼ cup solid shortening (such as Crisco)
1 egg yolk

Combine flour, sugar, lemon and orange peels, and vanilla in a large bowl. Add butter and shortening and blend with pastry blender to a texture of coarse crumbs. Stir in egg yolk until all flour is moistened. Chill at least 1 hour.

Roll out pastry to fit an 8- or 9-inch-round by 2½-inch-high cake pan. Pat into bottom and lower sides of pan.

Cook on High power (600–700 watts) for 5–6 minutes, just until pastry is crisp and a few brown spots begin to appear.

Note: For a more attractive crust, brush it with a beaten egg before cooking.

CRUMB CRUST
Makes 1 9-inch pie shell

When my children were growing up, we were fortunate to have a wonderful friend who would stay with the children so we could run away on a holiday. She was an older woman—a born cook who never purchased cookies or other sweets.

Her cookies and cakes went fast, and left the cookie jar with a marvelous assortment of big crumbs, filled with raisins, nuts, whatever she had cooked.

I well remember her crumb crusts—she saved all of the crumbs in a jar in the refrigerator; and when she had enough, patted them into a pie plate as a base for pies.

Although this recipe lists some specific wafers to turn into crumbs, substitute whatever pleases you—or start your own supply of crumbs (from cookies, cakes, coffee cakes, Danish, or whatever).

5 tablespoons butter or margarine
1½ cups fine crumbs (from vanilla wafers, graham crackers, gingersnaps, chocolate wafers, chocolate sandwich cookies [yes, they do work], or your favorite cookie)

In a 9-inch pie plate, melt butter on High (600–700 watts) for 1 minute. Blend in crumbs. If you wish, set aside 2 tablespoons of crumb mixture to sprinkle over top of pie. Press firmly and evenly over bottom and sides of plate. You can cook it on High for about 30 seconds to set (optional). Cool before filling.

CREAM CHEESE PIE WITH SOUR CREAM TOPPING
Serves 8

2 8-ounce packages cream cheese, at room temperature
2 eggs
½ cup sugar
1 tablespoon grated lemon peel
1½ teaspoons vanilla
Pinch salt
2 cups sour cream
1 9-inch graham cracker crust
¼ cup sugar

Combine cream cheese and eggs in small bowl and beat until fluffy. Add sugar, lemon peel, vanilla, and salt and blend well. Add 1 cup sour cream and mix thoroughly. Cook on Medium (300–350 watts) 8 minutes, stopping every 2 minutes to mix with whisk. Pour into graham cracker crust and let cool.

Combine remaining cup of sour cream and sugar and blend well. Spread over pie. Chill thoroughly before serving.

BANANA CREAM PIE
Serves 6

If bananas are not one of your favorites, make it anyway and substitute your favorite fruit — or just serve it as a not too sweet creamy custard pie. The sugar has been cut to a minimum for better taste.

It is so simple to prepare a silky custard in your microwave with cornstarch, milk, and egg yolks that there is no need to ever use an overly sweet prepared mix.

Remember, if you eat a banana each day, you are filling your body's need for potassium!

Crust

⅓ **cup butter**
1½ **cups vanilla wafer crumbs (approximately 35 cookies)**
¼ **cup sugar**

Filling

⅔ **cup sugar**
⅓ **cup cornstarch**
½ **teaspoon salt**
2½ **cups milk**
4 **egg yolks**
2 **tablespoons butter**
2 **teaspoons vanilla**
½ **teaspoon banana extract (optional)**
3 **large firm bananas**
Sweetened whipped cream (optional, but a nice touch)

To make crust, place butter in a 9-inch pie plate. Melt on High (600–700 watts) for ¾–1 minute. Stir crumbs and sugar together until well combined, then press into the pie plate to form a pie shell. Refrigerate until set. (Cooking this crust will make it too hard — and there is no need.)

Combine sugar, cornstarch, and salt in 2-quart glass measure or bowl. Add milk a bit at a time, stirring until cornstarch is completely dissolved. Add egg yolks, using a whisk to combine well. Cook on High for 6–7½ minutes, stirring once or twice, until mixture comes to a boil. Stir in the butter and vanilla (and banana extract if using). Allow to cool to room temperature. The mixture will thicken, but can be whisked together after it has cooled and before you pour it into the pie shell. (If you layer the custard and bananas in the shell while the custard is still warm, the layers tend to separate.)

After the custard has cooled to room temperature, peel and slice 2 bananas about ⅛ to ¼ inch thick. Arrange ½ the slices in the pie shell. Cover with half the custard. Place a second layer of sliced bananas over custard, and top with remaining custard. Chill thoroughly.

Just before serving, slice remaining banana and arrange over top. Spoon whipped cream over top of pie, or over each individual slice when serving.

BLUEBERRY PIE
Serves 6–8

Every season brings with it glorious fruit. In addition, you now have the option of fresh-frozen fruit in the freezer sections, many without the addition of sugar or preservatives. Either variety — fresh or frozen — works well in fruit pies.

My frustration with making fruit pies in my microwave ended when I used the same technique I used for making raspberry sauce: cooking the fruit with cornstarch to thicken. At that point it was perfect in texture and "baking" was stopped immediately to retain that lovely fresh taste.

I have always found fruit pie recipes too sweet. After all, if you are eating blueberries or a fresh peach, you don't coat it with sugar before tasting. Nature does a great job of sweetening. All of my recipes use a minimum amount of sugar; if you prefer a sweeter taste, increase the sugar to ¾ cup, which is what most fruit pie recipes use.

1 **9-inch prebaked pie shell (see index)**
5 **cups blueberries, fresh or frozen**
½ **cup sugar**
3 **tablespoons cornstarch**
1 **cup water**
1 **teaspoon lemon juice**
1 **teaspoon lemon peel, finely shredded**

Prebake pie shell and set aside to cool. If blueberries are frozen, place in a 2-quart bowl and cook on High (600–700 watts) for 3 minutes. Stir and set aside. If using fresh blueberries, rinse in a colander, and remove any that appear spoiled. Set aside.

Combine sugar, cornstarch, and water. Stir until cornstarch is completely dissolved. Cook on High 3 minutes, stirring once with a wire whisk. Stir in blueberries, lemon juice, and lemon peel. Cook on High 2–3 minutes, or until sauce begins to thicken slightly.

Stir mixture gently. Continue to cook 1 minute, or just until mixture appears thick. Remember, overcooking cornstarch makes it break down.

Set aside to cool slightly before pouring into pie shell. Allow to cool completely before serving. Fruit pies taste better at room temperature than chilled.

Serve with whipped cream or a scoop of vanilla ice cream.

PIÑA COLADA PIE
Serves 6–8

A Piña Colada, in case you have not discovered it, is a drink of rum, pineapple juice, and coconut. A pie version of these ingredients appeared as a favorite recipe sent in to the *Los Angeles Times*. Aha, I thought, sounds like a microwave winner to me—and since I had all the necessary ingredients I tried it immediately. It adapted the first time it was tried.

A short time later, Fern Storer, a microwave columnist, printed her adaptation of the pie with a story similar to mine. It seems that microwave people think alike.

Here is my adaptation of the conventional recipe. I decided to make my own pie crust out of coconut, instead of using the graham cracker crust from the original recipe. It is quite simple, but you must stir frequently to avoid scorching.

Crust

3 tablespoons butter
1½ cups coconut

Filling

2 envelopes unflavored gelatin
½ cup sugar
¼ teaspoon salt
1 20-ounce can crushed pineapple (in its natural juices)
1½ cups buttermilk
¼ cup lemon juice
1 teaspoon vanilla
½ cup flaked coconut
2 cups whipped cream, or 1 9-ounce container of nondairy whipped topping, thawed

To make coconut crusts, place butter in a 9-inch pie plate. Melt on High (600–700 watts) for 45 seconds–1 minute. Stir in coconut. Cook on High 4–5 minutes, stirring every minute. When coconut is toasted, pat into the pie plate to form a shell, and allow to cool while you prepare the filling. (Reserve 1 tablespoon toasted coconut to sprinkle over pie).

Combine gelatin, sugar, and salt in a 2-quart batter bowl; blend in the pineapple and its juice. Heat on High 3 minutes. Stir well, then stir in buttermilk, lemon juice, and vanilla. Chill until thickened but not set. Beat with mixer until fluffy. Fold in coconut and whipped cream or nondairy topping. Pour into pie shell. Sprinkle toasted coconut over top. Chill until set.

Note: If you do not wish to use a coconut crust, a 9-inch graham cracker crust works very well.

PECAN PIE
Serves 6

Definitely not for dieters—but worth every calorie. Great with vanilla ice cream or a touch of whipped cream.

¼ cup (½ stick) unsalted butter
2 cups whole pecans
1 cup sugar
1 cup light or dark corn syrup
3 eggs, lightly beaten
1 teaspoon vanilla
1 baked 9-inch pie shell (in glass or ceramic pie plate)

Melt butter in 2-quart measure on High (600–700 watts). Add nuts, sugar, corn syrup, eggs, and vanilla and blend well. Pour into pie shell. Cook on Medium High (400–500 watts) until center is set, about 11–12 minutes. Turn pie if it appears to be cooking unevenly.

Serve at either room temperature or chilled.

FLUFFY TAPIOCA
Serves 4

This recipe will absolutely change the minds of those who experienced lumpy tapioca pudding at camp and vowed never to try it again.

This recipe was never printed for students in class because I took it right off the back of the box. By reducing the sugar in the recipe and adding a bit more vanilla, which we have done, it becomes a lower calorie version and tastes just as sweet.

2 cups milk (may use skim or low-fat)
3 rounded tablespoons quick-cooking tapioca
4 tablespoons sugar, divided
1 egg, separated
⅛ teaspoon salt
1 tablespoon vanilla

In a 1-quart glass measure, combine milk, tapioca, 2 tablespoons sugar, egg yolk, and salt and mix well. Let stand 5 minutes. Cook on High (600–700 watts) for 8–10 minutes, or until boiling. Meanwhile, beat egg white in small bowl until foamy. Gradually add remaining sugar and continue to beat until soft peaks form. Use a wire whip to fold egg white mixture into cooked tapioca a little at a time until just blended. Mix in vanilla. Top with your favorite sauce and serve either warm or cold.

Note: You might like to add an extra egg white to the beaten white for more volume.

PERFECT JELLO

Have you ever wondered why some Jello tastes so creamy and clear, and at other times rubbery and without flavor? The difference is in the way it is cooked.

For me the learning experience came while visiting Canada. In many ways, the Canadian women have retained practices of the old world. In the family we met, the women did all their own baking, cooked from scratch, and were marvelous homemakers. They did it with a passion; it is a way of life for them.

Watching a jello mold being prepared, I learned the difference: Instead of just adding hot water and stirring the jello, they completely cooked all the water and all the jello mixture on the cook-top until every little granule was completely dissolved. *That* is the difference.

Now I do all my jello cooking in a 4-cup glass measure in the microwave. Once you know how long it takes for your microwave to bring 2 cups of liquid to a boil (it should be about 2½–3 minutes per cup), you can judge how long to set the timer. Stir once after a few minutes to be sure the mixture is dispersed through the water. Let it come to a boil and you will see the liquid clarify in front of your eyes.

This is also a great technique for preparing chocolate pudding mixes. However, milk needs to be watched more carefully so that it does not boil over (stirring helps).

CRÈME CARAMEL
Serves 6–8

This microwave adaptation of a classic French dessert is designed for ovens with low power settings. It is also important to have the proper dish. Since the high temperature needed to caramelize sugar requires tempered glass, you should use the 1½-quart brioche dish (or other similar fluted dish) made of Pyrex.

12 tablespoons sugar, divided
2 tablespoons water
2 cups milk
3 eggs
3 egg yolks
1 teaspoon vanilla

Combine 6 tablespoons sugar with water in 1½-quart glass brioche dish and blend well. Cook on High (600–700 watts) until mixture just turns brown, about 4 minutes; do not overcook or caramel will be bitter. Remove from microwave and carefully tilt dish to coat bottom and sides evenly.

Pour milk into 4-cup measuring bowl and cook on High until scalded, about 3–4 minutes, watching closely so milk does not boil. In 2-quart bowl, whisk together eggs, egg yolks, remaining sugar, and vanilla until well blended. Slowly add hot milk, whisking constantly until thoroughly mixed. Pour into caramelized mixture. Cook on Medium (300–350 watts) until custard begins to set, about 17–20 minutes. (Custard is starting to set when it begins to shrink from sides of dish.) Custard will be liquid in center when removed from oven since, like all custards, it will set as it cools. Cool completely. To serve, run knife along edge of custard before inverting and unmolding on small platter.

PEARS POACHED IN RED WINE
Serves 4

A truly elegant dessert—and just the right touch after a heavy meal. The microwave does this beautifully.

4 firm, ripe pears
3 cups water
3 tablespoons fresh lemon juice
2 cups dry red wine
½ cup sugar
1 cinnamon stick, plus ¼ teaspoon ground cinnamon
Peel of ½ lemon
Mint for garnish (optional)

Peel pears, leaving stem intact. Place in large bowl with 3 cups water and lemon juice to keep pears from turning dark.

Combine wine, sugar, cinnamon, and lemon peel in a 2-quart round baking dish. Cook on High (600–700 watts) for 5 minutes. Add pears, turning them in the wine to coat completely. Cover with wax paper and cook on High about 9–10 minutes, until pears are just fork tender. Turn pears once or twice during cooking to keep them nicely colored.

When pears are tender, spoon juices over them while they cool (pears should remain in liquid until ready to serve). Serve at room temperature, or chilled.

Add a piece of mint to the stem before serving.

BREAKFAST PRUNES
Serves 2

We all know why prunes are good for you. This was the way I introduced my mother to microwave cooking! She became an instant convert—the prunes are delightful.

The amount can vary—just add enough water to cover and increase the timing. For me, the best taste comes with a minimum of cooking—just long enough

to bring it to a simmer and cook about 2 minutes. Then let it sit covered for about 5 minutes before eating to complete the softening process and increase the flavor of the liquid.

You may wish to add raisins for additional sweetness.

1 cup prunes
3 slices lemon
Sprinkle of cinnamon, or small section of cinnamon stick

Place prunes in small casserole, just large enough to contain recipe. Add water to cover. Add lemon and cinnamon.

Cover and cook on High (600–700 watts) about 5 minutes. Timing will depend upon the amount of moisture in the fruit. Cook just until they are plump and tender, and allow to sit covered for a few minutes before eating. May also be chilled and served cold; however, fruit does taste better at room temperature.

MIXED FRUIT COMPOTE
Serves 6–8

This is a popular holiday offering, particularly after a heavy meal. Although the fresh orange and lemon can be left out if not in season, the orange does add a natural sweetness and color that is appealing and the lemon a touch of tartness.

All fruit is at its best when served at room temperature. I usually remove it from the refrigerator about 1 hour before serving.

1–1½ pounds fancy mixed dry fruit (peaches, pears, apricots, prunes)
¼ pound golden raisins
1 small orange, sliced into rings
1 small lemon, thinly sliced
1 cinnamon stick, or ¼ teaspoon ground cinnamon
2½ cups water

Place all ingredients into a 1½-quart casserole. Cover. Cook on High (600–700 watts) about 10 minutes, until fruit is plump and tender. Stir; allow to remain covered until it cools. (The liquid will become "fruitier" as it stands.) Refrigerate until ready to use—it will keep well in the refrigerator for about 1 week. Freezes well.

If more fruit is added, increase the water sparingly.

FRESH PEACH IN CHAMPAGNE
Serves 2

During my early years of pioneering new recipes, I attended an elegant wedding brunch at Scandia's restaurant on the Sunset Strip in Los Angeles. First course was a beautiful poached peach in a champagne glass, made more interesting when the waiter appeared with a bottle of champagne which he poured over each peach at the table. I could not wait until it was over, since I realized it was definitely a microwave recipe! After stopping at the market and experimenting that very afternoon, it soon became apparent that adding water to fresh fruit was unnecessary—it had enough of its own.

You can use this method to cook any fresh fruit or combination of fruits. Do not use glassware that contains lead. Inexpensive glassware from your local market works well.

Rather than give a timing for this, it is best to use your eyes. After all, fruit will vary with size and juice content.

2 large, ripe, firm peaches with good color, cut in half and seeded
Champagne, or Raspberry Sauce (see index)

Place peach (with halves placed back together) in individual wine glasses or champagne goblets. Cook on High (600–700 watts) until juices come to a boil and begin to cover fruit. Remove from microwave as each one boils and turn halves over, using wooden spoon to prevent bruising. Let stand in juices several minutes to complete cooking. Fill each glass with champagne, or pass Raspberry Sauce separately, or enjoy it just as is.

FRESH PEACH IN RASPBERRY LIQUEUR
Serves 2

Another variation to help you enjoy the fresh taste of peaches in season. Also a nice touch for plums, nectarines, apricots, or a combination of any of these. Use 1 tablespoon of liqueur for each large fruit added.

3 tablespoons raspberry liqueur

2 large peaches, halved and seeded
Whipped cream (optional)
Mint leaf for garnish (optional)

Place the liqueur in an inexpensive glass goblet. Add peaches. Cook on High (600–700 watts) until juices come to a complete boil. Stir gently to coat peaches with juices. Allow to cool slightly.

Serve as is, or serve hot over vanilla ice cream topped with a touch of whipped cream and mint leaf.

APPLESAUCE
Serves 4

This is microwave performance at its best. Of course your apple selection depends upon the seasons and your own taste buds. I love the tart green apples, like Granny Smith, and use very little sugar. Use a potato masher to break up the apples, because it leaves you some chunks to chew on and savor.

6 cups green tart apples, peeled, cored, and sliced (5–6 medium apples)
½ cup water
1 tablespoon lemon juice
2 tablespoons sugar
½ teaspoon cinnamon

Quarter the apples and slice ½-inch thick. Place in a casserole just large enough to contain recipe. Add remaining ingredients. Cover. Cook on High (600–700 watts) for 10–12 minutes until apples are fork tender. Allow to cool slightly, then mash with a potato masher.

APPLES SWEET AND GOLDEN
Serves 4

Preparing fruit is what the microwave does best. When you notice the fruit you purchased is showing a bit of age because it was not eaten in time, try cooking it with a touch of sugar and cinnamon.

If you prefer, do as I do: simply use the cinnamon and perhaps a touch of vanilla for flavor, instead of sugar. Easy to prepare just a serving for one. In my home, I prepare it without sugar for myself, and use this recipe for my husband—he loves the sweet flavor. Strangely enough, he is tall and thin and I am fighting weight! It is all so unfair!

4 **large cooking apples, peeled, cored, and cut into quarters**
¼ **cup brown sugar**
1 **teaspoon cinnamon**
1 **teaspoon vanilla**
2 **tablespoons butter**

Place apples in a casserole just large enough to contain recipe. Combine sugar and cinnamon and sprinkle over the apples. Place vanilla and butter on top. Cover and cook on High (600–700 watts) about 8 minutes, stirring after 4 minutes. Timing will depend upon the size of the apples. Cut the time if using less—notice I am using 2 minutes cooking time for each apple.

You may wish to add raisins to this dish. If so, add from the beginning.

CHERRIES JUBILEE
Serves 3–4

Sounds exciting—you can visualize the head waiter in full dress flaming the elegant dessert at your table—and like many mysterious-until-tried recipes, this one is so simple you should not wait for a special occasion to try it. If you are serving 4, you should have an extra pint of ice cream, just in case.

1 **pint vanilla ice cream**
1 **17-ounce can pitted dark sweet cherries (in extra-heavy sauce)**
½ **cup light rum**
2 **teaspoons cornstarch**
2 **tablespoons water**
¼ **cup brandy**
Whipped cream (optional)

Scoop ice cream in large balls into parfait glasses; cover and freeze. Drain the cherries, reserving ½ cup of syrup.

Mix reserved syrup with light rum. Heat syrup and rum mixture on High (600–700 watts) for 3 minutes.

Dissolve cornstarch in water. Stir gradually into the heated syrup. Heat on High for 2 minutes, or until just thickened. Stir briskly with wire whisk. Add cherries and heat on High until hot, about 1–2 minutes.

Pour brandy into heat-proof glass cup. Heat on High for 1 minute. At the table, spoon warm brandy over the hot cherry sauce and carefully ignite with match. Spoon sauce over ice cream.

May be served with whipped cream on the side.

FRESH FRUIT COMPOTE
Serves 4–6

2 **peaches, quartered and pitted**
4 **apricots, halved and pitted**
4 **plums, halved and pitted**
10 **cherries, halved and pitted**
1 **small bunch of grapes**

Combine all ingredients in a 2-quart bowl. Cook, uncovered, on High (600–700 watts) until juices come to a boil, about 10–12 minutes. Stir through. Serve warm, at room temperature, or chilled.

CRANBERRY FLUFF
Serves 6

A holiday treatment for cranberries that is light and different. Before I did it on purpose, I used to blend leftover cranberry sauce with whipped cream to get my family to eat the holiday leftovers.

2 **cups fresh cranberries**
1 **cup water**
¾ **cup sugar (or 1 cup if you want it sweeter)**
1 **3-ounce package orange-flavored gelatin**
½ **pint whipping cream, whipped**

In a 2-quart casserole combine cranberries, water, and sugar. Cook on High (600–700 watts) for 6–8 minutes or until berries pop open. Drain cranberries and reserve liquid; add enough hot water to make 2 cups. Stir the gelatin into hot liquid until it dissolves, and bring to boiling point. Stir well.

Add berries. Allow to cool, then place in refrigerator to chill until thickened. Whip cream until firm, and fold into cooled cranberry mixture. Spoon into an attractive 6-cup serving dish and garnish with additional cream. Refrigerate until ready to serve.

CARROT CAKE
Serves 10

Moist and rich, it makes a birthday party festive or could become a family favorite. It is a nice way to treat a carrot.

Microwave time of 12–14 minutes—instead of 1 hour 15 minutes in a conventional oven—is a good reason to prepare this in your microwave. You can, if you wish, substitute another vegetable for the carrots; the remaining ingredients stay the same.

1½ **cups all-purpose flour, sifted**
2 **teaspoons cinnamon**
1½ **teaspoons baking soda**
1 **teaspoon nutmeg**
½ **teaspoon salt**
3 **cups grated carrot**
1½ **cups sugar**
1 **cup oil**
1 **cup chopped walnuts**
3 **eggs, beaten**

Sift together first 5 ingredients. Combine carrot, sugar, oil, walnuts, and eggs, and blend well. Add dry ingredients and mix thoroughly. Turn into 10-inch ceramic, plastic, or glass Bundt pan. Cook on High (600–700 watts) for 10–11 minutes, turning pan if cake appears to be cooking unevenly. (When done, cake will pull away slightly from pan.) Cool slightly before inverting onto serving plate.

CREAM CHEESE FROSTING
Makes enough frosting for 2-layer cake, or 9-inch tube cake

If you would like a complementary frosting for carrot cake or zucchini bread, try this one.

1 **8-ounce package cream cheese, softened**
½ **cup butter, softened**
2 **teaspoons vanilla**
¼ **cup chopped nuts**
¾ **box confectioner's sugar (approximately 3 cups), sifted**
Additional chopped nuts for topping

Whip cream cheese until smooth. Add butter and whip thoroughly. Add vanilla and chopped nuts; stir to blend. Add confectioner's sugar and mix until well blended.

Transfer cake to serving platter and frost. Sprinkle with additional chopped nuts.

MISSISSIPPI MUD CAKE
Serves 8–12

From Martha Green's kitchen comes this rich, sinful cake.

Cake

1½ **cups sugar**
1½ **tablespoons cocoa**
¾ **cup (1½ sticks) margarine**
3 **eggs, well beaten**
1¼ **cups all-purpose flour**
1½ **teaspoons baking powder**
1¼ **cups coconut**
1¼ **cups chopped walnuts**
1 **teaspoon vanilla**

Frosting

1 **7-ounce jar marshmallow creme**
¼ **cup (½ stick) margarine**
¼ **cup evaporated milk**
¼ **cup cocoa**
2 **cups (½ box) powdered sugar**

To make cake, combine sugar and cocoa until well blended. Cream with margarine. Add eggs, flour, and baking powder, and stir until batter is well mixed. Batter will be very stiff.

Stir in coconut, walnuts, and vanilla. Pour batter into a greased 10-inch quiche or deep dish pie plate. Cook on High (600–700 watts) 10–11 minutes, turning if it appears to be cooking unevenly.

Spread hot cake with marshmallow creme by adding marshmallow in dollops, and then spreading.

To complete frosting, combine margarine, milk, and cocoa in a 2-quart bowl. Heat on High (600–700 watts) for 1½–2 minutes, until heated through. Stir in powdered sugar. Mix well and spread on top of marshmallow creme.

15

CHOCOLATE, CHOCOLATE, CHOCOLATE

Chocolate Cake with Almond Custard Filling

Chocolate Mousse Pie

Chocolate Nut Brownies

Chocolate Pudding

Steamed Chocolate Pudding

Fudge

Milk Chocolate Fudge

Chocolate Taffy

Chocolate-Covered Strawberries

Chocolate Lemon Creams

Rocky Road

White Chocolate Almond Bark

Honeycomb

Kahlua Chocolate Velvet

Chocolate Fondue

Perfect Hot Chocolate Sauce

Chocolate Marshmallow Sauce

Cappuccino

I have never met a chocoholic I didn't like, and I always felt that when it came to going out of my way to sample chocolate, I was on a par with anyone. After all, it was I who always made a Chocolate Mousse Pie in my first session with new students because I knew instinctively if you give students chocolate, they will love you forever.

Also it was I who said it was my greatest fear that one day long after I am gone from this earth, "they" will suddenly discover that a pound bar of chocolate each day prolongs life!

Also, it was I who told my students about my love affair with McFarlane's Rocky Road candy, to the extent that if I were driving and my car was hit by a truck and I discovered I was alone and that my main artery had been severed and, if while driving myself to the nearest hospital, I happened to notice a McFarlane's candy sign, I would stop! Therefore, there was not a doubt in my mind—I was a true chocoholic.

That was until I met what I consider the chocoholic—bar none. Slim and trim, with not so much as a blemish on her fair skin, she scanned the menu for chocolate desserts. Her eyes wandered to the cart to size up their chocolate offerings. She looked at the waiter with disdain when he suggested she make "A" selection—she smiled mischievously, looked him in the eye, and said, "I'll take one of each!" Not to share, you understand! In the true tradition of chocolate lovers, we do not share. Well, maybe a little taste here and there, but to pass my plate and leave you and your fork to your own devices—never!

My involvement started with this chocoholic when I began to work with Sanyo. It was sometimes necessary to work long hours at various shows like the Builders or Consumer Electronic shows in Las Vegas or other large cities. I did not know this about Pat Rienze immediately—although it was obvious when we had dinner together that she adored chocolate desserts, I thought it was in a normal fashion. It was not until we met accidentally about 1:30 A.M. in a hotel lobby. She was obviously exhausted from meetings, meetings, meetings. I was blindly making my way to the nearest elevator hoping I could stay awake long enough to find my room—when she spotted me, grabbed my arm, and said, *"Hot Fudge Sundae"?* That was when I knew for sure.

One would expect this sophisticated, exquisitely groomed, successful executive to head for the nearest bar. Not on your life! To find Patricia after a hard day at the office or away at the many business shows and conventions, look in the closest restaurant, dessert factory, or wherever they take their chocolate seriously. There you will see a pro at work: no vacillating for choices, no hesitation, no allowing anyone to intimidate—just simply, "I'll take one of each!" That is a chocoholic with class. To her I dedicate this chapter.

TERMINOLOGY

Unsweetened chocolate: Known as baking, cooking, or bitter chocolate. It is intended primarily for baking. I often add it to sweetened chocolate because it adds a rich quality and cuts the sweetness.

Bittersweet chocolate: Slightly sweetened, dark chocolate. It is used for desserts, for some baking, and is the confectioner's choice for dipping.

Semisweet chocolate: Sometimes called sweet chocolate. It is the choice of French chefs for baking. It is also used for frosting, fillings, sauces, creams, and mousses.

Milk chocolate: America's favorite. It works best for pies, puddings, and some steamed desserts.

White chocolate: Called chocolate but has only one chocolate component—cocoa butter. It is used for mousses, frostings, fillings, cakes, and for dipping.

Compound coatings: Not real chocolate—made of a hardened vegetable fat base, they are also called "Summer Coatings." Perfect for molding, because it is easy to work with. Comes in a rainbow of colors. It was this development that made it possible for everyone to use molds at home to make their own favorite decorative shapes, without providing the unique environment so necessary for "real chocolate" molding as done by professionals.

BASIC TECHNIQUES FOR CHOCOLATE

(Portions of this article previously appeared in my microwave column in *Bon Appetit* magazine, October 1981.)

When chocolate was first discovered in the new world by Cortez during his conquest of Mexico, he found the Aztec Indians using cacao beans in the preparation of the royal drink of the realm, *chocolatl.* It was known as the "Food of the Gods." For many of us that is the proper description for the love we have developed for this delightful dessert.

Like fine wines, the final product has everything to do with the way it is handled from its inception. What amount of cocoa butter is removed and replaced with substitute fats will have everything to do with the melting of the chocolate later. What flavorings are added will make the taste of each chocolate unique to its manufacturer. Since the original product is not sweetened and is very bitter, sweetening was added to make it more agreeable, and became a way of making it into the ambrosia we find today.

It was first used only as a drink—sometimes cinnamon was added, sometimes a dash of vanilla, sometimes it was tried hot—and during all of this experimenting it was acclaimed throughout Europe as a delicious health-giving food. Chocolate houses began to appear in England in the 1600s, and at the end of the 1800s Switzerland invented a way of making milk chocolate for eating. In the 1700s the first chocolate factory was established in this country. So much importance was placed on the chocolate bar that it became part of the Allied Armed Forces food allocation to our soldiers during World War II (taking valuable shipping space).

Chocolate varies in texture and therefore timings may vary when it is melted. If it is "cooked" rather than melted, the damage to the quality is beyond repair—It will become grainy and hard.

For best results microwave melting of chocolate is ideal, since you do not direct heat underneath the pan, which could cause scorching. Just remember to look for this clue that the chocolate has softened: The chocolate will change from a dull color to a shiny surface, but will *not appear melted* until you stir. Cooking is stopped before chocolate becomes runny or melted.

The recipes following use High power (600–700 watts) for about 2 minutes for 12 ounces of chocolate, then are stirred until chocolate is dissolved. Most recipes call for chocolate bits, which encourage quick melting. It is always best to break large bars into pieces, or to grate the chocolate in your food processor. The smaller the pieces, the quicker the melting. Adding a liquid like milk to the chocolate may change the cooking pattern, since milk heats rapidly and also tends to boil over. It may be best to use Medium (300–350 watts) when making hot chocolate drinks with milk.

Once the chocolate is dissolved after stirring, if you need to reheat a small amount it is best to use Medium power for small periods of time. Begin with 30 seconds, stir, then add seconds of timing rather than minutes to avoid bruising the chocolate.

Substitutions

For baking chocolate: 3 tablespoons cocoa plus 1 tablespoon shortening equals 1 ounce baking chocolate.

For semisweet chocolate: 6 tablespoons cocoa plus 7 tablespoons sugar plus ¼ cup solid shortening equals one 6-ounce package (1 cup) semisweet chocolate chips, or 6 ounces semisweet chocolate.

For sweet cooking chocolate: 4 tablespoons cocoa plus 4⅔ tablespoons sugar plus 2⅔ tablespoons shortening equals one 4-ounce bar sweet cooking chocolate.

Chocolate Tips

Recently Lee Gelfond, a chocolatier who was opening her own shop in Beverly Hills and wanted to avoid the installation of heavy-duty fans and equipment to abide by that city's codes, came to me for advice. Could she use a microwave—eliminate the conventional methods of tempering chocolate for forming her delightful chocolate designs? She visited my test kitchen with a variety of samples. By the end of the day and a few pounds heavier (we had to be certain the texture stayed intact) she decided to order her first microwave. After opening, she called to say that in all of her experience she had not been able to achieve the product she was able to produce in her microwave: it cut down hours of preparation; she was better able to control temperature; and because of its speed, she was able to work in small, controlled quantities.

For all of the chocoholics in the world, let me assure you: you do not need to be a professional to experience good results.

- Chocolate chips, bits, or chunks will become shiny but will *not* lose their shape when "melted"—they will not melt in the traditional sense. Stir through several times with a wooden spoon until chocolate is smooth to complete melting.
- Break up chocolate into smaller pieces to speed up the softening. Use High power for small amounts. For large amounts of chocolate used with liquid, High power is still best, since it speeds up the process. With large amounts of chocolate only, either melt in small batches or use a lower setting to avoid overheating.
- The temperature of the room is a crucial factor when you are dipping or working with melted chocolate. The ideal temperature is 65–68 degrees—a cooler room is always better than a warm, humid room.

- Never cover chocolate when melting since it will cause moisture to form on the inside, and even one drop of moisture can cause the chocolate to ball up and stiffen.
- Although you can add a tablespoon or so of vegetable oil to melted chocolate, it will affect the texture and taste.
- A good quality chocolate with cocoa butter retained is ideal to work with, and experimenting with different chocolate products will give you greater insight into quality and taste. Try taking the wrappers off different products and tasting each one slowly. You can then get a feeling for the differences in texture and taste. Then read the labels to understand the differences in the product. It will make it easier to judge chocolate products before purchasing.
- Problems can occur when temperature changes. It can cause chocolate to turn color, or a grayish-white mottling on the finished chocolate can occur. Although it is unattractive, it does not affect the taste.

CHOCOLATE CAKE WITH ALMOND CUSTARD FILLING

Serves 10–12

Be very gentle when moving this delicate cake as it crumbles easily.

Cake

2 cups sugar
1¾ cups all-purpose flour
¾ cup unsweetened cocoa powder
2 teaspoons baking soda
1 teaspoon baking powder
1 teaspoon salt
1 teaspoon instant coffee powder
2 eggs, room temperature
¾ cup strong coffee
¾ cup buttermilk
½ cup vegetable oil
1 teaspoon vanilla

Almond Custard Filling

2 eggs, room temperature
2 egg yolks
1 cup sugar
1 cup milk, scalded
¼ cup all-purpose flour
3 tablespoons unsalted butter

½ cup finely chopped toasted almonds
2 teaspoons vanilla
½ teaspoon amaretto

Frosting

¾ cup (1½ sticks) butter
1¼ cups unsweetened cocoa powder
3½ cups powdered sugar
½ cup milk
2 teaspoons vanilla

For cake: Line bottom of 8 x 2½-inch round microwave-safe cake pan with parchment paper. Spray sides of pan with vegetable spray. Combine sugar, flour, cocoa powder, baking soda, baking powder, salt, and instant coffee powder in large bowl. Combine eggs, coffee, buttermilk, oil, and vanilla in another large bowl and beat well. Add egg mixture to dry ingredients and mix thoroughly. Pour half of batter into prepared pan. Cook on High (600–700 watts), 6–6½ minutes, turning several times if cake begins cooking unevenly. Set pan on rack and let cool 10 minutes. Invert cake onto rack and let cool completely. Repeat with remaining batter. When cool, cut each cake in half horizontally to make four layers. Set aside.

For filling: Combine eggs, egg yolks, sugar, milk, and flour in 1-quart measure and cook on High 2 minutes. Stir through several times. Continue cooking on High 30 seconds. Repeat cooking and stirring at 30-second intervals until mixture is thick, about 2 minutes. Blend in butter. Add chopped almonds, vanilla, and amaretto and beat until smooth, about 1 minute.

For frosting: Melt butter in 2-quart measure on High 45 seconds. Stir in cocoa and cook on High 30 seconds. Let cool. Add sugar and milk alternately to mixture, beating until smooth and thick, about 3 minutes. Stir in vanilla.

To assemble: Set one cake layer on serving platter. Spread with ⅓ of filling. Top with second layer and spread with another ⅓ of filling. Add third layer and cover with remaining filling. Set fourth layer on top. Cover top and sides of cake with frosting. Serve at room temperature or chilled.

CHOCOLATE MOUSSE PIE

Serves 6–8

I have always known instinctively that the best way to convince my students of the value of microwave cooking was to include an easy chocolate recipe that was a "to die for." This was my selection for the first class session.

When I first started using this recipe, I would prepare a pie ahead of the class session so that it would be firm for the class—until I realized that that left me with an extra pie which I would devour the next day. No more of that, I thought, and from then on made only one pie—in class—which I put in the freezer to set up.

In fact, I recommend that your pie be placed there immediately after preparing. (It is the only safe place to store it!) Place it in uncovered, then when frozen wrap it in foil. To use, take it out about one hour before serving to thaw at room temperature.

¾ **cup milk**
3 **cups miniature marshmallows**
1 **8-ounce chocolate almond bar (like Hershey's), broken into pieces**
3 **ounces unsweetened baking chocolate, broken into pieces**
3 **tablespoons unsweetened cocoa powder**
1 **pint whipping cream, whipped; or 2 10-ounce cartons solid whipped topping**
1 **prepared crumb crust using chocolate cookie crumbs, chocolate toasted coconut, or chocolate wafer crumbs (see index)**

In a 2-quart bowl, place milk, marshmallows, chocolate bar, and baking chocolate. Cook on High (600–700 watts) for 3–4 minutes. Stir until chocolate is melted and marshmallows are completely dissolved. Stir in the cocoa powder. If necessary, place back in to heat on High for another 30 seconds. Set aside to cool completely.

For best results, cooled chocolate mixture should be at room temperature, otherwise the chocolate may be too stiff to fold in the whipped cream. If you place it into the refrigerator to cool, allow it to remain at room temperature for a short time before going to next stage.

Fold in all but ½ cup of whipped cream. Place filling into crumb crust, and garnish with whipped cream and a bit of chocolate sprinkles. Chill until firm.

CHOCOLATE NUT BROWNIES
Makes about 20 brownies

2 **ounces unsweetened baking chocolate**
½ **cup (1 stick) unsalted butter**

2 **eggs**
¾ **cup sugar**
½ **cup all-purpose flour**
1 **tablespoon vanilla**
1 **teaspoon baking powder**
¼ **teaspoon salt**
1 **cup walnuts, coarsely chopped**
1 **cup chocolate chips**
Powdered sugar (optional)

Combine chocolate and butter in 2-quart measuring cup and cook on High (600–700 watts) until butter is melted, about 1½ minutes. Stir to blend (chocolate will not appear melted until you stir).

Beat eggs in large bowl until well mixed. Add chocolate mixture, sugar, flour, vanilla, baking powder, and salt and blend thoroughly. Stir in nuts and chocolate chips. Turn into 9-inch pie plate or quiche dish. Cook on High 6 minutes. (Mixture will still be moist, but will firm as it cools.) Sprinkle with powdered sugar. Let cool completely before cutting into squares.

CHOCOLATE PUDDING
Serves 4

You may never purchase a package mix again, this is so easy to prepare and so delicious. I have cut the sugar to the minimum. If you prefer a sweeter taste, increase the sugar to ⅔ cup. Stirring helps to keep mixture smooth and to keep the milk from boiling over.

Best of all—no scorched pan bottom!

½ **cup sugar**
¼ **cup cocoa (unsweetened powdered variety)**
3 **tablespoons cornstarch**
¼ **teaspoon salt**
2¼ **cups milk (may use low-fat)**
2 **tablespoons butter**
1 **teaspoon vanilla**

Combine sugar, cocoa, cornstarch, and salt in 8-cup glass measure. Gradually stir in milk, stirring until cornstarch is completely dissolved.

Cook on High (600–700 watts) for 7–10 minutes, stirring every 2 minutes. Cooking is finished when mixture is cooked through and thickened. Stir in butter and vanilla. Pour into individual serving dishes. Cover with plastic wrap pressed down on pudding surface to prevent skin from forming over top. Refrigerate.

STEAMED CHOCOLATE PUDDING
Serves 8

This uses a traditional method of steaming in a water bath. It produces a lovely, moist, cakelike pudding. If you already own a 6-cup ring mold and a rack which can be placed inside a shallow dish to hold the water—and are a chocolate lover—this is a recipe you might enjoy.

1 cup (2 sticks) butter, at room temperature
1 cup sugar
3 eggs, separated
1½ cups all-purpose flour
1 teaspoon baking powder
¾ cup milk
4 ounces unsweetened baking chocolate
2 teaspoons vanilla
2 tablespoons sugar
½ cup boiling water
1 cup whipping cream
2 tablespoons Kahlua liqueur (optional)
Toasted walnuts or almonds, chopped

Lightly grease a 6-cup ceramic ring mold. Cream butter with sugar in large bowl. Add egg yolks and beat well. Combine flour and baking powder and add to creamed mixture alternately with milk, beating well each time.

Heat chocolate on High (600–700 watts) in small bowl for 2 minutes, or just until chocolate turns shiny (do not wait for it to appear melted). Stir through until melted. Blend into flour mixture. Stir in vanilla.

Beat egg whites until soft peaks form. Sprinkle with 2 tablespoons sugar and continue beating until whites are stiff and glossy. Fold into chocolate mixture, blending completely. Spoon into mold. Place large shallow dish into microwave and pour in boiling water. Set microwave rack over or into dish (depending upon design). Set mold on top. Cover and cook on Medium (300–350 watts) about 12 minutes, until pudding appears set (top will be moist, but pudding will firm as it stands). Let rest 20 minutes.

Meanwhile, whip cream with Kahlua liqueur to desired consistency. Unmold pudding onto platter. Sprinkle with nuts. Serve warm with whipped cream on the side.

Pudding can be prepared ahead and reheated on High for 15–20 seconds per slice.

FUDGE
Makes about 1½ pounds

This was a popular recipe for beginners many years ago. It is fun because all the ingredients are simply dumped into a bowl, and you don't have to stir until the ingredients are heated. Several years ago I increased the amount of cocoa and added the marshmallows, which cuts the sweetness of the taste. The marshmallows are optional; in either case, it tastes just as good.

If you are planning to visit a friend, this can be prepared in an attractive dish, then wrapped as a present with cellophane and ribbon. Not only have you taken the time to make a special candy for a gift, but the enjoyment of the dish remains.

1 pound powdered sugar
1 cup cocoa, unsweetened
⅓ cup milk
¼ pound butter or margarine
1 cup walnuts, coarsely chopped
1½ cups miniature marshmallows (optional)
1 tablespoon vanilla

Place sugar, cocoa, milk, and butter in a 2-quart bowl. Cook on High (600–700 watts) for 2 minutes. Stir well to completely blend ingredients. Stir in walnuts, marshmallows, and vanilla. Immediately pour into a greased 8-inch dish and allow to cool completely in refrigerator before cutting into squares.

MILK CHOCOLATE FUDGE
Makes about 1 pound

This recipe came about when son Paul was left with some extra maraschino cherries from a recipe-testing session. To him, it seemed perfectly natural to start with a package of chocolate. (It seems to run in the family.)

This makes a nice holiday gift recipe.

1 12-ounce package milk chocolate chips
¼ cup evaporated milk
⅛ teaspoon salt
½ teaspoon vanilla
10 maraschino cherries, drained and coarsely chopped
¾ cup walnuts, coarsely chopped

Lightly butter 8-inch square baking pan. Combine chocolate chips, milk, and salt in 1-quart glass measure. Cook on High (600–700 watts) until chocolate appears shiny, about 2 minutes. Add vanilla and stir until chocolate melts. Blend in cherries and walnuts. Pour into prepared pan and allow to cool until firm. Cut into ½- to 1-inch squares.

CHOCOLATE TAFFY
Makes about ¼ pound

1 cup sugar
¾ cup light corn syrup
½ cup water
¼ teaspoon cream of tartar
**1 ounce (1 square) unsweetened baking
    chocolate, coarsely chopped**

Generously grease 9-inch square baking pan. Combine sugar, corn syrup, water, and cream of tartar in 2-quart measuring cup or bowl and mix well. Cook on High (600–700 watts) until mixture boils, stirring once, about 5–10 minutes. Continue cooking on High without stirring until candy thermometer registers 266°F. or until small amount of mixture forms ball hard enough to hold its shape but still pliable when dropped into very cold water; it will take about 12 minutes. Stir in chocolate, blending well. Pour into prepared pan. Set pan on a rack. Allow to cool at least 30 minutes.

Grease hands well and pull taffy until satiny and elastic. Cut into pieces. Wrap in waxed paper, twisting ends closed. Store in airtight container.

CHOCOLATE-COVERED STRAWBERRIES
Serves 2

Although this is a recipe for the romantic combination of chocolate and strawberries, I have dipped dried apricots the same way. These touches will make your favorite person feel special.

The chocolate holds up well in the refrigerator, but remember strawberries have a short life—for best results, dip them the day they are to be served, or if they are very firm, the day before. The apricots can be stored for several days without any loss in quality.

12 large strawberries
½ pound white or semisweet dark chocolate
**If using dark chocolate, add 1 ounce baking
    chocolate**

Wash strawberries with stem in and dry well. Place chocolate in glass measure (if in large pieces break apart). Melt on High (600–700 watts) for 2–3 minutes, just until chocolate appears shiny. Stir until melted.

Place a toothpick into the stem end of each strawberry. Dip each berry into the melted chocolate, coating the lower ⅔ part only. Let the excess chocolate drip back into the cup.

As strawberries are coating, stick the strawberries, on their toothpicks, onto a large piece of styrofoam to dry. Place strawberry-filled styrofoam into the refrigerator until chocolate is firm.

CHOCOLATE LEMON CREAMS
Makes about 7 dozen

3 tablespoons unsalted butter
2 tablespoons milk
2 tablespoons fresh lemon juice
1 15-ounce box white creamy frosting mix
1 tablespoon lemon peel, finely grated
1 teaspoon lemon extract
Yellow food coloring
**2 12-ounce packages semisweet real chocolate
    chips**
6 tablespoons solid vegetable shortening

Combine butter, milk, and lemon juice in 2-quart measuring cup and cook on High (600–700 watts) until butter is melted, about 45–60 seconds. Blend in frosting mix. Continue cooking on High, whisking through several times, until mixture is creamy, about 2–3 minutes. Whisk in lemon peel, lemon extract, and food coloring, mixing thoroughly. Drop by teaspoons onto wax paper. Let cool, then refrigerate until firm.

Combine chocolate chips and shortening in bowl and cook on High 1½–2 minutes. Using wooden spoon, stir through to melt thoroughly. Dip chilled creams into chocolate, covering completely. Let cool on wax paper, then refrigerate in airtight container.

ROCKY ROAD
Makes about 4 pounds

Here are two recipes from my articles in *Bon Appetit*. Enjoy—they are both fattening!!!!

3 12-ounce packages semisweet real chocolate chips
3 ounces (3 squares) unsweetened baking chocolate, broken into pieces
9 tablespoons solid vegetable shortening (like Crisco)
40 large marshmallows
2 cups whole toasted walnuts

Grease deep casserole dish or a 1½- to 2-quart soufflé dish. Combine 1 package chocolate chips, 1 ounce baking chocolate, and 3 tablespoons shortening in 1-quart measuring cup and cook on High (600–700 watts) for 2 minutes. Stir until smooth. Pour into prepared dish. Sprinkle with half of the marshmallows and half of nuts. Repeat layers, ending with final layer of chocolate. Allow to firm at room temperature before refrigerating. When firm and cool, cut or break into large pieces before serving.

WHITE CHOCOLATE ALMOND BARK
Makes 1½ pounds

We now have chocolate designed for home use that is easier to work with. It has a variety of names depending on the manufacturer.

1 cup whole blanched almonds
1 tablespoon butter
1 pound white chocolate, broken into pieces

Place almonds and butter on a 9-inch glass plate. Cook on High (600–700 watts) for 4–5 minutes, stirring once or twice, until almonds are toasted. Set aside.

Place chocolate in a 2-quart bowl. Melt on High 2–2½ minutes, just until it becomes shiny and appears softened. It will not melt and appear runny until you stir. Do not "cook" the chocolate or it will become grainy. Stir until completely melted.

Stir in almonds. Pour onto a waxed or parchment-lined baking sheet. Spread to desired thickness and refrigerate until set. Break into pieces to serve.

HONEYCOMB
Makes about 1 pound

1 cup sugar
1 cup dark corn syrup
1 tablespoon white vinegar
1 tablespoon baking soda

Chocolate Coating

1 12-ounce package semisweet real chocolate chips
3 tablespoons solid vegetable shortening (like Crisco)
1 ounce (1 square) unsweetened baking chocolate, broken into small pieces

Line 8″ x 8″ baking dish with foil; grease generously. Combine sugar, corn syrup, and vinegar in 2-quart bowl and cook on High (600–700 watts) 3 minutes. Stir through several times. Continue cooking on High until mixture has thickened and candy thermometer registers 300°F. (or until small amount of mixture separates into hard and brittle threads when dropped into very cold water), about 7–10 minutes. Quickly stir in baking soda (mixture will foam), blending completely. Pour into baking dish, tilting to cover bottom evenly. Let cool at room temperature until firm, about 1 hour (do not refrigerate). Break honeycomb into pieces and set aside.

Combine chocolate chips, shortening, and baking chocolate in a 2-quart bowl; cook on High 2 minutes. Using wooden spoon, stir through to melt thoroughly. (Chocolate will not appear melted until stirred; do not cook chocolate, just heat long enough to soften.) Dip honeycomb pieces into chocolate, covering completely. Place on wax paper. Let cool at room temperature.

Note: Chocolate coating can also be used to dip marshmallows. One recipe is enough for about 40 marshmallows.

KAHLUA CHOCOLATE VELVET
Serves 6–8

M-mmmmmmm!

⅓ **cup Kahlua liqueur**
½ **teaspoon instant coffee granules**
½ **teaspoon vanilla**
2 **1-ounce squares unsweetened chocolate**
4 **ounces semisweet chocolate**
5 **large eggs, separated**
¼ **teaspoon cream of tartar**
⅓ **cup sugar**

Place Kahlua, coffee granules, vanilla, and chocolate into a 1-quart bowl. Cook on High (600–700 watts) for 2–2½ minutes until chocolate appears shiny. Stir until melted.

Beat egg yolks well in small mixer bowl. Beat in chocolate mixture. When mixture is cool, beat egg whites with cream of tartar to soft peaks. Gradually beat in sugar to make meringue. Beat half the meringue into chocolate mixture until smooth; fold in remaining meringue. Turn into 1-quart serving dish, or individual dishes. Cover and chill until firm.

CHOCOLATE FONDUE
Serves 4–6

A fun way to serve fresh fruit. Each person selects a chunk of fruit and, using a fondue fork, regular fork, or long wooden skewers, dips it into the warm chocolate. You could also serve pastry chunks, or an assortment of both.

1 **12 ounce package semisweet chocolate bits**
3 **ounces baking chocolate**
½ **cup heavy cream**
2 **tablespoons Kahlua liqueur (optional)**

Place all ingredients into an attractive bowl suitable for serving. Heat on High (600–700 watts) for 2–2½ minutes, until chocolate appears shiny. Stir until smooth. Serve immediately. If reheating is necessary, use Medium (300–350 watts).

You can also melt the mixture in the microwave and transfer it to a fondue pot.

PERFECT HOT CHOCOLATE SAUCE
Makes 2 cups

Use over cake or ice cream, or as a frosting, since it will become firm when cold. This is a smooth and silky melt-in-your-mouth sauce.

1 **cup sugar**
½ **cup light cream**
4 **ounces unsweetened baking chocolate**
½ **cup butter, cut into pieces**
2 **egg yolks, beaten**
1 **teaspoon vanilla**

Combine sugar and cream in a 4-cup measure. Cook on High (600–700 watts), uncovered, 4 minutes, or until sugar dissolves and mixture boils. Add chocolate and butter. Stir to blend; cook an additional minute. Add half the chocolate mixture to beaten egg yolks. Stir egg yolk mixture into remaining chocolate mixture in measuring cup. Cook on Medium (300–350 watts) for 2 minutes. Whisk in the vanilla. Serve hot or cold.

To reheat, use Medium power beginning with 30 seconds. Timing for reheating will depend on the amount of chocolate. Just heat until liquid—do not cook. Sauce will store well in the refrigerator, covered.

CHOCOLATE MARSHMALLOW SAUCE
Makes about 2 cups

Marshmallow sauce for a chocoholic.

¾ **cup water**
1 **cup sugar**
20 **large marshmallows**
½ **cup cocoa powder**
1 **teaspoon vanilla**

Place water and sugar in a 2-quart measure. Cook on High (600–700 watts) 7–8 minutes, until 220°F. is reached on candy thermometer.

Add marshmallows. Cook on High power 1 minute and 30 seconds. Stir in cocoa; add vanilla. Allow to stand at room temperature until bottom of bowl is cool. Beat until thick. Serve on ice cream or pound cake.

CAPPUCCINO
Serves 4

For coffee and chocolate lovers, a combination of both with a touch of brandy to bring you warmth on a cold, brisk evening. If you travel to the snow for weekends, throw your microwave in the car. It can be a tremendous money-saver to prepare easy snacks in your room—or even breakfast, lunch, and dinner. Just take plenty of paper plates, some of the heavy-duty kind now available for cooking, serving, and storing. To keep your perishables cold, an insulated cold box will hold overnight—or you can place them outside in nature's refrigerator.

2 cups milk

¼ cup semisweet chocolate chips
2 teaspoons instant coffee
8 tablespoons brandy
Whipped cream
2 teaspoons sugar (optional)

Combine milk and chocolate in a 1-quart glass measure. Cook on High (600–700 watts) 3–4 minutes, until hot; do not allow it to boil. Stir in coffee and stir until dissolved. Divide among 4 mugs. Stir 2 tablespoons brandy into each mug. Top with whipped cream and serve immediately.

Add sugar to the milk if you would like a sweeter drink. The chocolate has sugar in it, and for some that is enough. You can always stir in the sugar at the end to your taste.

16
CANDY

Marshmallows
Divinity
Peanut Brittle
Quick Party Mints
Lollipops
Caramel Nut Candy
Chocolate-Coffee Truffles

CANDY MADE EASY

Microwave cooking has taken the mystery out of candy-making, and budding chocolatiers no longer have to spend hours slaving over a hot stove to produce tasty results that are better than store-bought. One taste of our Carmel Nut Candy, or crisp chocolate-coated Honeycomb, rich Rocky Road, or Chocolate Taffy (in Chocolate chapter) will convince you of the versatility of your microwave.

Perhaps the greatest advantage of the microwave for candy-making is the absence of direct heat. There is less chance of overcooking or scorching, the most frequent pitfalls of the novice. Microwave heat is more uniform (around top, bottom, and sides of bowl) and since microwave energy keeps the mixture constantly in motion, there is no need to stir continually as required for many conventional candy recipes (usually over a double boiler).

Temperature and the ratio of ingredients are important factors in both conventional and microwave candy-making. The temperature of the basic syrup controls the moisture content of the finished candy, which in turn determines its characteristics, such as the difference between taffy and peanut brittle. Microwave cooking does not reduce moisture as quickly as conventional cooking, and since reducing moisture is the key to success, it is sometimes a good idea to cut back a bit on the amount of water specified when adapting your favorite recipes to microwave.

You will also find that most of my microwave recipes use sugar and corn syrup in combination. Corn syrup controls crystalization and gives more flexibility in timing when a thermometer is not available. It contains sugar in the form of dextrose and maltose that do not crystalize readily, yet do interfere with the crystalization of other sugars.

Candy-making Tips

- Use the 2-quart glass measuring cup for preparing candy. The handle stays cool even though the sugar mixture is very hot, so you can remove it from the microwave at just the right moment.
- Simple cleanup: If the syrup remaining in the measuring cup hardens before washing, add some water to it and bring to a boil in microwave on High (600–700 watts). Any sticky nonmetal utensils can be added to the cup and cleaned at the same time.
- In most instances, solid vegetable shortening is more reliable for candy-making than butter or margarine with their unspecified water content, which can upset moisture balance.

Testing the Temperature

New candy thermometers designed for microwave use take the guesswork out of preparation. But if you don't want to invest in one, here is a standard test to determine the approximate temperature and firmness of candy mixtures:

Drop a small amount of the boiling syrup into a cup of very cold water (without ice), being sure to take the remaining candy mixture out of the microwave during testing to prevent overcooking. Shape syrup gently with fingertips, then remove from water.

Soft Ball (234°F. to 240°F.)
Shapes into soft ball that flattens when removed from water.

Firm Ball (244°F. to 248°F.)
Shapes into firm ball that does not flatten when removed from water.

Hard Ball (250°F. to 255°F.)
Forms ball that is hard enough to hold its shape but is still pliable.

Soft Crack (270°F. to 290°F.)
Syrup separates into threads that are hard but not brittle.

Hard Crack (300°F. to 310°F.)
Syrup separates into hard and brittle threads.

MARSHMALLOWS
Makes about 36 marshmallows

This is definitely a must for the true tender-tasting marshmallow. Adapted from my old battered *Joy of Cooking* bible, it is easy as long as you have an electric mixer. I cannot tell you how long they can be stored—each time I have made it, they disappear while drying.

1   envelope unflavored gelatin
⅓ cup water
⅔ cup granulated sugar
½ cup light corn syrup
Pinch salt
1   teaspoon vanilla
2   tablespoons cornstarch
3   tablespoons powdered sugar, sifted

In a 2-quart glass measure, stir in the gelatin and water. Let soften for 10 minutes. Stir in the granulated sugar. Cook on Medium (300–350 watts) for 5–6 minutes until the sugar dissolves. Stir at 4 minutes to keep the mixture from boiling over. (This is the reason for using such a large container for such a small amount of liquid.)

Place the corn syrup, salt, and vanilla in an electric mixer bowl. Add the cooked gelatin and sugar mixture and beat at high speed for 12–14 minutes until mixture is thick and begins to hold its shape.

Combine the cornstarch and powdered sugar in a bowl.

Dust an 8″ x 8″ pan with cornstarch mixture. Spread the fluffy marshmallow mixture in pan. Let it set for several hours to dry so that it can be cut into squares.

Sprinkle the remaining cornstarch mixture onto a flat cookie sheet. Loosen edges of marshmallow with sharp knife dipped into the cornstarch mixure. Cut in half. Place pieces on cookie sheet. Cut into squares with knife or scissors dipped into cornstarch mixture. Dust each square in cornstarch mixture. Allow to dry about 1 hour before storing in an airtight container.

DIVINITY
Makes about 3 dozen pieces

2⅔ cups sugar
⅔ cup light corn syrup
½ cup water
3 egg whites
Pinch salt
1 teaspoon vanilla
1 cup chopped unsalted nuts

Combine sugar, corn syrup, and water in 2-quart measuring cup or bowl and cook on High (600–700 watts) until candy thermometer registers 260°F. (or until a small amount of mixture forms ball hard enough to hold its shape but still pliable when dropped into bowl of very cold water), about 12–15 minutes.

Meanwhile, beat egg whites with salt in large bowl until stiff. Beat in vanilla. Gradually pour hot syrup into egg whites, beating constantly until mixture is very stiff, about 2–3 minutes. Stir in nuts. Drop by tablespoons onto wax paper. Cool completely before storing in airtight container in cool place.

PEANUT BRITTLE
Makes about 1 pound

Don't let the instructions stop you from trying this one; it is quite easy and very popular with young microwave cooks.

1 cup sugar
½ cup dark or light corn syrup
2 cups dry-roasted unsalted peanuts
1 teaspoon unsalted butter
1 teaspoon vanilla
1 teaspoon baking soda

Generously grease baking sheet. Combine sugar and corn syrup in 2-quart measuring cup or bowl and cook on High (600–700 watts) for 4 minutes. Stir in peanuts using wooden spoon. Continue cooking on High 3 minutes. Stir in butter and vanilla and cook until candy thermometer registers 300°F. (or until small amount of mixture separates into hard and brittle threads when dropped into very cold water), about 2–2½ minutes. Blend in baking soda and stir until mixture is light and foamy. Pour onto prepared sheet; spread quickly to edges with back of wooden spoon. As candy cools, stretch into thin sheet using moistened palms of hands. Let cool completely. Break into pieces. Store in cool place.

QUICK PARTY MINTS
Makes about 6 dozen

3 tablespoons unsalted butter
3 tablespoons milk
1 15-ounce box white creamy frosting mix
1 teaspoon peppermint extract
Green food coloring

Combine butter and milk in 2-quart measuring cup and cook on High (600–700 watts) until butter is melted, about 45–60 seconds. Blend in frosting mix. Continue cooking on High, whisking through several times, until mixture is creamy, about 2–3 minutes. Whisk in peppermint extract and enough food coloring to give mixture a light green hue. Drop by teaspoonfuls onto wax paper. Let cool, then refrigerate until firm. Store in refrigerator in airtight container.

LOLLIPOPS
Makes 10 2½- to 3-inch lollipops

10 lollipop or popsickle sticks
¾ cup sugar
½ cup light corn syrup
¼ cup (½ stick) unsalted butter
1   teaspoon flavoring or extract (peppermint,
    orange, vanilla, cinnamon, etc.)
Food coloring
Cinnamon candies or other miniature candies
    for decoration

Arrange sticks on parchment paper, spacing at least 4 inches apart. Combine sugar, corn syrup, and butter in 2-quart measuring cup and cook on High (600–700 watts) for 2 minutes. Stir in flavoring and food coloring. Continue cooking on High until candy thermometer registers 270°F. (or until small amount of mixture separates into threads that are hard but not brittle when dropped into very cold water), about 5–7 minutes. Drop syrup by tablespoon over one end of each stick. Press candies gently into place. Let cool completely. Wrap each lollipop in plastic. Store in airtight container.

CARAMEL NUT CANDY
Makes about 7 dozen

1   pound light caramels
3   tablespoons water
1   12-ounce can mixed nuts (about 2 cups)

Lightly butter 9″ x 9″ baking pan. Combine caramels and water in 2-quart measuring cup and cook on High (600–700 watts) until caramels soften slightly, about 2–3 minutes. Using wooden spoon, stir through to melt completely. Blend in nuts, mixing well. Pour into prepared pan. Refrigerate until firm. Cut into 1-inch squares before serving.

CHOCOLATE-COFFEE TRUFFLES
Makes about 4–5 dozen

This is one recipe that justifies the term "food of the Gods." Use a good quality chocolate.

12 ounces semisweet chocolate
4   egg yolks
½ cup coffee liqueur (Kahlua)
⅔ cup unsalted butter (softened)
Unsweetened cocoa powder, ground almonds, or
    powdered sugar as garnish

If using bars of chocolate instead of bits, break the bar into pieces. Place into a 1-quart glass measure. Melt on High (600–700 watts) for 1½–2 minutes, just until chocolate appears shiny. It will not melt until you stir. Stir thoroughly until smooth. Let cool to room temperature.

Beat in egg yolks one at a time. Blend in liqueur. Cook on High 30 seconds. Add softened butter to mixture one tablespoon at a time, beating well after each addition. Continue beating until mixture is light and fluffy, about 4–5 minutes. Cover with plastic wrap and refrigerate 4–5 hours.

To make the candies, roll mixture into ¾-inch balls. Coat with desired garnish. I like to roll the truffles in cocoa powder. Then use ground almonds or powdered sugar, if desired.

Chocolate truffles can be frozen. Arrange between sheets of wax paper and place in a container that will hold them without crowding. Use foil as an overwrap to eliminate any possibility of moisture getting into the package.

17
KID'S CORNER

Eggs in a Basket
Hot Dog
Bacon Sticks
Tuna-Noodle Casserole with Cashews
Chicken-Potato Chip Casserole
Chili/Cheese/Corn Chip Casserole
English Muffin Pizza
Pita Pizza
Chocolate Cake with Pecan Frosting
Cocoa Cookies
Lemon Bars
Snackin' Cake
Caramel Penuche
Somemores
Caramel Nut Sauce
Dog Bisuits

FAMILY MEALS IN A HURRY

Many years ago a woman revolutionized cooking by writing a cookbook called *I Hate to Cook*. It was funny, but it also made people realize that it was possible to take a "can of this" and a "can of that" and put together a fairly attractive meal that also tasted good.

You can thumb through this book and find ingredients you like to eat and make the recipes from what we call *scratch* — which means using uncooked foods and putting them together yourself.

However, in this chapter, we have included some quickly prepared things that can serve more people for less money than TV dinners. It will also provide you with some microwave experiences so that you will be able to experiment on your own. After a busy day at work, it is not always possible for mothers to shop, cook, and clean up afterwards. How nice it would be to come home and find dinner on the table!

I was very fortunate that both my sons, Paul and Richard, enjoyed food and found preparing meals rather fun. I wish I could honestly say they felt the same about cleaning up. However, they were always good sports and usually left the kitchen in better shape than they found it. They have become good cooks, and Paul's experimentation with microwave cooking in his teens resulted in many of the original concepts you now see in microwave cookbooks. He has worked professionally in this special field, and in my opinion (a bit prejudiced of course) he is the best microwave cook I know. (He can make the best scratch pizza in a regular oven as well.)

So you see, there is room for all types of cooking, and cooking with all methods available to you. If you enjoy eating — and who doesn't? — now is your chance to be creative. Don't sit around waiting to be served. Why not do it yourself!

EGGS IN A BASKET (HOLE IN ONE)
Serves 1

If you toast the slice of bread first, you can have a fun breakfast cooked right on your serving plate.

1 slice whole grain toast (or your favorite bread toasted)
1 egg
Salt and pepper to taste

Remove a small circle from the center of toast with a small glass. Place on paper plate. Break an egg into the center of the circle. With a toothpick, break through the yolk of the egg three times. Use just enough pressure to break the yolk's membrane — it will not run. Sprinkle with salt and pepper.

Cover dish with a piece of wax paper. Cook on High (600 – 700 watts) for 45 seconds – 1 minute, until it looks almost done. Then allow it to sit for 1 minute to finish cooking.

Note: You may butter the toast before cutting the circle, if you wish.

HOT DOG
Serves 1

My family always insisted the only reason I went to the ball games was to eat the hot dogs. But that was before they stopped *cooking* them. I refuse to purchase a hot dog that is skewered on a slightly heated roller and then placed in a cold bun. I feel the same way about the timing and procedure for hot dogs in the microwave cookbooks. Just because you can place a hot dog in a bun and heat it in the microwave does not mean it is the best way to get the flavor from the hot dog.

It is just this type of "cutesy" cooking that makes people turn away from the microwave — because done that way it tastes "funny."

Let us think together for a moment. Microwave energy cooks the food from the outside in. When you place the hot dog inside the bun, the bun cooks first, and if you continue to cook long enough to heat the hot dog, the bun turns to stone (after it first turns to rubber, that is).

So to really enjoy a perfect, hot, steamy dog with a fresh-tasting bun try the following recipe.

1 hot dog
1 bun
Mustard, catsup, relish to your taste

Place hot dog on cutting board; lightly slash at angle several times. Place on paper plate. Cook on High (600 – 700 watts) for 45 seconds – 1 minute (depending on size and temperature of dog). Place bun around it. Cook on High 15 – 20 seconds, until heated through.

Add mustard or your choice of spreads.

BACON STICKS
Makes 4 bacon sticks

Cook these and place them in a mug. Fun to serve—your friends will love these tasty treats. Or invite your parents in the kitchen to join you.

2 slices bacon
4 bread sticks

Cut each slice of bacon in half lengthwise to make 4 strips. Wrap bacon around each bread stick barber-pole fashion. Place on a paper towel on a paper plate. Cover with a paper towel. Cook on High (600–700 watts) for 1½–2 minutes, just until the bacon is crisp.

TUNA-NOODLE CASSEROLE WITH CASHEWS
Serves 4

To make this tasty dish, you must first have cooked noodles. They are cooked according to the directions on the package. I prefer to cook noodles in a large pot of water on the cook-top rather than the microwave, because you do not save any time, and handling boiling water in a microwave can be difficult. Right after you drain the noodles in a colander, add the soup and milk so that the noodles do not stick together.

3 **cups cooked noodles, drained**
1 **10¾-ounce can cream of mushroom soup**
¾ **cup milk**
1 **6½-ounce can tuna**
½ **cup sliced celery**
1 **cup cashews, broken into pieces**
1 **scallion, sliced**
½ **cup crushed potato chips**

Cook noodles; drain well. Place them in a 2-quart casserole. Stir in the soup and milk, making sure it is well blended. Stir in all the rest of the ingredients except the potato chips.

Cook on High (600–700 watts) for 5 minutes. Stir the mixture from the outside toward the center, because the outside portion of the food cooks more than the center. Sprinkle potato chips on top. Continue to cook on High 2–3 minutes, until it is hot in the center. Serve hot.

CHICKEN–POTATO CHIP CASSEROLE
Serves 3

Use leftover chicken if you have it on hand; if not, it is now possible to purchase chunk chicken in a can.

2 **cups crushed potato chips**
1 **10¾-ounce can cream of chicken soup**
1 **6¾-ounce can chunk breast of chicken, or 1 cup leftover cooked chicken**
1 **4-ounce can of mushrooms, drained; or 6 fresh mushrooms, sliced**
1 **cup shredded cheddar cheese**
½ **cup mayonnaise**
¼ **cup sliced green onion**

Divide one cup of potato chips in thirds; place in the bottom of three deep soup bowls. Combine all the remaining ingredients except the remaining potato chips in a large bowl and stir until they are well mixed. Divide the mixture among the three bowls, and sprinkle with remaining potato chips. Heat in the microwave on High (600–700 watts) for 2–3 minutes, or until mixture bubbles. If not serving immediately, refrigerate.

CHILI/CHEESE/CORN CHIP CASSEROLE
Serves 1

Makes an easy, hearty snack or meal. You can find these small vacuum-packed cans in your market. The can will read *chili con carne with beans*, which translated means *chili with meat with beans*. The cheese can be Monterey Jack as well as cheddar. Chopped onions add a nice flavor—we like to add them after the chili is heated.

½ **cup corn chips**
1 **7-ounce can chili con carne with beans**
½ **cup shredded cheddar cheese**
1 **green scallion, sliced thin**

Place corn chips in a 2-cup cereal bowl. Spoon chili over top. Heat on High (600–700 watts) for 2 minutes. Stir. Add cheese to top. Heat on Medium 45–60 seconds, just until cheese is melted. Sprinkle onion over top, if desired.

PIZZA

Because the microwave does not have a hot, dry environment, we use a different method to make a tasty pizza. It has the flavor of traditional pizza and won't become soggy. Here are a few pizza recipe suggestions. If you have a microwave rack, the pizzas will turn out even better.

ENGLISH MUFFIN PIZZA

1 muffin makes 2 servings

First toast the muffin or it will become soggy. Place the opened jar of sauce in the refrigerator after using.

1 English muffin, halved and toasted
1 14-ounce jar Pizza Quick sauce, chunky style, or 4-ounce can pizza sauce
6 pepperoni pieces, thinly sliced
½ cup shredded jack cheese or mozzarella cheese
Parmesan cheese

Place muffin halves on a paper plate. Spoon about 1 tablespoon of sauce on each muffin. Place pepperoni over top of sauce, sprinkle with cheese and parmesan. Heat on High just until cheese is bubbling, about 45–60 seconds.

PITA PIZZA

1 pita makes 2 servings

Pita bread, also known as pocket bread because it can become a pocket for fillings, has been around for over two thousand years. It is popular in the Mideast and is available in supermarkets across the country. My son Paul began making this recipe 10 years ago because he loved pizza and this was the only way he could cook one in the microwave that would stay crisp.

To make a Pita Pizza use the same toppings given in the English Muffin Pizza recipe or any topping of your choice. It is not necessary to toast the pita bread. Either pull the two pieces of the pocket apart carefully or cut them apart with a scissors. Place each half on a paper plate. Add the toppings. Place in the microwave and heat on High just until cheese is bubbling, about 45–60 seconds. Be careful not to taste it too quickly, it will be very hot.

CHOCOLATE CAKE WITH PECAN FROSTING

Serves

Children love to prepare this cake mix. It comes out frosted!

1 box German chocolate cake mix
⅓ cup oil
3 eggs, beaten
1 box coconut pecan frosting mix

Combine German chocolate cake mix with oil and eggs. Mix by hand until well blended. Set aside.

Prepare frosting as directed on box. Spoon frosting into bottom of a 10- or 12-cup tube pan. Pour cake batter over frosting. Cook on High (600–700 watts) for 10–12 minutes; turn pan once or twice if cooking unevenly.

Cake is finished cooking when it begins to move away from the sides and a wooden pick comes out clean. Do not overcook. Allow to cool 10–15 minutes before turning onto a serving platter.

COCOA COOKIES

Makes about 30 cookies

You may make the dough ahead of time and refrigerate—then microwave these delectable treats only as you need them. The dough can be wrapped tightly in plastic wrap, and refrigerated for up to three days.

¾ cup (1½ sticks) butter or margarine at room temperature
¾ cup sugar
1 egg
1¾ cups all-purpose flour
¼ cup unsweetened cocoa powder
1 teaspoon baking powder
½ teaspoon salt
1 teaspoon vanilla
½ cup chopped walnuts
Sugar for coating

Combine butter, ¾ cup sugar, and egg in an electric mixer and blend until the mixture is light and fluffy. In a bowl mix together flour, cocoa, baking powder, and salt; mix it until everything is blended.

Put it into the butter mixture and beat together, just until it is mixed. Do not overbeat. Stir in vanilla and nuts.

Divide dough and roll in 1-inch balls. Put a little sugar into a plate. Roll the balls in the sugar. Place in a dish and cover. Leave in the refrigerator until ready to bake.

To bake, place balls of dough 1½ inches apart on a paper plate. Flatten tops slightly with a spoon. Cook on High (600–700 watts) until cookies are puffed: about 1 minute for 2 cookies; 1¼ minutes for 4 cookies; 2 minutes for 8 cookies; and 3 minutes for 12 cookies. For crisper cookies, let cook an additional few seconds. Let cool slightly before removing from plate (they will get firm as they stand). Transfer to rack and cool completely.

LEMON BARS

Makes 12–16 bars (depending on how you cut them)

This is my son Paul's recipe. When there is nothing "good" to eat in the cookie jar, he can prepare these fast. They have a nice lemon flavor and are delicious to share with friends and a glass of milk.

Crust

1 cup all-purpose flour
⅓ cup powdered sugar
½ cup butter or margarine, softened

Filling

2 eggs
1 cup sugar
1½ teaspoons cornstarch
½ teaspoon baking powder
1 tablespoon lemon rind, grated
3½ tablespoons lemon juice
Powdered sugar to sprinkle on top

To make crust, combine flour and sugar in a 9-inch round microwave baking dish. Place butter or margarine on plate. Place in the microwave on High (600–700 watts) for 45 seconds to soften. Add it to the flour and sugar in baking dish; stir all ingredients together until mixture is crumbly. Press the mixture into the bottom of the dish. Cook on High 4 minutes. Set crust aside while you prepare the filling.

In a 1-quart glass measure, combine the eggs and sugar; beat until mixture is fluffy. Add all the rest of the ingredients, and stir well until the cornstarch is completely dissolved.

Pour this mixture over the baked crust. Cook on High for 3½–4½ minutes, just until the center begins to look "set." Remove from microwave, and let it stand at least 10 minutes before cutting so that the custard can set completely.

Sprinkle powdered sugar over the top and cut into 12–16 bars.

SNACKIN' CAKE

Serves 6–8

1 Snackin' Cake mix (for a single layer cake)
1 9-ounce container solid whip topping

Prepare cake mix as directed on package, using the cardboard cooking container inside package.

Cook on High (600–700 watts) for 6–7 minutes, just until sides appear barely cooked. Allow to cool, then coat with whipped topping frosting.

CARAMEL PENUCHE

Makes

Instead of just eating the caramels, try this delicious candy.

1½ cups sugar
⅓ cup milk
¼ cup margarine
50 caramels (a 14-ounce bag)
¾ cup chopped walnuts

Place the sugar, milk, and margarine in a 2-quart glass measure or bowl that is heat-resistant so that it is strong enough to handle the high temperatures of melted sugar.

Cook on High (600–700 watts) for 7 minutes, stirring once. While this is cooking, unwrap the caramels. Add them to the hot liquid; stir. Cook on High 1 minute. Beat vigorously until mixture is smooth (I like to use a strong wooden spoon). Add the nuts. Stir again.

Pour into a lightly greased 8-inch square pan. Let it cool before cutting into squares.

SOMEMORES
Serves 1

This popular snack got its name because whenever it was served to a child (or an adult for that matter), they always said "Some more."

1 **graham cracker, or 2 vanilla wafers**
1 **milk chocolate candy bar**
1 **marshmallow, regular size**

Break graham cracker in half, or use 1 vanilla wafer cookie. Place on paper plate. Top with piece of chocolate, then marshmallow. Heat on High (600–700 watts) for 20–30 seconds (watch the marshmallow puff up). Remove from microwave, place second half of graham cracker or a vanilla wafer cookie on top, and *eat*.

For two or more, increase the time about 15 seconds for each Somemore.

CARAMEL NUT SAUCE
Makes about 1¼ cups

Delicious over ice cream, pound cake, or baked apples.

½ **pound (28) caramels**
⅓ **cup water**
½ **cup almond topping (chopped nuts in packages found near ice cream)**

Unwrap caramels and place in a 1½-quart bowl. Add water and melt on High (600–700 watts) for 2–3 minutes. Stir until smooth. Stir in the nuts. Serve warm.

To reheat, place the amount you want in a glass measure. Heat on Medium (300–350 watts) just until warm, start with 45 seconds. If caramels become too thick, add a tablespoon of water.

DOG BISQUITS
Makes about 20 treats

And what is a kid without a dog?

This recipe was given to me by one of my students who noticed a box of dog bisquits in my shopping cart at the market. Her dog, she said, would only eat the ones she made.

After serving these to our favorite dog, I can understand why. My advice is, don't start unless you intend to continue — your dogs definitely will let you know they can tell the difference.

½ **pound whole wheat flour (about 2 cups)**
1 **egg**
½ **cup liquid (beef broth, chicken broth, or gravy)**
2 **tablespoons wheat germ (optional)**
½ **teaspoon garlic salt**
½ **teaspoon onion salt**
½ **teaspoon garlic powder**
A bit of kasha, or oatmeal (optional)

Place flour in bowl; add egg and enough liquid to moisten. Add remaining ingredients.

Roll dough into a ball. Sprinkle flour on a board, and roll dough into dog bisquits, either ring shaped or rolls, to equal about 20 individual servings. Place on large baking dish in a single layer. Bake on High (600–700 watts) for 10 minutes, or until firm.

INDEX